THE ASCENT OF SELF

THE ASCENT OF SELF

A Reinterpretation of the Mystical Poetry of Lalla-Ded

Translation and Commentary by

B.N. Parimoo

Foreword by

K.L. Shrimali

MOTILAL BANARSIDASS PUBLISHERS PRIVATE LIMITED • DELHI

Reprint: Delhi, 2013
Second Revised Edition 1987
First Edition 1978

ISBN: 978-81-208-0305-3 (Cloth)
ISBN: 978-81-208-3641-9 (Paper)

MOTILAL BANARSIDASS
41 U.A. Bungalow Road, Jawahar Nagar, Delhi 110 007
8 Mahalaxmi Chamber, 22 Bhulabhai Desai Road, Mumbai 400 026
203 Royapettah High Road, Mylapore, Chennai 600 004
236, 9th Main III Block, Jayanagar, Bengaluru 560 011
Sanas Plaza, 1302 Baji Rao Road, Pune 411 002
8 Camac Street, Kolkata 700 017
Ashok Rajpath, Patna 800 004
Chowk, Varanasi 221 001

Printed in India
by RP Jain at NAB Printing Unit,
A-44, Naraina Industrial Area, Phase I, New Delhi–110028
and published by JP Jain for Motilal Banarsidass Publishers (P) Ltd,
41 U.A. Bungalow Road, Jawahar Nagar, Delhi-110007

If we remember that all life is one, there is no reason why we should treat one another as enemies.—MAHATMA GANDHI

To My Father

PANDIT BHAGWAN DASS
PARIMOO

An Emancipated Soul

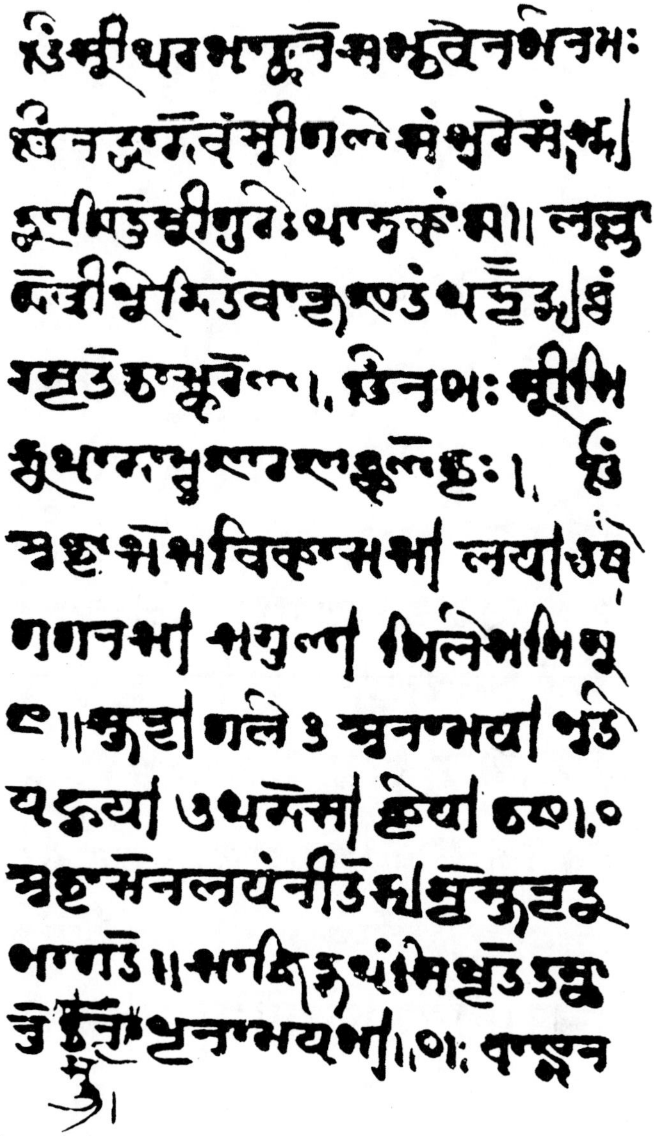

Lalla-Vakhs in Sharda Script (old MS.) Bhaskar Razdan

1] (MS-Private possession of Pandit Dina Nath Yach).

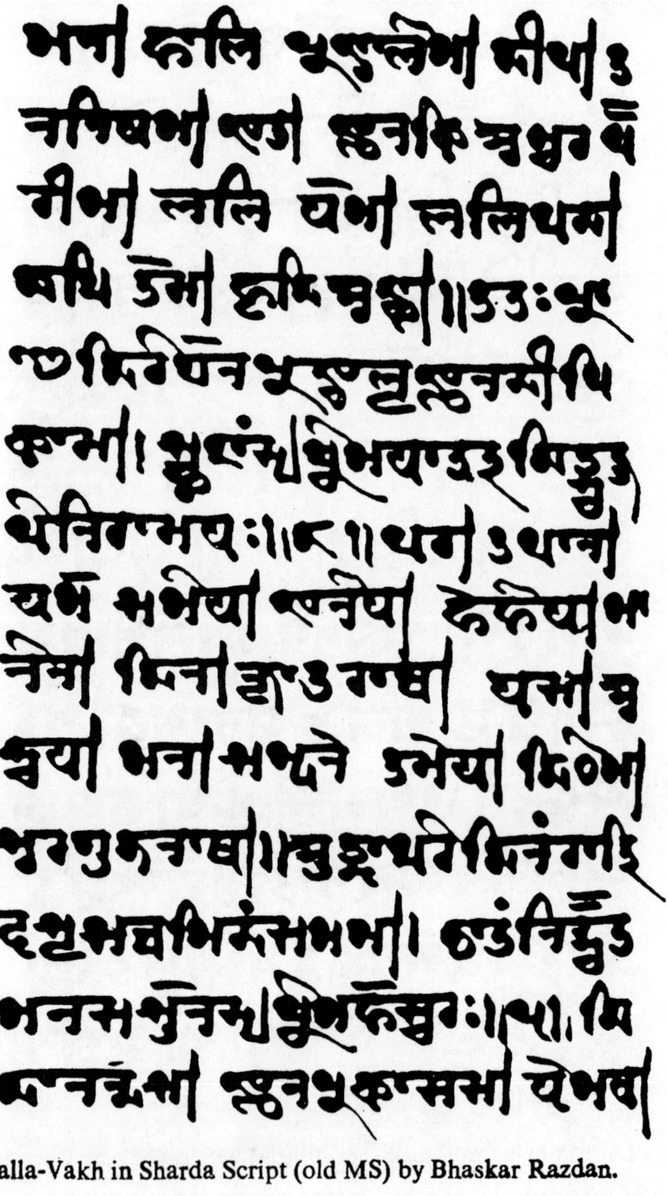

Lalla-Vakh in Sharda Script (old MS) by Bhaskar Razdan.

SWAMI MUKTANANDA

BLESSINGS

For centuries Kashmir has been the land of spiritual seeking for many Siddhas. Among them was the Siddha Yogini Lalleshwari, a great devotee of Lord Shiva. People of Kashmir were much influenced by her. Her philosophical poems were sung in every home. Hindus as well as Muslims have respected her. To her the truth was above any sect, creed or religion. In her poems she has narrated openly the experiences of her spiritual seeking and the final attainment.

It is a matter of great joy that the words of such a great being are now available in English in book form with explanations.

May the readers benefit greatly by its reading, and ascend the Self.

SWAMI MUKTANANDA

I am happy to learn that an attempt has been made by Shri Badri Nath Parimoo to re-interpret the poetry of the mystical genius of Kashmir, Lalla-ded. Way back in the 14th century she perfected Kuṇḍalinī Yoga, and the present volume, I am told, demonstrates the evolution of her soul. I append my blessings and commend it to the readers, especially those of the spiritual bent of mind.

GOPI NATH KAVIRAJ
Mahāmahopādhyāya

FOREWORD

The book, *The Ascent of Self*, deals with the spiritual evolution of a mystic saint-poetess of Kashmir, of the 14th century. The work is based on the verses of the poetess collected from old manuscripts and other sources. The verses have been re-arranged, translated and commented upon and the thesis made out that Lalla-děd, as the poetess is called, attained yogic perfection.

The verses have not only been rendered into English but also critically analysed and examined. The commentary on each quatrain has been supported extensively by quotations and texts from the Indian Scriptures such as the *Bhagavad Gītā*, the *Upaniṣads*, the *Brahma Sūtras*, the *Śaiva-Tantras of Kashmir*, etc., besides references to sacred books and philosophies of the West. In a way it may be considered as a treatise on practical yoga—the 'ascent' of the individual self through subtle planes of consciousness, and its final dissolution in the consciousness of the Absolute Being.

The teaching of Lalla-děd has a great bearing and significance today, as ever. The spiritual salvation helps rise above the narrow considerations of selfishness, greed and, more than anything else, above religious bigotry. In this respect, this book will be highly valuable in fostering human understanding and bringing about emotional integration of our people irrespective of their caste, creed and colour.

Persons with spiritual predilections will find the book particularly interesting and useful.

It is hoped that it will be appreciated by those for whom it is intended.

Banaras Hindu University,
Varanasi,
17th January, 1976.

K. L. SHRIMALI

CONTENTS

INTRODUCTION

(*i*) *Relevance of Mysticism today*

The snow-capped mountain peaks, the undulating glaciers, the placid lakes of emerald green water, the dense forests of dark-green firs and pines, the meandering rivulets making music on their pebbly beds, the willow-groves and the majestic chinars, one and all seem to have something to do with giving human consciousness an expansive dimension. One does not know by what mysterious process the apparently inert, though awe-inspiring, aspects of Nature influence the mind of man. Out in the open, away from the circumscribed social environment, he is imaginatively elevated to regions of subtle consciousness, in the presence of her august forms. The valley of Kashmir has been endowed with Nature's abundance and it is no wonder that we have had the benefit of a long line of saints, sages and seers cradled by benign Nature in her fertile lap. To the Kashmiri she provides not only fullness of sensuous pleasure by her superb attractions but also informs him with a spirit of mystical quest which tries to see into the heart of things. Cosmic consciousness may be an inevitable product of fascinating natural surroundings, bracing atmosphere and scenic beauty.

The puzzling phenomenon, however, is that, in spite of such inviting and exalting surroundings, the mystic saints should have chosen to withdraw from external Nature and to look for the Truth within themselves. Instinctively, the caterpiller shuts itself in the cocoon in order to emerge as a perfected butterfly with bright, variegated wings. There may be some law of Nature operating behind the scenes and prompting the mind to withdraw into itself in order to attain perfection. Whatever the mysterious impulse may be, the age-old aphorism KNOW THYSELF[1] has been accepted as the gateway to the knowledge of the Source of Life by mystics the world over.

The specific hallmark of the Kashmiri mystic has been his great capacity, 'to withdraw into oneself', like the caterpillar. On the anvil of subtle self-experience, he has shaped the sterling of

1. Gnothi seauton (know thyself): Socrates. The Story of Philosophy: Will Durant; p. 6.

knowledge and come at the eternal Truth. He has discovered the spirit of Nature in its most potential form within himself. The presence of Nature, as the Divine Spirit, has been realized within and without the mind as one all-pervading Being, knitting the whole existence into the all-encompassing fabric of Unity. Mysticism sums up the recognition and realization of the self in man and the Macrocosmic Self and the identification of the two as One. Self-realization and God-realization are one and the same thing. The mystic aims at the dissolution of the individual self into the Universal Self so as to attain Truth-Consciousness-Bliss.

Mysticism is a practical discipline and the goal is achieved after a hard struggle. Kashmir has had a conspicuous advantage in producing mystics of a high accomplishment at close intervals. The discipline helps purging the mind of evil influences. The song sung out of realization of the ultimate Truth is the rich legacy left behind by our mystical poets. Kashmiris can well boast of a rich treasure of poetry of this denomination. It is sublime, exalted poetry which elevates thought, purifies emotions and brings plenitude of peace to the mind.

Apart from being an integral part of our literature,—one would say the first and the best part of it, without fear of contradiction—mystical poetry has left an indelible mark on the thought and conduct of a normal Kashmiri. The socio-cultural heritage of Kashmiris bears a clear imprint of this branch of literature, and its strong impact can be guaged by the fact that much of the pithy, mystical verse of Lalla-yogeśvari, Sheikh Noor-uddin (Vali), Krishnajoo Razdan, Parmānanda, Wahāb Khār, Shamas Faqir and others has been committed to memory and is sung with gusto by all—Hindu, Muslim and Sikh—alike. The mystical poetry has the efficacy of generating the blessed mood in which the pettinesses of mundane interests are shelved and forgotten. This particular stream of literature brings rippling waters to the Kashmiri doorstep which have, over the centuries, helped produce and nourish a spirit of understanding, tolerance, fellow-feeling and an acute sensibility of religious humanism.

If, in the history of Kashmir, there appear some dark patches of intolerance and religious zeal, we may attribute these to temporal lust and spiritual ignorance. The salutary thing is that Muslim Sufism found its counterpart in the indigenous Advaita (non-dualistic) Śaivism and the fusion of the two issued forth in superb mystical poetry. So Kashmiri culture was dyed fast in a rich saffron of mystical consciousness which has formed the sub-stratum of the Kashmiri mind. It is this consciousness which forms the bed-rock of the conception of Brotherhood of Man.

A humble attempt is, therefore, being made to interpret the mystical verse of Lalla-dĕd and to open the conduits of the pure, crystalline reservoirs of her spiritual poetry to remind Kashmiris in particular that we are the inheritors of a great tradition and it would be but mockery of our common sense and sanity to allow ourselves get drowned in the flooding current of narrow-mindedness and ignorance. Mystical poetry has a broader significance too. It brings a message of hope to mankind in general. In the warring world of today mysticism has a relevance, more than ever before.

(ii) Raison d'être

Not a few translations of Lalla-vakhs, as the mystical verses of Lalla-yogeśvari are popularly called in Kashmiri, are extant, some in free verse and some in poetic prose. All these are laudable attempts in their own way because their authors have unearthed the buried treasure of the Vakhs and preserved it for posterity against the ravages of time. Besides, by their translations, the Vakhs have been made available to English and Urdu knowing readers. Naturally we owe these authors a great debt of gratitude for the significant work they have done.

Nevertheless, one thing seems to have escaped the notice of these admirers and scholars of Lalla-yogeśvari, viz., that there is a sequence of thought in the Vakhs which deserves being looked into. So far the Vakhs have been taken at random and translated as such. But a little care makes it evident that there is a palpable growth in the temper of the Vakhs. When arranged in a particular order, they construct themselves into a mystical edifice at the same time awe-inspiring and imposing and fascinating. To help building that mystical mansion is the *raison d'être* of the present volume. And the peculiarity of the attempt is that the whole structure is raised with the material of the Vakhs joined together in an ascending order with the cement of the *internal evidence*.

In isolation, the Vakhs pose a problem to the reader as the disjointed limbs of any organism would naturally do. Each Vakh appears intricately involved in a maze of occult knowledge and to get at the root of the Vakh is a job. By itself each Vakh becomes a riddle. But arranged brick upon brick together they unfold a new perspective, not at all discovered so far. They unravel a regular growth of mystical thought and experience. On the infra-structure of experience, on the material plane, rises the colossal super-structure of the highest spiritual knowledge that may ever have been acquired. When studied in an orderly, graded form, as envisaged in the present volume, the Vakhs raise the reader higher and higher imaginatively. The Vakhs stand one above the other like terraced fields on a mountain slope, the inner edge of the lower one giving the basal support to the outer projecting ledge of the one stretching above it. The ascent is conical, all round the base, till the fields of limiting vision dug out into the slope become narrower and narrower, and simultaneously open out broader and broader vistas of enveloping aerial space until finally the limited patches of ego-consciousness taper into a point at the top beyond which stands out the consciousness of Unlimited—The Ethereal Void, The Nothingness! Lalla calls it the *Shunyah* which is the same thing as Parama Śiva, The Absolute Being.

The cue to the arrangement of thought in the verses is taken from the "I-ness", not amounting to or smacking of egotism, but categorically denoting personal experience. In fact, the personal element in the poetry of the Yogeśvari is intriguing. The verses are the poetical expression of the spiritual changes she undergoes in her life with the passage of time. The conspicuous first person, singular number, of the subject in each sentence catches our attention. It impresses us as a poetical element, uniquely individual. The subjectiveness carries along with it the flavour of lyrical emotion. The element of personal experience lends itself to an arrangement of a developing or evolving process which is surely autobiographical. Through her

Vakhs, the Yogeśvari writes the autobiography of her soul. The following examples may be cited to illustrate the point.

(i) Gātulāh akh vuchhum...verse 2. (I saw a wise man...)

(ii) Āyas ti syŏduy, ta gatsha ti syŏduy.....v. 3. (I came by the straight path, so shall I go by the straight path...)

(iii) Āmi pana sŏdras nāvi chĕs lamān......verse 4. (I am towing the boat......).

(iv) Zanam prävith vĕbhav na tshoṅḍum......v. 2. (In this life I did not hanker after pomp and pelf........

(v) Lalith, Lalith vaday bŏh vāy.....v. 14. (I shall lament after thy state, O Mind!......).

(vi) Gwaras pritshām sāsi late...... v. 26. (I asked the Guru a thousand times.....

(vii) Gwaran vŏnunam kunuy vatsun......v. 27. (The Guru gave me the word.....).

(viii) Dihici lari dāri bar trŏprim, Prāna-tsūr rŏṭum...v. 31 (Closing fast the windows and doors of my body. I caught hold of the thief—Prāṇa......)

(ix) Damāh dam kŏrmas damanhāle.....v. 33. (For a moment, I suppressed the bellows of my respiration...).

(x) Mal vŏṅdi zolum, jigar morum......v. 37. (I burnt up the impurities of my mind...)

(xi) Lal *bŏh* tsāyas swaman bāgabaras, Vuchum Shivas Shakt mīlith ta vāh...v. 44. (I, Lalla, willingly entered through the garden gate...), etc., etc.

Obviously her vakhs denote a series of spiritual evolution moving with a regulated pace from the outer to the inner world of knowledge—the knowledge of the Self. A number of concentric circles may help conjuring up the picture of the movement. At the periphery of the outermost circle stands the world of material phenomena, with all its attractions and repulsions, from where the Yogeśvari is driven, as it were, by the compulsion of her past karmas, her vāsanās and saṁskāras, to look for the Truth inwards, hidden as it is at the centre. A born yoginī, she becomes a seeker very early in life.

(iii) Synopsis

Naturally shy and demure, as all otherworldly people needs must be, Lalla is misunderstood by those with whom it was her lot to live. She becomes a victim of slander and calumny. But she does not swerve from her path. Dead earnest as she is to realize her self, she finds that patience and perseverance are her only weapons to ward off external pressures. She bears her domestic opposition with proverbial fortitude. The vakhs provide an evidence that she has moments of stark despair. Her despair, however, is not so much due to the uncongenial domestic atmosphere as to the fear lest her present life should run to waste without perfecting yoga. Born a spiritual prodigy, she has her voices that she is born to realize the self and meet her Lord face to face (v.3). But she does not know how to find the highway of salvation. (v. 19). To the domestic difficulties she finds an easy solution; she becomes deaf and dumb to her incriminators and carries on with her meditation (v. 10).

She is, however, in the doldrums in spite of her indifference to the onslaughts of the world of sense-perceptions. She is uncertain about her spiritual success. Her destination seems to be too far off. She wonders whether after all she would be ferried across the ocean of existence to the shore of salvation, to lead an immortal life in the lap of the Lord (v. 4).

The internal evidence points to the fact that, with the passage of time, her yogic practice becomes more and more intensive. She employs the paraphernalia as enjoined on the aspirants for mystical knowledge. Continence in food is stressed upon as the first pre-requisite, though she does not uphold fasting or physical mortification (vv. 11,80,81). The indriyas or organs of sense-perception must be brought under control (vv. 10,30, 31,34,70). Prāṇāyāma or regulation and control of breath is referred to in many verses (vv. 30,31,60,84). One cannot be too cautious against the deadly evils—Lust, Anger and Greed. She understands their inevitable, instinctive potentiality and teaches that they should be given proper consideration and be sublimated by being redirected to the thought of the Self within, (vv. 82,83). Of great importance is right action (v. 85). Lastly. mention must be made of her unshakable faith in the omniscience of the Lord (v. 22).

The Yogeśvari upholds the time-honoured injunctions of the Aṣṭāṅga or the Eight Limbs of the Yoga Discipline, viz., śama, dama niyama, pratyāhāra, prāṇāyāma, dhāraṇā and dhyāna,—as the preliminary means to the end of attainment of yoga. She does not preach what she did not practise. So the distinctive feature of her teaching is that she stresses the practical aspect of yoga and supports her precept by personal example (v. 31).

Śrī Śrīkaṇṭha, a Siddha i.e. an emancipated yogi of perfection, has been observing her from close quarters all the time and at the appropriate, propitious hour whispers the Word of initiation into her ear. The Guru's Word brings about a complete change in her. Demureness and secrecy are cast to the four winds, and rapturously she sings of her spiritual metamorphosis (v. 27).

Henceforth she concentrates on the inner world of Self and shuts the external world completely out. She fixes her mind on the Praṇava at the Nābhisthāna and practises the Kuṇḍalinī Yoga. The telling distinction of her approach to yoga is the importance she attaches to the Ādi-Bīja-mantra, OM. But it is the grace of the Lord—*Anugraha*—which is resorted to as the final key to salvation (v. 37). Continuous practice leads to the realization of the Self, as the most effulgent Light, within. (v. 33).

But the realization of the Self is not the end of her yoga. Her mystical ambition does not stop short of perfection, which is the dissolution of the individualized Self in the macrocosmic Self or Parama Śiva. Lalla concedes that it is not a child's play. She sees no end to warning the aspirant: "Shiv chuy krūṭh ta tsen vŏpadīsh"—Śiva is difficult (to attain), learn thou the lesson (v. 29).

Intensive practice culminates in perfection (v. 39). The Śakti is raised through the Six Cakras and the Śaśikalā sends down the stream of nectar (amrita). Verses 40,41,42, and 43 are adequate evidence of her attainment of perfection. She becomes a Jīvanmukta.

The merger of the individualized Self with the Absolute Being is an ineffable experience. Through her own "Ascent", the Yogeśvari carries us higher and higher helping us leave plane after plane of consciousness behind, till we are face to face with 'Shunyāh!' It must be an awful mystical state, indeed! The subtle planes of experience defy description. She sings: "Shunĕs

Shunyāh milith gav"—the Void mingled with the Void. What that adds up to is hard to explain and may well be left to yogis and mystics to unravel.

(*iv*) *Lalla's Teaching In A Nutshell*

Lalla-děd teaches the people to rise above the plane of sensory perceptions to the subtle plane of recognition and true knowledge. That is the plane of correct understanding. Once man rises to that height, narrow-mindedness and stubborn discrimination between man and man on the basis of accidents of birth, race, caste and creed are wiped out.

Her teaching has a devastating effect on the religious bigotry of man whose understanding is warped by misconceived notions of the ultimate Truth.

Her philosophy is simple. God-realization is an act of self-realization and recognition of the fact that though apparently cast in different moulds, we are all made of the same stuff. The Essence of creation is one and the same. The Mighty Being pervades us all.

Her teaching boils down to the basic tenet of all religious teaching,—The Universal Spirit is One, and we are but His earthly tabernacles. We must realize Him whose manifestations we are. The following vakh sums up her teaching:

Shiv chuy thali thali rav zān
Mav zān Hyŏnd ta Mussalmān
Trukhay chukh ta pananuy pān parzān
Ada chay Sāhibas sạtiy zäniyzān.

Lallavakya, shloka 88.
MS. Acc. No. 961.Research Lib. Srinagar.

Śiva, like the sun, shines everywhere;
Do not discriminate between a Hindu and a Muslim:
If thou art wise, recognize thy self;
That is the way of knowing the Lord.

(*v*) *Kashmir Śaivism And Lalla's Poetry*

The Key to Lalla's mysticism, from the evidence of the vakhs, is the Śivādvaita or the Trika philosophy of Kashmir. According to this school: "The Ātman, that is the true and innermost Self in everything and every being, is a changeless reality of the nature of a purely experiencing principle, as distinguished from whatever *may assume the form* of either the experience or of the means of experience."[1] In fact this philosophy of the Trinity (Śiva-Śakti-Aṇu) holds that there is no second Reality. The experiencing principle, the means of experience and the object of experience are, in essence, modes of one and the same Truth. The experiencer, the medium of experience and the object of experience are different aspects of the same all-pervading Śiva, in so much as it is He who assumes the forms simultaneously of the Experiencer and the experienced.

This Reality or Ātman has been given different names such as the Supreme Lord, Caitanya or Citi, Parmeśvara or Parama Śiva. Lalla calls It Śiva. In other religious philosophies too this same Eternal Reality, which is beyond the limitations of Time, Space and other dimensions, has been called variously according to the genius of each age and clime. "This Caitanya or Parama Śiva is the Reality which underlies as its innermost and true self not only every experiencing being but also everything else in the universe, both separately, i.e. individually, as well as a totality, i.e., as the entire universe as a whole."[2] Lalla yogeśvari contributes to this view, unequivocally. She says:

> Gagan tsay, bhūtal tsay,
> Tsay chukh dĕn, pavan ta rāth,
> Arg, tsaṅdun, posh, poñi tsay;
> Tsay chukh soruy ta lägizi kyāh? (v. 57)

and

> Aṅdriy āyas tsaṅdray gārān
> Gārān āyas hihĕn hih;
> Tsay hai Nārān, tsay hay Nārān, ,
> Tsay hai Nārān, yim kam vih? (v. 64)

and

> Tari salila khŏta tai tare
> Hĕmi trĕ gay bêŏn-abĕŏn vĕmarsha
> Tsetani rav bhāti sab same:
> Shivamai tsarātsar zag pashya. (v. 84)

1. *Kashmīr Shaivaism* J.C. Chatterjee, p. 43.
2. *Ibid* p. 44.

"As the underlying reality in everything and every being in the universe, Parama Śiva is one and the same in them all—undivided and unlimited by any of them, however much they may be separated either in time or in space. In other words, Parama Śiva is beyond the limits of time, space and form; and as such is Eternal and Infinite. ... He is all-pervading and at the same time He is also all-transcending. That is to say, His nature has primarily a twofold aspect—an immanent aspect in which He pervades the Universe and a transcendental aspect in which He is beyond all Universal manifestations. Indeed the Universe with all its infinite variety of objects, and means of experience, is nothing but a manifestation of the immanent aspect of Parama Śiva Himself. It has no other basis or ingredient in it."[1] The immanent aspect, in the Trika terminology, is called the Śakti. Thus *Śiva and Śakti are but two aspects of the same Absolute Being.* In the state of samādhi, the Yogeśvari recognizes the oneness of the two aspects. She says:

Lal bŏh tsāyas swamana bāgabaras,
Vuchum Shivas Shakt· mīlith ta vāh!
Tati lai karmas amritsaras,
Zindai maras ta mĕ kari kiyāh? (v.44)

In the exalted state of samādhi, all the apparent differences are effaced and blotted out. She says:

Bān gŏl tay, prakāsh āv zūne,
Tsaṅdar gŏl tay mwŏtuy tsĕth,
Tsĕth gŏl tay kĕṅh ti nā kune,
Gay Bhoor, Bhwāh, Swāh vĕsarzith kĕth. (v. 45)

The descent of Śakti or manifestation recognizes 36 tattvas or principles. Parama Śiva manifests Himself as the Universe of His own free will and without the use of any other material save His own power or Śakti, and in Himself as the basis of the Universe. (For details reference may be made to *Kashmir Shaivaism* by J.C. Chatterjee and *Abhinavagupta* by Dr. K. C. Pandey).

On this systematic theological base stands the structure of yoga, or the concept of the merger of the individuated Self and the Absolute Being. An individuated Self, as a manifestation of the Parama Śiva, is part and parcel of the Supreme Being. The

1. *Ibid.* pp. 44, 45. Also cf. *Praty. Hṛ.* Leidecker p. 28.

evil lies in the consciousness of the state of separation, i.e., the state of individuation and bliss accrues from the supreme consciousness of oneness of the microcosmic and the Macrocosmic Being.

Being a philosophy of positive acceptance of the immanent existence as an essential aspect of the Ultimate Being, *it is not the philosophy of escapism.* God is not to be looked for outside one's self. Self-realization is tantamount to God-realization. The external world is not an illusion or an unreality. Māyā-Śakti is only one of the powers of Śiva, as a force of obscuration which conceals the Reality of the manifested existence from the individual mind. Tearing away the veil of Māyā through true knowledge (Jñāna) one can recognize the Reality of the manifested things.

Lalla affirms this view. She does not consider it necessary to abandon hearth and home in search of the Lord. In fact, it is useless.

Kaṅděv gěh těza kaṇděv vanvās
Věphōl...... (v. 76)

Spiritual attainment boils down to a twofold process : *firstly*, discovering one's own self. As the individual is but a manifestation of the Lord, the yogi's attainment lies in discovering the self within. Lalla's joy knows no bounds when she is told to look for Him within herself (vv. 27, 31). She declares :

Pānas lägith rovukh mě tsa
Mě tsě tshāṅḍān lūstum dōh
Pānas maṅz yěli dyūṅṭhukh mě tsa
Mě tsě ta pānas dyutum tshōh. (v. 50)

Again in verse 51 she says :

"Suh yěli dyūṅtḥum nishi Pānas,
Soruy Suy ta bōh na kěṅh."

The fact that the Lord is witḥin you is amply substantiated by the verses 46 and 61.

Tshāṅḍān lūsas päni pānas,
Tshěpith jñānas votum na kūṅtsh...
Ase pōṅde zwase zāme...Nishi chuy ta parzāntan.

Secondly, yoga is perfected when the individual self is recognized as the Universal Self, when the consciousness of the union of the manifested and the unmanifested Self is brought about by a mystical discipline under the guidance of an adept in yoga, a master in mystical knowledge (a Jñāna-yogi). After discovering her Self, (cf. verse 33. Prazalyom däph ta nañyayam Zāth...) Lalla carries on intensive practice of yoga and by virtue of that realizes the Oneness (cf. v. 39. Abhyāsi Svavikās layi vŏthu, Gaganas sagun myūl samitsrāṭāh...Also, see vv. 40, to 45).

Yoga has been set down as of different forms such as : Rāja Yoga, Haṭha Yoga, Mantra Yoga, Jñāna Yoga, Bhakti Yoga, Laya Yoga etc. It is the last mentioned form of Yoga which Lalla Yogeśvari takes to, under the guidance of her preceptor. This yoga-krama or methodology seems to have suited the temperament, mood and traditional base of the Yogeśvari. Siddhmol, as her preceptor is popularly called, might have been himself a yogi of this order. The Yogeśvari, consequently, follows the path of Laya-yoga or Kuṇḍalinī Yoga.

There is a sprinkling of verses which bear out that Lalla was well acquainted with the Tantra-śāstras. What formal education she may have received in the field of Tantric lore cannot be ascertained with any certainty. But the internal evidence is that she was pretty well up in the esoteric formulae laid down in them. It is said that the Kashmiris, before the advent of Islam, were staunch adherents of Śākta-mata, or worshippers of the Goddess Śakti and did their Pūjā in accordance with the Tantric rituals. (cf. v. 13). At the least, Lalla appears to have received sufficient grounding in assimilating the knowledge propounded in the Ṣaṭ-cakra-nirūpaṇa or the six centres of the Cosmic Power in the human body. She may have received lessons from her Guru as to how to rouse Kuṇḍalinī Śakti lying coiled round the Svayambhū-Liṅga at the Mūlādhāra Cakra, and how to manage the Śakti on the subtle plane and bring Her up through the Six Centres to the highest of the Centres, Sahasrāra, which is said to be the Abode of Śiva.

The Yogeśvari refers to the Cakras in several verses which confirms our thesis. In verse 28, she says :

Akuy Oṁkār yus *Nābhi* dare
Kumbhai Brahmāṇḍas sum gare...

Concentrating on the Praṇava at the *Nābhi-padma* is a means to building a bridge up to *Sahasrāra* (Brahmāṇḍa), and she stresses the need of *Kumbhaka* or control of the breath. What is the bridge for ? We can conclude that the bridge is to make it possible for the Kuṇḍalinī Śakti to rise to the highest of the cakras. The Śakti is to be raised through the Sushumnā Nāḍī and it is a veritable problem to get hold of this subtle nāḍī. She admits her difficulty. She says in verse 29:

Zānha nāḍidal raṭith.....

She refers to the vṛttis or characteristic attributes of the cakras. She says.

Nābhisthānas chai prakrath zalvañi
Hridistām yati Prān vatagŏt
Brahmāṅḍas pĕṭh shīt nad vahavani......

Other relevant verses in this connection are 53 and 54. But the most significant reference which finally seals the conclusion that she had been taught the Kuṇḍalinī yoga and took to Laya-krama is the following verse :

Shĕ van tsaṭith Shĕshikal vuzam,
Prakrath huṅzam pavana säti......(v. 38).

This is an affirmation of the fact that she had successfully raised the Śakti up through the six Cakras, and made Her lick the Nectar oozing from the Shĕshikala. Also in v. 42., she says : "Tavai Shĕshikal vĕgalith vatsham..." In v. 44., we are told categorically that her yoga was of this style. She says, "Tati lai karmas amritsaras." A quotation from *The Serpent Power* may help us to understand this. "The union of the Śakti-Kuṇḍalinī with Śiva in the body of the Sādhaka is that coition of the Sāttvik Pañca-tattva which the *Yoginī-tantra* says is the best of all unions for those who have already controlled their passions", and are thus 'Yati' (यति).

Of this the Bṛhat-Śrīkrama says : "They with the eye of knowledge see the stainless Kalā united with Cidānanda on Nāda. He is the Mahādeva, white like a pure crystal, and is the effulgent cause (Bimbarūpa-nidāna) and She is the lovely woman of beauteous limbs which are listless by reason of her great passion." "On their union nectar flows which in ambrosial stream runs from Brahmarandhra to the Mūlādhāra, flooding the Kṣudra-brahmāṇḍa or microcosm and satisfying the Devatas of its Cakras. It is then that the sādhaka, forgetful of all in this world, is immersed in the ineffable Bliss. Refreshment, increased power and enjoyment follows upon each visit to the well of life."[1]

Verses 39, 44 and 45 strongly support the view that Lalla attained the mystical state of samādhi and was 'liberated' from the bondage of life and death by the yoga of Laya-krama. Her ascending vakhs culminate on the note of perfection, as described in the Tantras. "Well concealed, and attainable only by great effort, is that subtle Bindu (Śūnya) which is the chief root of liberation and which manifests the pure Nirvāna-kalā with Amā-kalā (the nectar-dropping digit of the Moon). He is the Brahman and the Ātman of all Beings. In Him are united both Rasa and Virasa (the bliss of liberation arising from the union of Śiva and Śakti), and He is the Sun which destroys the darkness of nescience and delusion."[2]

[Also for details on the evolution of self by awakening the 'sleeping' Kuṇḍalinī Power, *Saundaryalaharī* and *Devātma Śakti* by Swami Vishnu Tirth Ji Maharaj may be usefully consulted].

(*vi*) *An Apology*

Holding me at the bar of conscience, a really curious observer, or even one inclined to pick a large, obvious hole in a seemingly patched garment, may pose a very pertinent question: Did Lalla-dĕd sing her vakhs in the sequence in which they have been arranged by me? Or, a still more quizzical query may be made as to whether she did intend that her vakhs should be presented to the world in this order. To these explosive questions which, to a superficial reader, may appear to shake the very foundation of this rickety frame-work, all that one can give by way of a reassuring reply with utmost humility is: WHO CAN TELL ? Rummaging all the available historical records, such as

1. Jona Rāja — *Rājatarangiṇī* edited by Prof. S.K. Kaul.

1. *Serpent Power*. pp. 274-275.
2. *Ibid*. p 481. *Ṣaṭ-Cakra-nirūpaṇa*, v. 42.

2. *Navadir-al-Akhbar*	History of Kashmir, microfilm, original in British Museum. Research Library, Srinagar. Acc. No. 69.
3. *Baharitani Shahi*	Microfilm; original in India Office, London. Size 20.26/4; Pages 212. R.L. Sgr. MS. Acc. No. 691. Dated 1023 H.
4. Malikh Haider Chadorvi	*History of Kashmir* written between 1605-27, in the time of the Mughal Emperor, Jehangir, R.L. Sgr. MS, Acc. No. 39.
5. Khwaja Mohammad A'zm, Dedamari	*History of Kashmir* entitled Waqaya Kashmir. Dated 1747.
6. Pir Ghulam Hassan Khuyihami	*Tarikhi-Hassan*, vol. 111 (Tazkirat-ul Avlia). Dated 1833-98.
7. Pandit Birbal Kachroo	*History of Kashmir* from early times upto 1846 A.D. R.L. Sgr. MS Acc. No. 14.
8. Mohammad-ud Din Fouq	*History of Kashmir* published from Lahore. Dated May 19, 1910.
9. Abdul Ahad Azad	Cultural Academy Publication, vol. I. Srinagar, 1959.

has been almost futile. In the historical archives nearer Lalla-dĕd's age, there is only a passing reference to a lady mystically absorbed, God-mad in her ways and possessing miraculous powers. A'zmi, Hassan, Kăchroo and all those who followed have taken their material information from the lap of tradition. Even the Rishi-nāmās and Noor-nāmās—extant manuscripts—have little light to throw on any organized body of the Lalla-vakhs. Not infrequently the vakhs of Lalla-dĕd and the 'shruks or verses of Sheikh Noor-uddin (Vali) have been mixed up, and only a very careful study and discerning sifting is necessary to disentangle the intertwined mystical poetry of the two. Under the circumstances, one has to fall back upon tradition and tradition is always a hotchpotch.

(*vii*) *Sources of the Lalla-Vakhs in the present text*

1. *Lalla Vākyāni*: Sir George Grierson & Lionel D. Barnett., 1920.

2. *Lalavākya*: Bhaskara: Kashmiri-Sanskrit: Śāradā Script C. P. Size—20 cm. by 15 cm.: Acc. No. 797. MS. Research Library, Srinagar.

3. *Lalavākya*: Country-paper: Śāradā Script: MS. Size 16 cm. by 12 cm. Acc. No. 961., Research Library, Srinagar.

4. *Lalavākya*: MS. Acc. No. 1335. Country-paper, No of Folios pages 6. Śāradā Script. Size 30 by 18., R.L. Srinagar.

5. *Sayings of Lalleshwari*: Pandit Anand Kaul Bamzai: Reprinted from the Indian Antiquary, vol. LX, 1931 and vol. LXI, 1932. Sri P. S. Public Library, Srinagar.

6. Lalla Number, *Käshur Samāchār*: January-February 1971, New Delhi.

(*viii*) *Acknowledgements*

I cannot omit acknowledgement of my debt of gratitude to Sir George Grierson, K.C.I.E., Ph.D., D.Litt., M.R.A. S., and Lionel D. Barnett, D. Lit., M.R.A.S. who took all the pains to dig out the vakhs of Lalla-dĕd and to purify them of the dross that had collected around them over the centuries. Grierson's *Lallā-Vākyāni* includes sixty vakhs rendered into Sanskrit by Shri Bhaskar Razdan. I am also grateful to Pandit Dina Nath, in charge of the Sanskrit Section of the Research Library, Srinagar, for reading to me the MSS. of *Lallāvākyas* written in Śāradā script.

My thanks are due to Shri P.N. Bhan, Headmaster, and to Pandit Vidh Lal Kaul Aima for encouraging me to take up the difficult task of writing this book, and for going through some parts of the manuscript.

I must acknowledge thanks to all those authors and their publishers whose books have been consulted in the preparation and presentation of this humble volume by one who has little pretension to Sanskrit scholarship and much less to any yogic practice. I owe my inspiration to William James, LL.D. etc., through his Gifford Lectures published in *The Varieties of Religious Experience—a study in human nature.* I am also indebted to the University Grants Commission, Government of India, New Delhi, who selected me under the scheme: "Utilization of the services of distinguished retired university teachers," (1972-77), and placed at my disposal some contingency grants.

I acknowledge my indebtedness to Professor S. K. Toshakhani, Chief Editor, *Kashmiri Dictionary*, Cultural Academy, Srinagar, for going through the text of Lalla-vakhs written in Devanagari script and helping me with his valuable suggestions, particularly in the preparation of the 'key'. I record my thanks to Shri Mohan Raina, a reputed artist, who prepared the jacket design for the book at a very short notice.

My acknowledgements would be incomplete without recording my deep sense of gratitude to Dr. K. L. Shrimali who wrote the Foreword to this book; to Swami Muktananda ji and revered Dr. Gopi Nath Kaviraj of Banaras for their blessings; and lastly to Professor S.L. Dar (Ex-Registrar B.H.U.) for his constant encouragement.

Srinagar, June 1978 **B. N. Parimoo**

AIDS TO PRONUNCIATION

ʌ	a	=अ	(as the short u sound in muster, duster)
a :	ā	=आ	(as the a sound in hall, fall)
i	i	=इ	(as the i sound in this, his)
i :	ī	=ई	(as the long e sound in geese, these)
u	u	=उ	(as the vowel sound in hook, brook, cook)
u :	ū	=ऊ	(as in cool, coop)
ɔ:	o	=ओ	(as in both, hope)
au	av	=औ	(as in bough, or cow)
ei=e		=ए	(as in they, gay, lay)
ai	ai,ay	=ऐ	(as in die, lie)
	ṅ	=अं	(For nasal sound of n as in sank, drank)
	ṁ	=म्	(as in drum, sum)
tʃ	c	=च	(as in choose, chicken)
	ch	=छ	(aspirate c)
ʃ	ś	=श	(as in shine, sheep)
	ṣ	=ष	

Note—In Kashmiri 'bh' is pronounced as 'b'. In transliteration into the Roman alphabet, the aspirate has ben indicated by 'bh'

Sounds peculiar to Kashmiri and the diacritical marks adopted:—

t=त, ṭ=ट, d=द, ḍ=ड, th=थ, ṭh=ठ, ñ=ञ

ts =च़ as in Kashmiri चास (cough) = tsās
चख (anger) = tsakh
चल । (run away) = tsal

tsh=छ़ as in Kashmiri छाया (shadow) = tshāy
छल (trick) = tshal
छठ (a gust of wind)=tshaṭh

ju : yū =यू as in university, universal and in Kashmiri
न्यूल (green) =nyūl
म्यूल (met) =myūl

ə: ä =आ़ as in Kashmiri आ़स (mouth) = äs = ə: s
का़म (work) =Käm = kə: m

a̤ =अ़ as in Kashmiri तअ़र (cold) =ta̤r
कअ़र (cruel) =ka̤r

ĕ = Restrained sound of e as in Macbeth, Elizabeth, taketh in English and in Kashmiri
Khĕth = ख्यथ tsĕth = चयथ
Dapinĕm = दपिन्यम

ŏ = Restrained sound of o, as in Kashmiri
gŏl = गो॒ल (melted)
hŏl = हो॒ल (curved)
bŏh = बो॒ह (I)

KEY TO THE PRONUNCIATION OF KASHMIRI WRITTEN IN SUITABLY MODIFIED DEVANAGARI SCRIPT

A. Vowels peculiar to Kashmiri:

1. अं or (') indicates the short sound of 'a' as in Kashmiri
   अंड = half;
   अंछ = eye;
   लंर = house.

2. आ॑ or (ॏ) is the long vowel sound of the above and is pronounced as 'u' in curd or surd (English words).
   In Kashmiri, we have आ॑स = mouth;
   ना॑र = jug;
   दा॑र = window;
   ला॑र = cucumber.

3. उ॒ or (˘) as in Kashmiri
   तॖर = tatter (singular)
   तॖरॖ = tatters (plural);
   खॖर = slip.

4. उ़ or (ॗ) long sound of the above.
   as in Kashmiri
   तॗर = cold;
   कॗर = hard-hearted;
   दॗफ = a kind of incense;
   (Hindi धूप)
   चॗन = bits; filings.

(*Note*: I have not been able to find vowel sounds corresponding to 3 and 4, either in English or any Indian language known to me).

5. ओ॒ or (ॊ) the sound of short 'o' as the first 'o' in 'opinion', or 'oppress.'
   In Kashmiri, we have
   ओ॒न = blind;
   सो॒न = deep;
   गो॒न = thick; dense; multiple.

B. Consonants :

1. च़ written as 'ts' in the Romanized script. This consonant is found in Marathi and Telugu also.

In Kashmiri, we have चम़=skin;
चास़=cough;
चल़=go away.

In Marathi, they say चाक़=knife;
चांदी=silver;
चटाई=mat;
चरखा=spinning-wheel;

In Telugu, they say चदु़उ=education;
चूचुट=seeing;
चप्पुन=immediately.

2. छ़ ='tsh' is the aspirated form of च़
In Kashmiri, we write छठ=wind;
छाय=shadow;
गछ़=go.

3. ज़ =English 'z'
In Kashmiri, जङ्ग=leg;
जल=water;
जाल=net;
रज़=rope.

C. Soft aspirates such as घ, झ, ढ, ध, भ are not found in Kashmiri, so that we write

गऱ	corresponding to	Hindi or Sanskrit	घर
जगडु	"	"	झगडा
दोब	"	"	धोबी
डकुन	"	"	ढकन
बगवान	"	"	भगवान
प्रबा	"	"	प्रभा

and so on.

1

HISTORICAL APATHY

Of the myriad springs which have fed the thought-channels of Kashmir over the centuries, fostering an emancipated, cosmopolitan outlook on life, that of the mystical poetry of Lalla-ded is the most profound. That her biography should be recorded only on the pages of oblivion is, therefore, a matter for regret. Quite a few versions are extant about the place of her birth. But, in the face of differences in these versions, no authenticity can be attached to them. However, the majority of evidence holds that she was born at Sempur, a village near Pampore, to a Kashmiri Brahman named Shri Cheda Bhat or Shri Chandra Bhat,[1] in the year 1382 Bikrami Samvat, corresponding approximately to 1326 A.D., i.e. about six hundred and forty six years ago. She saw the light of the day on the auspicious night of the full moon in the Bikrami month, Bhadoon, corresponding to September.

1. Shri Ramjoo Pandit Malla, a revenue official who functioned as a Patwari at Pampore for some time and whose address is given as Peerbagh Hyderpore, has written an interesting booklet, Lalla A'rifa Saheba, in Urdu on the biography of Lalleshwari and the actual authorship and source have been ascribed to one Mahatma Devi Bhagat Ji Maharaj. This is a recent publication and does not quote any authority in support of the biographical or other data put forward by him. All the same the names of the father, father-in-law and the husband of Lalla-ded have been adopted from this booklet, because these names do not tilt the balance of the purpose of this book in any way, and because there is no other source to tap, known so far.

Khawaja Mohammad A'zam Dedmari, Kashmiri,[1] makes no mention of the birthplace of Lalla-ded. He mentions her only as a God-mad, "self-absorbed", wandering saint with miraculous powers. He places her in the time of Sultan Ala-ud-Din who breathed his last in 758 Hijri. This historian relates an interesting anecdote about Lalla-ded who helped Sultan Shahabud-Din ascend the throne of his father, by making him drink two cups of milk. Shri A'zam does not throw any light on the parental nest of this mystical lark of Kashmir. All that Hassan,[2] a well known later historian of Kashmir, has to tell us is : "(this Saint) is known by many names, such as Lalla-ded, Lalla-moj, Lalleshwari etc. She was born in the 8th century Hijri, at the village of Sempore, in the house of a Kashmiri Pandit. The date and day of her birth is not correctly known. From her very childhood her ways were extraordinary. She heard voices from

Note:— Shri J. N. Bhan, Shri Nand Lal Chatta and Shri P. N. Kaul Bamzai locate her birth-place at Pandrethan or Purāṇādhisṭhāna of yore. Their articles were published in *Kashur Samāchār*, February 1971, New Delhi.

1.

واقعات تاریخ کشمیر - اعظمی - 1747A.D.

"سلطان علاء الدین در سنه هفتصد و پنجاه و هشت به بیماری در گذشت ....
سلطان شهاب الدین پسر سلطان علاء الدین بعد فوت پدر بزرگوار بمشوره امرای نامدار بر تخت نشست
که پیش از جلوس در زمان پدر عالی مقدار طرف جنگلی بتقریب شکار رفته بود و از مجذوبه کامله دو پیالهٔ شیر
خورده و بشارت سلطنت یافته بود. گویند که آن مجذوبه لله عارفه است. و دو رفیق همراه داشت یکی
چندارو دوم اوشه را اول آن مجذوبه این هر دو کس را بدستور بعد عطای حصهٔ شیر و بشارت وزارت داده
فرموده که علامت این اخبار آنست که آخته جی سلطان که بهره شیر نیافته بود پیش از رسیدن بخانه خواهد مرد .....
ذکر عارفه کامله لله مجذوبه ظهورش در زمان سلطان علاء الدین بود (هفتصد و چهل و هشت هجری). اوائل گرفت اهل
قید عقد شخصی شده و تاهل و خانداری در افتاده در همان اثنا جذبه الهی او را داده دل بانقطاع و انزوا نهاده چندی
بسیر و خفائی بیگذرانید و کسی از خویش و پیوندی بحالت باطنی آن مجذوبه در دمند نمیبرد ....."

This historian uses the word " گویند " (they say). Obviously, his brief account of Lalla-ded is based on hearsay and tradition. No mention is made of the names of the parents or the husband of Lalla-ded, nor of any sources of his information.

2. *History of Kashmir* by Hassan, in Urdu, Vol. 3. p. 447.

the unknown and had holy visions..." Tradition and history tell us that she lived at the time of the visit to Kashmir by Syed Ali Hamdani, popularly known Shahi-Hamdan, who came from Bukhara in 1379-80. That does place Lalla-ded somewhere in the middle of the 14th century, without any shadow of doubt.

Apart from circumstantial evidence, we have no definite, authoritative information to fall back upon. Sir Richard Temple, in *The Word of Lalla, the Prophetess,* in spite of his long, erudite introduction, does not help us in regard to the family antecedents of Lalla-ded. If, therefore, anything helps us today to reconstruct the story of her life, and, more than that, the story of the evolution of her spiritual life, it is the *internal evidence* of her poetry, and the tradition which has preserved not only the "vakhs" but also titbits about her life, passed on by word of mouth from generation to generation down the dark corridors of Time. Social upheavals and political vicissitudes that Kashmir has been subject to over the centuries have not rubbed out the memory of this "Realized-soul", the depth and magnitude of whose mystical poetry beggars description. On the contrary, she is remembered today as if she were with us the other day.

As already said, history has been callously silent about the pedigree, the occupations and the predilections of both Shri Chandra Bhat (father) and Shri Shiva Bhat (father-in-law of Lalleshwari) of Pampore. What little is known of Shri Soma Bhat, son of Shri Shiva Bhat, is entirely founded on traditional folk-tales. That it was an unequal marriage is corroborated by subsequent events and Lalla's verses. It appears that he was a molly and held on to the apron-strings of his mother.

2

CHILDHOOD

Perhaps nobody took note of Lalla as a child. The parents generally take their children for granted and, more often than not, even precocious children are neglected. The introverts suffer particularly, insomuch as they do not demand attention like the extroverts. How long Lalla lay buried in the unfathomable depths of her own musings nobody knows.

Shri Chandra Bhat was a big landowner and lived at Khona-Moha[1] for sometime. He must have been a pious, religious man, of course, for the Lord in the *Bhagvadgītā* says that those who do not accomplish yoga in their lifetime, despite their best efforts, take birth in the house of a yogi or a pious man.[2] Yoga continues to be practised birth after birth until perfection is reached. The environment and the parentage obtained for this purpose are said to be congenial. Of the two types of favourable

1. Malla tells us that Chandra Bhat was a devotee of Mahādeva and paid frequent visits to the cave of Harshishwar. We are also told that he and his wife knew of the "lion" who carried their young daughter to the cave for pūjā and brought her back. But what they did about it, he does not tell us. Under the circumstances, should they have considered and carried out ner marriage ? There is no internal evidence to support Shri Malla. The legendary "lion" may be symbolical. Shri Malla also tells us that two springs, one at Khona-Moha and the other at Chasmashahi welled up on the day Lalla was born.

2. *Bhagavadgītā*, VI, 41, 42.

families, that of the wise yogis is superior to that of the pure and prosperous.[1] A close study of Lalla's verse leaves one in no doubt that her parental home had been a veritable yogic school and a spiritual seminary for the budding, enthusiastic child. Her verse is replete with evidence that she had made intensive study of the Gītā and the Upaniṣads.[2] In the Brahmin families of Kashmir around-the-hearth discussions on topics relating to Śaivaism,[3] could not have flown over her head. And it is not unlikely that she sponged up theoretical Śaivaism as it flowed around her.

Abhinavagupta,[4] in the long line of yogi-philosophers of Kashmir Śaivaism beginning with Vasugupta who, it is said, received the Śiva Sūtras inspirationally, lived towards the end of the tenth and the beginning of the eleventh century of the Christian Era. Kṣemrāja, Yogrāja and Jayaratha continued and carried forward, with commentaries, the Śaiva philosophy of the masters. We can safely hazard a guess that, being nearer to the heyday of Śaivaism than we are by about six hundred years, Lalla must have strongly felt the impact of that great philosophy. As the translation of and commentary on her verse will show, her yoga stands poised on the kingpin of this philosophy. Śaivaism and Vedānta have much meeting ground and Lalla's thought and discipline must have made the best of both the philosophies. It is said that she met Siddha Śrīkaṇṭha or Siddhamol[5] while she was only seven : he was the family Guru. If that be so, we

1. *Bhagavadgītā* by Swami Chidbhavananda, p. 405.

2. References in the foot-notes are a clear testimony to this claim.

3. Lalla-ded hails her Lord by the name of Śiva, throughout her verse.

4. Abhinavagupta (933 to 1015 A. D.):

"A great Shaiva Yogi of Kashmir, and author of commentaries on Utpalacharya's works and on the Para-Trimishka (Tantra). He also composed the great work Tantraloka, which is an independent treatise, and the Tantrasara, besides numerous other works. He thus became the one dominant influence of his own and subsequent ages in all matters relating to Kashmir Shaivaism." J. C. Chatterjee. *Kashmir Shaivism* pp. 38, 42. 1962.

5. Malla. p. 4.

cannot but conclude that she had the benefit of the guidance of a great scholar and yogi early in life.[1]

Lalla's hold on Sanskrit is pretty strong, and it is obvious that the Kashmiri language of her time had a substratum of Sanskrit to support it. Persian, which later became the court language and also the language of the elite, and in course of time was profusely sucked into the Kashmiri vocabulary and syntax, does not seem to have seeped into the Kashmiri homes yet.

Aside of learning Sanskrit, Lalla, a born yogeśvarī, may have pursued study of the Hindu scriptures under the able guidance of her father and the family Guru.

It is said that she was married when she was hardly between ten and eleven and her new haven was a Brahmin family of Pampore (Padmanpora of old),[2] only a few miles away from Sempura. At her in-laws, she was named Padmānded (or Padmâvati).

So passed her early years unobserved and unrecorded. And we are the poorer for all that.

1. Sheikh Nur-ud-din (Vali), a great mystic saint and junior contemporary of Lalla-ded, says:

"Totḥyokh Siddha Shrikanṭhas siddhas
Tyuthuy mĕ var dito Dīva."

It is taken from a long prayer of the Sheikh for God's grace.

MS. by Mir Haqir Abdullah, Mutvatni Kashmir. 1256 H.

2. Sheikh Nur-ud-din (Vali) says:

Tas Padmānporaci Lalle
Tami gale amrit pivā
Sŏh säni avtār lŏle
Tyuthuy mĕ var dito Divā.

MS. *Nur-Nama* (Mir Abdullah).

3

THE ORDEAL

Lalla's age was less sophisticated and more disciplined than ours. The family unit was a small kingdom where the mother-in-law reigned supreme. Tradition paints Lalla's mother-in-law in the darkest colours. A termagant and a shrew : a veritable ogress ! Short of eating the plum of a daughter-in-law, she did everything to make her miserable. They say she went even to the length of starving her. A round, white stone was placed in her eating-bowl. The stone was covered with rice to give it the semblance of a big lump of food. This information is based on an incident and we hang it on the peg of a verse current to this day. It is said that on a day of feasting, a neighbouring lady, — as is the wont among ladies of Kashmir even today — asked her what she had had for dinner. Pat came the reply:[1]

I. Hŏnd māran yā Kaṭh
Lali nīlvath tsali na zāṅh

हों_ड मारन या कठ
लल्लि नीलुवठ चलि नु जांह ॥१॥

Whether they killed a large sheep or a small one,
Lalla had her round stone (as her usual fare).

1. This 'vakh' has become proverbial for expression of resentment against ill treatment and poor food.

It is said that Shri Shiva Bhat somehow came to know of the episode of the round stone and, for once at least, asserted his authority as head of the family and Lalla's bowl lost the companionship of that stone for good. But this did not usher in a new era of domestic peace for her. On the other hand, thwarted in her manipulation, the elder lady racked her brain for fresh manoeuvres. There was no end to taunts and gibes the child-bride received from her mother-in-law. She was even scandalized and her husband's ears were poisoned.

But that is, *prima facie,* a lopsided assessment. There must be two to a quarrel. What was after all Lalla's fault ? What was the source of the mother-in-law's bile and pique ? Mothers-in-law have always been maligned. Nobody pays heed to their version of the case, to their tale of woe. Tradition has gone out of the way to disfigure the image of Shri Shiva Bhat's wife. Not a word is mentioned to extenuate her guilt. Lalla is painted as an ideal daughter-in-law, by the standards of the fourteenth century. She would meticulously attend to the needs of the father-in-law, helping him with water; washing the floors of the house with cowdung and yellow clay; preparing the vegetables and attending to a hundred odd jobs of the household. But a description of absolute correctness smacks of dollishness or a fairy tale. Very often the woe of mothers-in-law springs out of sheer misunderstanding of things or an affront to their acute awareness of self-respect.

It is quite probable that Lalla's foible was her other-worldly demeanour. *That* did not fit in with the exclusively 'this worldly', material view of the folk around her. The residual imprints of the actions of her past lives — her saṁskāras and vāsanās[1] — had predisposed her in a way which her mother-in-law failed to grasp. Spiritual predilections, garnered by her during her

1. Cf. Cosmic Dissolution and Evolution: "At the time of Dissolution (Pralaya) there is in consciousness as Mahā-kuṇḍalī, though undistinguishable from its general mass, the potentiality or seed of the universe to be. Māyā, as the worldly, potentially exists, as Mahākuṇḍali, who is Herself one with consciousness or Śiva. This Māyā contains, and is, in fact, constituted by the collective Saṁskāra and Vāsanā — i.e., the mental impressions and tendencies produced by Karma accomplished in previously existing worlds."
The Serpent Power—Woodroffe. p. 43. Also: *Bhagavadgītā*, VI 43.

sojourn through life after life, may have coloured her conduct so as to make it appear strange and abnormal to the mother-in-law. Lalla's extraordinary patience and forbearance; her practice of penance and self-mortification; her endurance with the stone in the bowl; and a thousand shades of difference between the approach to life of the two, may have set her mother-in-law at her wit's end, much the same way as was the case with the shrewish wife of Socrates.[1] Sages and mystics are often misunderstood.

Lalla had chosen her path or, we might say, that it had been chosen for her by the spiritual momentum of her past lives. Her *will* and *destiny* joined hands to carve a surer way up the climb. Like Prince Siddhārtha, she came across chance incidents to brood upon. She naturally desired to break off the bonds of attachment of the limited self to the worldly things. She says:

2. Gātulāh akh vuchum bŏcha säty marān
Pan zan harān Pŏhani vāva lāh
Nĕshibodh akh vuchum vāzas mārān
Tana Lalla bŏh prārān tshĕnĕm-na prāh.

गादुलाह् अख वुछुम ब्वछि स़ूत्य मरान
पन ज़न हरान पोह्नि वावुलाह
न्यशबो़द अख वुछुम वाज़स मारान
तनु लल बो़ह प्रारान छ़यन्यम ना प्राह ॥२॥

I saw a wise man starving for want of food.
Emaciated, he seemed to wither and fall like autumn leaves.
I saw a fool beating his cook !
Since then have I, Lalla, been waiting for the bonds to break off.

The event of seeing a wise man starving, and a fool feeding sumptuously and still not satisfied with his cook, was an eye-

1. It is related that when the Greek philosopher refused to be drawn into a verbal bout and when his wife's vituperation fell upon deaf ears, fretting and fuming she poured a jug of water over his head. The story goes that instead of fulminating back, the sage quietly observed: "After thunder comes the rain!"

opener for her. She was convinced that the order of the world was fortuitous and some mysterious power managed life. She looked forward to the day when the chains of the earthly cares and worldly ambitions and attachments should break and allow her freedom to devote herself to self-realization, exclusively.

Her acute observation of the facts of life was not, however, incidental. The pricked ears and wide-open eyes and, above all, a discerning mind had, in the background, a deep-seated conviction of the value and goal of human life. Imbued with the teachings of the Lord in the *Bhagavadgītā* and other scriptures, she well knew she could not swerve from the path destined for her. Realization of the self was the end she would strive for, and no obstacle, however great, would deflect her from that path. She says:

3. Āyas ti syŏduy ta gatsha ti syŏduy
Sĕdis hŏl mĕ karem kyāh
Bŏh tas āsas āgarai vĕzay
Vĕdis ta vĕndis karĕm kyāh.

आयस ति स्यो_दुय त गछु ति स्यो_दुय
स्यदिस हो_ल म्यं कर्यम क्याह
बो_ह तस आंसस आगरय व्यं.जय
व्यदिस त व्यंदिस कर्यम क्याह ॥३॥

I have come straight and straight shall I go back;
Who can warp me out of my shape ?
I knew Him from the source (or beginning),
Oh ! who can harm one acquainted with and familiar to Him ?

This vakh springs from the conviction that her longing to see her Lord was not a passing fancy. Since success in yoga is not a matter of a day and not even a matter of several births in this world, she had made up her mind to cling to the straight path and make the most of her present life. She was conscious of the direction her spiritual boat was to sail in, and nothing could deflect the needle of the compass guiding her. She could not be warped out of shape by external forces and pressures, however vehement and antagonistic they might be. Embedded in the faith that in the phase of Śiva-tattva, the Lord as the All-Experiencer knew her, and in the phase of Śakti-tattva she had been born as an individual, she was determined to make up and see that this life was the last of the cycles. Her faith was buttressed by her inborn hope that one, who is already acquainted with the Lord, is not deserted by Him in the hour of need. She was sure that the ignorant and the crooked could bring the righteous to no harm. It is not a case of self-righteousness but one of self-confidence. The mortar of faith combined with hope becomes stronger than granite, impregnable.

Lalla seems to have picked up, even at this early stage, the essentials of Kashmir Śaivaism. In the Śiva-tattva, the All Experiencer sees All this, in the ideal state. That is, at the source (Āgrai) Lalla was known to Śiva.[1] In the immanent world, we only get limited and individualized. She wanted to get out of the world of manifestation and merge with the Transcendental Absolute.

Towing the boat of her soul by herself was a problem to reckon with. She must have had moments of forlorn wretchedness. Self-assurance is an attribute of the yogis. But Lalla had miles to go to that destination. As yet her boat of the soul was tossing on the billows of uncertainty. And uncertainty is not far short of affliction. Her prayer has, therefore, an undertone of a wail and a sob. She says:—

4. Āmi pana sŏdaras nāvi chĕs lamān,
Kati bozi Dai myon mĕti diyi tār
Āmĕn ṭākĕn poñ zan shĕmān
Zuv chum bramān gara gatshaha.

1. "The world is nothing other than the objectified content of the consciousness of the divine soul, and as such identical with it. God is cause as well as effect and is the *Causa Efficiens* and *Causa Materialis* of the world at one and the same time. . . ."

Pratyabhijñāhṛdayam, Kṣemarāja. Intr. by Leidecker, p. 12.

Also cf. *Īśāvāsya-Upaniṣad.* Mantra 4.

The Lord having been there before anything else knows everything from the beginning.

आँमि पन संदरस नावि छुस लमान
कति बोज़ि दय म्योन म्यंति दियि तार
आँम्यन टाक्यन पोञ जन शमान
.जुव छुम ब्रमान गर ग.छु हा ॥४॥

I am towing the bark on the river[1] with a rope of untwined yarn,
How I wish my God were to help ferry me across !
(My efforts are wasting away) like water poured in an unbaked earthen dish, getting absorbed or leaking with a frizzling sound;
How I long for return Home !

Deep down her soul, there was a burning desire to meet her Lord, the eternal Home. Metaphorically speaking, Parama Śiva is the 'Home' of man, for the immanent world is said to be His expression, the shining forth. Lalla's longing, therefore, is based on knowledge of the Truth. But knowledge alone would not suffice. There were not a few obstacles in her way. Her social environment was not at all congenial for spiritual practice. Her efforts at concentration and yogic practice appeared to her as difficult and vain as the attempt of a sailor to pull a boat across an ocean with a rope of untwined yarn. Without the rudder of a guide and the oars of yogic practice, she felt, as it were, lost on a stormy sea. Her efforts seemed to go to waste as water poured into an unbaked earthen dish. In that condition of despondence, she seeks God's benign grace to ferry her boat of spirit across the ocean of existence. Fain would she merge her little self in the Cosmic Self, which was its home.

A student of Indian mysticism may trace the developed individual form back to its seed. By and large, we hold the view that a Jīvanmukta or a perfected soul is not a freak. It is held that it takes quite a few life-times to evolve spiritually and ascend back Home. Birth after birth, the self strives to give up

1. Boats are towed with a rope along the bank of a river. The ocean has no bank, as such. But in mystical parlance, it is conventional to use the word, 'ocean' instead of 'river'. We say: the ocean of existence, of ignorance, etc.

the material clothing for good. Transmigration,[1] in that sense, is a necessity, not only as it is natural owing to the law of Karma but also as it affords an opportunity to those who choose to break off the chains and throw away the clothes for ever and ever and return 'home' never to roam apart until He wills.

We cannot make out the meaning of the following vakh without assuming that she had to bear a heavy burden of ill-treatment. Her unworthy husband behaved like a screech-owl blinking at the light of truth. Instigated by his mother, he too was on the rampage. However that may be, she would not turn back as Christian does not in the *Pilgrim's Progress*. Lalla had planted her feet firmly and she knew that the path of knowledge was not strewn with roses. She says:

5. Tsālani chaĭ vuzamala ta traṭai
   Tsālun chu mandiñan gaṭakār
   Tsālun chu pān- paṇun kaḍun graṭai
   Hĕti māli santūsh' vāti pānai.

चालनि छय वुज़मल त त्रटय
चालुन छु मंदिन्यन गटकार
चालुन छु पान पनुन कडुन ग्रटय
ह्यति मालि संतूष वाति पानय ॥५॥

One has to bear lightning flashes and thunderbolts.
One has to put up with pitch darkness at mid-day:
Forbearance is tantamount to getting ground to powder between the mill-stones,
(If one can stand all this), contentment and peace attend on you.

A terrible ordeal could not be couched in an apter language. She had to face a storm of flashing lightning and deafening thunder. The mid-day sun would get veiled in a cloak of darkness. Lalla was patience incarnate. She was a Job. Patience is like getting ground between two mill-stones; the lower one the immovable strength of faith and the upper one of the antagonistic forces

1. *Bhagavadgītā*, II, 13, 22.

bent upon pulverizing you. Her patience seems to have been the compound of faith and hope. Optimism is her hallmark. Patience would pave the way to contentment and peace, she says.

Esoterically the vakh may be interpreted to signify terrific flashes of lightning and thundering vibrations she experienced during her attempts at yogic practice, all by herself. Suddenly the abnormal light she experienced switched off into pitch darkness. Perhaps she dabbled with Kuṇḍalinī in the basal centre (Mūlādhāra)[1] and had the experience of flashing lightning; she may have disturbed the vital breaths in the Nāḍīs and heard the awful thundering vibrations on the subtle plane.

But the last line of the vakh does not imply mystical visions and the next vakh supports this view.

6. Ösā bol parinĕmsāsā
Mĕ mani wāsā khīd na hĕye;
Bŏh yŏd sahaza Shaṅkar-bakts āsā,
Makris sāsā mal kyāh pĕye.

श्रोसा बोल पंडिन्यम सासा
म्यं मनिवासा खीद न ह्यये
बोह योद सहज शंकर बखच श्रासा
मकुरिस सासा मल क्याह प्यये ॥६॥

He hurled a thousand abuses at me,
But I did not take it to heart.
Or, (The Lord seated in my heart did not get disturbed).
If I am a true devotee of Śaṅkar (Śiva),
How can the mirror of my mind get defiled with ashes and dust ?

Clearly, her husband remonstrated with her a thousand times using even strong, unbecoming language but she did not take it to heart. She did not identify herself with her body. The Self

1. Sir John Woodroffe—*The Serpent Power*, pp. 7, 24. cf. "Serpent Fire" — *The Inner Life* by C. W. Leadbeater.

2. Parinĕm is a dialectical variation of Kashmiri Parinam, and dapinĕm of dapinam. The former is used in the southern valley.

within the body was not affected by the harangue. She would not lose her mental equipoise, for her devotion to Śiva was too earnest and too deep to be shaken. The mirror of her heart, pure and clean, could not be defiled by the ashes and dust of false accusations and baseless charges. The fortress of her soul was steeled against inroads of folk-criticism. She cherished the image of her Lord within the sanctuary of her heart: awake or asleep she worshipped Him and relied entirely on His help. The Self, being invlulnerable, was immune to slander.[1]

This vakh is an indication that she had reached the stage of differentiation between the body and the self within. Her urge to realize the self within her was growing apace. She stuck to her guns and carried on her spiritual quest, trying her utmost to get behind the veil of Māyā,[2] — the appearance of the phenomenal world. She did not pay any heed to the abuses and ill-treatment of the people around her. Devoted with undivided attention to the search for Truth and conscious of her impeccable and immaculate conduct, she could easily withstand the onslaughts of criticism and calumny. She says:

7. Gāl gaṅḍiněm ta bol pariměn (paḍiněm),
Dapiněm tiy yas yih rŏtse,
Sahaza-kusamav pūz kariněṁ,
Bŏh amalöñ ta kas kyāh mŏtse.

गाल गंन्डिन्यम त बोल पंडिन्यम
दपिन्यम तिय यस यि रो.चे
सह.ज क्वसमौ पूज कंरिन्यम
बोह अमलांञ त कस क्याह म्व.चे ॥७॥

Let them reproach and call me names,
Let them say | whatever suits their individual inclination;
Let them even worship me with real flowers,
Since I am pure and faultless, let them reap whatever benefit they may.

1. *The Bhagavadgītā*, II, 22, 23.

2. For detailed study of Māyā, refer to *The Concept of Maya* by Ruth Reyana.

She had attained the state of mental equilibrium and equipoise. Abuse had lost its barb, and praise its elating power. The prerequisites[1] of mystical knowledge were establishing themselves in full strength. The emotions of grief and joy were gradually losing their punch. If some had begun appreciating her ways, her 'other-worldly' character, it did not shake the rhythm of her life, the same way as reproaches fell flat on her ears.

Nevertheless, there is a limit to forbearance. She does not pretend to be superhuman. Placed in precarious conditions, particularly in regard to her inner life, it is quite likely that she may have approached some relatives and women in the neighbourhood unburdening herself of her tale of woe and misunderstanding at home. But, it appears, she was quite dismayed to find that none supported her. Those to whom she talked lashed at her, too. She says:

8. Dod kyāh zāni yas no bane
Gamaki jāma ha valith tane
Gara gara phīras pĕyam kane
Dyūṅṭhum na kāṅh-ti panani kane.

दोद क्याह ज़ानि यस नो बने
गमुक्य जामु हा वॅलिथ तने
गरु गरु फीरुस प्यॅयम कने
ड्यूंठुम न काँहति पनुनि कने ॥८॥

Only the wearer knows where the shoe pinches !
I went door to door, in my robes of sorrow,

1. अथातो ब्रह्मजिज्ञासा ॥

"Now therefore the inquiry (into the real nature) of Brahman."

"'*Now*' assumes "certain spiritual requisites. The spiritual requisites are: (1) discrimination between things permanent and transient, (2) renunciation of the enjoyment of fruits of action in this world and the next, (3) the six treasures, viz., not allowing the mind to externalize and checking the external instruments of sense-organs (Śama and Dama); not thinking of things of the senses (Uparati), ideal forbearance (Titikṣa), constant practice to fix the mind in God (Samādhāna), and faith (Śraddhā); and the intense desire to be free (Mumukṣutvam)."

Swami Vireshwarananda, *Brahma-sūtra* 1. p. 19.

> Nothing did I receive but stones;
> I did not find any one supporting me.

If she was not patted and encouraged by anybody, it may have been quite in tune with the norms of social discipline of the times. A young daughter-in-law should not be pampered, they might have said. But why she was misunderstood and nagged can easily be attributed to the fact that she was looking for something different from what the common man, floating aimlessly on the current of life, seeks. Her soft silence and dumb expostulation was to them an anathema.

In good time she realized that it was impossible to make others understand the turmoil of her soul. It is likely that her entreaties, her supplication, her efforts to make them understand her ailment had all been in vain. She says:

9. Swayikul no dwada säti sagize
Sarpini thūlan dizi no phāh
Sĕki shāthas phal no vavize
Rāviy kŏm-yājan tīl.
Muḍas jñānac kath no vanize
Kharas gor dina rāviy dŏh.
Yus yuth kare su tyuth sware
Krere karizina panun pān.

स्वयिकुल नो द्वद् सूत्य संगिज़्
संयंपिनि ठूलन दिज़ि नो फाह
स्यंकि-शाठस फल नो वंविज़्
रा़विय को़मयाजन तील ॥
मुडस ज्ञानुच कथ नो वंनिज़्
खरस गोर दिनु राविय दोह
युस युथ करे सु त्युथ स्वरे
क्रेरे करिज़िनु पनुन पान ॥९॥

It does one no good watering the nettle with milk;
Hatching the eggs of a snake should be eschewed;
Sow not the seed on a sandy dune;
Using oil to fry bread made of paddy-husk flour is sheer waste;

To make a numskull grasp true knowledge is a vain attempt.
Feeding an ass on lumps of brown sugar and molasses is but waste of time.
One's thoughts are the offspring of one's deeds;
It is not wise to harm oneself (by engaging in unfruitful talk and discussions).

These verses are evidence enough to confirm the tradition that her domestic life was not happy. She was constrained to conclude that in the immanent world diversity of character could not be changed by human effort. 'A thing is what it is, rather than otherwise', lays down the law of Sufficient Reason. It is in the nature of things to possess peculiar characteristics, their 'differentia', which they cannot shed off. A snake is a snake and poison its characteristic quality. A donkey without its stubbornness will lose its identity. Though the self, pervading every animate and inanimate object, is one and the same, each individual thing or class of things is bound down by its own specific traits, as a result of the Law of Karmic Cause and Effect. Thoughts are born of actions. If the people, opposed to her way of life, thought in a particular way, their past and present actions were responsible for it. The last but one line of the vakh may also mean that 'they would reap as they sow now'. It was, therefore, futile to try to bring about a change in their thought and deed.

Note: The Buddha was pestered by evil spirits as he meditated under the Bodhi-tree. Lord Jesus Christ was nailed to the cross for voicing the dictates of conscience. In the field of science, those who knew better were not given any quarter. Giordino Bruno was burnt at the stake and Galileo suffered terribly. Pioneers of true knowledge had to pay the price, to whatever field they belonged. The Inquisition dogged the Protestants. The names of Mahatma Gandhi and Socrates have become immortal as Martyrs for Truth.

4

THE PREPARATION

But Lalla was neither a prophetess,[1] nor a reformer. She was just an aspirant seeking the Truth. Therefore, the only course left to her in this blind alley without an exit was to retreat into herself.

About Amir Khusru, it is said that "when Khusru was a child, his father looked after him as his mother had died very early. The father would notice daily in the morning, when he would change Khusru's shirt after he woke from his sleep, that the portion of the shirt which covered the child's breast was scorched as if by contact with fire. Such was the fire of Love that was constantly burning in the heart of Khusru."[2] Whatever one may infer from this, it testifies to the statement that nobody turned into a mystic overnight. Lalla's inherent seed of transcendental mysticism was gradually maturing as she grew in years. Her trying domestic circumstances proved a boon for her, as it led to a conscious adoption of an attitude of indifference and nonchalance. Her bones were full of spiritual marrow and her stamina of faith was unshakably strong. She says:

1. Sir Richard Temple in *The Word of Lalla* calls her a 'prophetess'.

2. *Nigaristan Faras* — p. 83. Quoted by Bankey Behari in *Sufis, Mystics and Yogis of India* — Bhavan's Book University.

10. Mūḍh zänith pashith ta ŏn
Kŏl shrutuvun zaḍ-rūpi ās,
Yus yih dapiy tas tiy bol (boz)
Yuhoy tattvavidis chuy abhyās.

मूड ज़ानिथ पशिथ त ओ̆न
को̆ल श्रुतवुन ज़डरूपी आस
युस यी दपिय तस तीय बोज़
यो̆हो̆य तत्त्व व्यदिस छुय अभ्यास ॥१०॥

Though thou hast knowledge, be thou as a fool;
Though thou canst see, be thou as blind;
Though thou canst hear, be thou as dumb;
Be thou, as it were, a non-sentient block;
Tell others what they like you to say.
(or) Listen to whatever a person talks to you.
This is the wont of one who knows the 'Tattvas[1].'

Henceforth, she turned a deaf ear and a blind eye to the taunts and jeers. The physical afflictions she bore as if she were an inanimate object, like wood or stone. She said 'yes' to whosoever asked her anything, lest contradicting others should involve her in fruitless, cold logic.

1. "When Shakti expands or opens herself out (unmishati), the Universe comes to be, and when she gathers or closes herself (nimishati), the Universe disappears as a manifestation, i.e., as 'predicable' in terms of discursive thought and speech". *Kashmir Shaivism*, J. C. Chatterjee, p. 48.

"A phase of manifestation or actuality of the Shakti is called an Udaya, Unmesha, Abhasana or Srishti, while a potential phase is termed a Pralaya (dissolution. ... " *Ibid.*, p. 49.

"Now, even though of an infinite variety, the things and beings of which the universe, thus produced by the 'opening out' of Shakti consists are built up really of *only a few Tattvas*, (lit. the *thatness* or *whatness*, namely, of everything that exists)...." *Ibid.*, p. 49.

तस्य भावस्तत्त्वमिति भिन्नानां वर्गाणां वर्गीकरणनिमित्तं यदेकमविभक्तं भाति तत् तत्त्वम्, यथा गिरिवृक्षपुरप्रभृतीनां नदीसरस्सागरादीनां च पृथ्वीरूपत्वात् अब्रूपत्वं चेति ।

Pratyabhijñā vimarśinī, Abhinavagupta, III, i. 2.

As already stated, Lalla had acquired the theoretical knowledge of the Cosmic Existence by the study of Hindu scriptures and she had learnt that the importance of human life was the opportunity to realize one's self. As a preliminary step to that end, the sense-organs had to be brought under control. The aspirant could not afford wasting breath and frittering away energy over inanities. He who knows the truth lives habitually in a state of perfect control over his sense-organs.[1] It was not merely a matter of book-knowledge for her: she lived upto what she had learnt. She says:

11. Zanam prävith vĕbhava na tshoṅḍum,
Lūbhan bhūgan baram na prai,
Sŏmuy āhār sĕṭhāh zonum,
Tsolum dwakha-vāv *polum* Dai.

जनम प्रोविथ व्यबव न छोंडुम
लूबन बूगन बरम न प्रय
सो_मुय आहार स्यठाह ज़ोनुम
चोलुम दुःख वाव पोलुम दय ।।११।।

In this life, I did not hanker after pelf and pomp,
I did not attach myself to greed and physical enjoyments;
Middling food was enough for me.
I faced the storms of adversity, but nurtured the thoughts of the Lord (within).

She had determined to make the most of this life as a means to the realization of her Self, the Lord within her. She would not let this opportunity go by pursuing the pleasures of the world. She ate to live: she did not live to eat. She put up with her uncongenial circumstances, but did not give up her way of nourishing the thoughts of the Lord. What amount and quality of courage it might have required and what strain it might have caused her is left to our imagination. In her eating, she adopted the Aristotelian golden mean. We are told that starvation is contrary to the rules of spiritual health, as is overeating.

1. *Bhagavadgītā*, III, 7. Also VI, 23,24.

"Once a mind succeeds in directing its energy towards the existence beyond the domain of intellect, and begins to realize and experience the magnitude, the grandeur and the novelty that are perceived and absorbed by the mind direct, without having recourse to the senses of the body, the person concerned becomes more and more unconcerned with his bodily requirements and surroundings. All his conscious energy is then naturally used in the course of his all-absorbing inner life, leaving the body and its sustenance to its own subconscious energy, and to the direct support from the very source of all energy — God."[1]

Lalla had by now arrived at the stage of her spiritual preparation for the '*Ascent*'.[2] It is said the Lord is ever ready to extend His helping hand to pull the devotees through.

"He who neither rejoices nor hates nor grieves nor desires, renouncing good and evil, full of devotion, he is dear to me."[3]

1. *The Wayfarers* by William Donkin; Foreword by Mehar Baba. p. 15.
2. Cf. footnote to v. 19.
3. *Bhagavadgitā* XII. 17. "God's presence cannot be felt in that heart which is given to attachment, aversion and fear". Sri Ramakrishna.

5

THE CROSS-ROADS

But she had not cast off the social slough yet. There were other problems which stared her in the face. Sectarian loyalties to different formalities of worship may have drawn her almost to the brink of a vortex of controversial issues. As sanity and steadfastness demanded it, she would fain sail clear of the vortex. She wanted to realize her Self and attain Kaivalya. The Kashmiris before her age had witnessed change after change in the approach to religious thought and practice. Buddhism had had a clean sweep over Kashmir for a long time. Śaṅkarācārya, repudiating Buddhism, had brought to the people here his Advaita Māyāvāda. Vedānta had struck deep roots, and become almost a household word for spiritual discourses. Rāmānuja had scattered seeds of his Vaiṣṇava philosophy in this religiously fertile ground. And lately, Islam had appeared on the religious firmament. Muslim saints and sūfis like Hazrat Syed Jalal-ud-Din,[1] Hazrat Syed Hussain Samnani and Amir-i-Kabir Syed Ali Hamdani, etc. preached their own convictions.

1. "Hazrat Syeed Jalal-ud-Din came to Kashmir. Lalla A'rifa went to receive him at Herapura. When they met, it was a great surprise that each enquired aftei the welfare of the other. Each made the enquiry in his or her own language and also replied in the same manner, and without an interpreter they understood each other well. . . . ."

History of Kashmir, Hassan (Urdu) vol. III. p. 448

However, there is no internal evidence in any form among Lalla's verses to confirm this account.

It is quite imaginable, therefore, that Lalla was at the cross-roads. Which of the formal paths should she tread ? But her moorings in yoga philosophy, — the *ascent* of the self so as not only to stand face to face with the Lord but also be absorbed in Him, — seem to have been too strong to yield to the winds of change. It appears to have been quite clear to her perspicacity that all roads lead to Rome. The storm of formal, institutional[1] religions, was too weak to waft her off her feet. She stood foursquare against the rival demands. She says:

12. Śiv vā Kishav vā Jinn[2] vā
Kamalajanāth nāmadhārin yuh,
Mĕ abali kästan bavarŏz,
Su vā su vā su vā suh.

शिव वा कीशव वा जिन वा
कमलजनाथ नामदारिन युह
म्यं अबलि कास्यतन बवरोज
सु वा सु वा सु वा सुह ॥१२॥

Shiva or Keshva or the Buddha,
Call Him what you may !
Let Him release me from the yoke of worldly
afflictions, weak and helpless as I am.

"What is there in a name ? A rose with any other name will smell as sweet." Śiva or Keśava or any other name would suit the Lord. "Mysticism is to be defined as the direct awareness of reality conceived as truth.... Mysticism discloses the truth which it has been the proud privilege of science as well as of philosophy to seek. The goal of the search has always been the same, though the methods have been different."[3] Lalla was a

1. *The Varieties of Religious Experience, A Study in Human Nature* (The Gifford Lectures). p. 6. William James calls all institutional religions "second-hand". That of the mystic is 'first-hand' religion.

2. Kishava or Viṣṇu, the god of the Vaiṣṇavites : Jinn is the name given to the Buddha, — the one who has conquered the sense-organs. Kamalazanath: One born of the lotus flower: Brahmā.

3. Mahendranath Sircar *Hindu Mysticism*: pp. 8, 9.

mystic to the core and every word of her poetry bears testimony to this claim. Aside of mysticism, she felt not the least interested in any dogmatic religion. 'Direct awareness' of the Lord was the be-all and end-all of her life. The walls which compartmentalize religions did not exist for her. 'Truth is one, without a second'.[1] This knowledge was a matter of conviction with her. As such, the religious pulls and pushes of the time did not upset her balance. She focused the torchlight of her attention on the realization of the Truth. She could not rest content with the second-hand knowledge about Him: she would not stop short of *'seeing'* Him. That is why she selected for herself the path of yoga, the path which leads to union with Him.[2] For her *religion* was not a subject of philosophical hairsplitting or abstruse knowledge, but a practical possibility of realizing the Truth and she had set her mind on it. She wanted to get rid of the affliction of worldly attachments.

She had not broken off with her hearth and home yet. Although formal religious practices and rituals seem to have ceased to be significant and meaningful to her as the ultimate instruments of perfection yet she accepts the religio-social set up in which she lived. She may have been taught that it was sacrilegious to revolt against the scriptures which were the repositories of wisdom and experience of savants, sages and seers, over thousands of years.[3] It was not in keeping with permissible tenets of

1. "Haqīqat yĕh hai ki Lalla 'Arifa vahdat ke samandar kī tairāk thī, jiskī lahreṅ mazhaboon kī dīvaroon ko girākar pāsh pāsh kartī hain, aur yĕh bāt iske kalạ̄m ke har lafaz se numāyān hai."

Hassan: *History of Kashmir* (Urdu), vol. III. p. 449.

2. "On the basis of the Shaiva, Yoga and Advaita learning, she teaches but one main idea with an infinite variety of illustration. Her object for herself and her hearers is to escape re-birth,.. , by securing union with the Supreme after death at the end of the present life...."

The Word of Lalla the Prophetess — p. 164.

Done into English verse by Sir Richard C. Temple (Principal Editor of the *Indian Antiquary*) Cambridge. At the University Press 1924.

3. भवतु निश्चयदार्ढ्यादूर्ध्वं शास्त्ररक्षणम् ॥

·*Bhakti Sūtras* of Devarṣi Nārada. Sūtra—12

"The injunctions of the Scriptures should be scrupulously respected." *The Philosophy of Love* by Hanuman Prasad Poddar.

(Footnote continued on next page)

social conduct to discard custom unless and until one had come upon a surer way of salvation. Perhaps her guru, too, observed her, and felt that time was not ripe for her to renounce the routine religious rituals of the household. She says:

13. Vŏth rañya artsun sakhar
Athi al-pal vakhur hĕth,
Yŏdvanay zānakh parma-pad akhĕr
Hishi Khŏsh-khŏr kĕtha-khĕth.[1]
Or, (Khishekhar Hishekhar hĕth).[2]

व्वथ रैन्या अ़र्चुन सखर
अथि अल-पल वखुर ह्यथ
यो॒दवनय ज़ानख परमुपद अक्षर
हिशी खो॒श ख्वर क्यथ्‌ ख्यथ
(क्षिशेक्षर हिशेक्षर ह्यथ) ॥१३॥

Arise, O Lady ! set out to make thine offering,
Bearing in thy hand, wine, flesh and bread;
If thou knowest the Syllable, which is the highest of words,
Then it is all the same, whether thou performest the rites according to the 'Left-foot' way or in any other way.

This vakh is suggestive of the fact that Lalla's duty of formal, ritualistic worship was becoming perfunctory and mechanical. There is a shade of the sentiment of abhorrence exuding from the first two lines. The address, 'Arise, O Lady !' to herself smacks of boredom. The second line confirms this conclusion. Carrying in her hand 'flesh' and 'wine' and 'bread' to worhip the Lord

अन्यथा पातित्याशङ्कया ॥ "Otherwise there is risk of a fall." *Ibid*, 13.

लोकोऽपि तावदेव किंतु भोजनादिव्यापारस्त्वाशरीरधारणावधिः ॥ *Ibid.*, 14.

"Worldly duties should also be scrupulously performed till there is consciousness of external world, but (bodily) actions such as taking of food, etc., will continue to be performed till the body persists."

Ibid., pp. 50-52.

1. Grierson. *Lalla-Vākyāni.* vakh 10.
2. R. Lib. MS. Bhaskara. Acc. No. 797. Shl. 10.

do not appear to be in line with her Buddhistic leanings,[1] as is amply borne out by other verses — particularly her teaching (v. 93) 'Atsītan vaṭas satsītan dikh āhār' —, and the Śaivite education that there is one Śiva present in everything.

The Kaula[2] method of worship may have been in vogue in

1. Cf. The use of the word 'Śūnya', the Buddhistic concept equivalent to the ultimate Reality (vs 41, 42, 43).

"The translation of *śūnyatā* as meaning 'void' which in English connotation equals 'nothingness' or 'emptiness' is unfortunate, for such a meaning of the term is not acceptably demonstrated in the teaching of Gautama the Buddha, and is more aptly defined as 'indeterminateness' in the Buddhistic implication...." Ruth Reyana: *The Concept of Māyā*; p. 9.

2. "The lady is a diligent worshipper of Shiva, with all the necessary rites, and is apparently a follower of the left-handed sect, that consumes wine, and flesh, and performs less reputable acts as a part of worship, which are not consonant with regular Hindu 'ācāra', or custom. ... Lalla points out that violation of her Hindu custom, by the performance of the Kaula sacraments, is unobjectionable, or, indeed, praiseworthy, provided she knows the mystic syllable, Om.... The 'lady' is probably the Śakti abiding in the speaker's own body." *Lalla Vākyāni*, Sir George Grierson.

The comment of Sir George Grierson, is illogical and he seems to have committed the error because of wrong interpretation of 'Arise, O Lady'. The 'Lady' is none but Lalla herself. When a person addresses himself in Kashmiri, usually the temper is one of 'compulsion'. It is a manner of grumbling; and voices the sentiment of listlessness and apathy. The meaning of this vakh becomes evident from later verses of Lalla in which she clearly expresses herself against slaughter of animals. Also the 'Vām-marg' could not probably agree with Lalla's method of self-realization, which was above all rituals. Also Grierson's misinterpretation becomes clear when we note the following quotation:

"Now to the other methods of Śākta worship: the Kaulas worship the Kuṇḍalinī' *without rousing her* from her sleep in the Mūlādhāra, which is called Kula; and hence Kaulas (Sans. Ku=earth, Prithvi; so Mūlādhāra). Beyond the Mūlādhāra they do not rise; they follow the Vāmācāra or black magic, and gain their temporal objects and joy; they are not liberated from birth and death; they do not go beyond this earth...."

Pandit R. Anantakrishna Shastri—*Saundarya Laharī*—cited by Woodrooffe p. 286. (Yoga: Laya-Krama).

Grierson's note: "The 'lady' is probably the Śakti abiding in the speaker's own body", is untenable, insomuch as Śakti is the object of worship. Rañya is a Kashmiri equivalent for a lady and is derived from Sanskrit राज्ञी a queen. Distinction must be made between Rañya (रॆञ्या) and Raina (रैना). The latter is a corruption of Rajanaka—a title given to distinguished scholars and poets.

Kashmir for long, long before Abhinavagupta came on the scene in the tenth century. It is said that Kaulism had originated from the top mouth of the five-faced Śiva and according to *Kulārṇavatantra* there is no higher system of philosophy than that presented in the literature on Kaulism. It is called Ūrdhvāmnāya because it is above the "Law" (Niyati) — (*Kulārṇavatantra*, Chap. III, 18). According to this mode of worship, a Yogin is admitted to be capable of producing everything by sheer force of will, independently of the physical things which are necessary for their production. But the Kaula practice is not pleasant and easy. From the *Kulārṇavatantra* (Chap. II, 123), we gather that following this path, though a sure means of salvation through direct knowledge, is yet "as difficult as walking on the edge of a sword and as risky as holding a lion by the ear, or holding a serpent in hand, because herein *wine*, *meat* and *woman* are to be used, not for the satisfaction of the sensuous desires, but for the realization of the highest spiritual value by ascending from the sensuous to the spiritual level. . . ."

"By the time the *Kulārṇava* was written, degeneration had already set in among the followers of Kaulism. There were many who did not inherit the tradition and, therefore, were ignorant of the secrets. They were preaching Kaulism as they thought and imagined it to be. They seem to have advocated the use of wine, woman and meat as a means of liberation, waiving aside the spiritual and psychological training as an antecedent condition and transcending the empirical level as the main objective of their use."[1]

"The *Kulārṇava* recognises that wine is not to be even looked at and touched, much less to be taken. It enjoins like the Dharmaśāstra, various forms of penance in case they are touched or taken. It forbids its use by the three higher castes."

As regards the meat, it holds that all those who permit, connive at, or take pleasure in killing animals, sell, purchase, prepare, help in preparation or eat the meat are morally guilty.[2]

But it enjoins the use of both, wine and meat, in the perform-

1. *Abhinavagupta* by Dr. K. C. Pandey. pp. 559-60. *Kulārṇavatantra* is said to have been written earlier than *Vāmakeśvaratantra*, as there are references to the former in the latter. *Kul. Ar.* Chap. II. 117-21.

2. *Ibid.*, *Kul. Ar.* Chap. II. 133.

ance of the Kaulika rituals. . . . It asserts that just as drinking of Soma by Brahmans in sacrifices (according to the Vedic Literature) does not mean a sin, so does not drinking of wine in the Kaula rituals.[1]

To justify the use of wine and meat, it emphasizes *the importance of motive* and says that the person who takes wine and meat for mere sensuous satisfaction is a sinner.[2]

The Kaulas or the followers of Vāmācāra[3] did offer wine and meat and cakes in their religious worship in Lalla's time and the vakh indicates that the family to which she belonged followed this particular mode of worshipping the goddess Śakti. But due to the degeneration which had set in, the worship had by the fourteenth century become a mere ritual bereft of the spiritual substance for which Lalla's heart pined. Mere formalism does not seem to have appealed to her. Or may be she had already risen above the stage of rituals and depended for her salvation on the direct perception of the Lord. The vakh does, beyond doubt, suggest a feeling of indifference to, if not positive disapproval of, the Vāmācāri ritual. Sāttvic by temperament, Lalla seems to express repugnance by her listlessness. She gets up to perform the 'pūjā' in accordance with the tradition of the family to which she belongs, because she must under the circumstances in which she is placed. It was not for her to rise in revolt against the orthodox family way of worship. She was neither an iconoclast nor a religious reformer.

Her sense of disapproval is evident from the unenthusiastic, passive, reluctant acquiescence. The paraphernalia of her spiritual march had been patience, self-abnegation and total tolerance. She seems to have added to her stock another item, viz., indifference. Little did it matter whether the 'pūjā' was performed according to this way or that.

The next two lines strengthen our view. The main thing *she bothered about* was the knowledge of the word Oṃ, the highest of syllables, the gateway to self-realization. So long as she chanted this syllable, it did not at all make any difference how she was

1. *Ibid., Kul. Ar.* Chap. V. 86.
2. *Ibid., Kul. Ar.* Chap. V. 82-83.
3. Cf. Description of 64 Tantras. Com. on *Saundaryalaharī*, Śloka 31. pp. 183-88. Swami Vishnu Tirthji.

called upon to perform her pūjā according to the family tradition. She had chosen the *Word*: she had not been taught its secret powers, though.[1]

The third line "Yodvanay zānakh Parama-pad Akhĕr" may also mean: If you know the "Parama-pad" which means the supreme state or the Brahman, who is 'Akhĕr' — imperishable, everlasting, the source and sustenance of all the manifested worlds — then the different paths of worship can be seen to converge at the same goal. The Tantric ritual would not appear merely a fetish and an exercise in the art of necromancy and enchantment. In the state of the True knowledge of the Lord, all forms of worship, irrespective of the methods adopted, blend into one condition of supplication to the Lord. The manner of worship was but secondary to the main and primary need of knowing Him. This vakh indicates that Lalla had risen spiritually above the stage of formal worship.

1. The last line of the quatrain has a variant. The version given above is from Grierson's text. The alternative is indefinite, taken from an old, anonymous manuscript of Lalla-vakhs available in the Research Library, Srinagar. Khishekhar. Hishekhar might either relate to the Bījamantra ह & क्ष. "In each of Cakras there is also a Bīja (seed) Mantra of each of the Tattvas therein. They are the seed of the Tattva, for the latter springs from and re-enters the former. ..." ह & क्ष indicate the Ājñā Cakra between the eyebrows. The *Serpent Power*. Woodroffe, p. 111.

Or, it might mean: If you know the highest of sacred syllables, Oṃ, you gain the key to the knowledge of both (the perishable world of sense perception, and the imperishable) the manifested and the transcendental Śiva. c.f. "Gargi said 'In what then is the ether woven, like warp and woof' ?"

"Yājñavalkya said: 'O Gārgī, the Brahmans call this the Akṣara (the imperishable). It is neither coarse nor fine, neither short nor long... without taste, without smell. . .having no within and no without, it devours nothing and no one devours it'." *Bṛhadāraṇyaka Upaniṣad*, III. 8. 8.

6

THE DARK NIGHT OF DESPAIR

The institutional religion having lost its significance as a necessary oar to the boat of her spiritual life, gradually Lalla seems to have drifted into a mood of despondence. It is a new phase, the state of the "Dark night of Despair". "In spite of the unquestionable fact that saints of the once-born type exist, there may be a gradual growth in holiness without a cataclysm, ... you must first be nailed on the cross of natural despair and agony[1]... ". "A glorious transformation .... ought of necessity be preceded by despair."[2] "The man's interior is a battle ground for what he feels to be two deadly hostile selves, one actual, the other ideal." "The normal evolution of (spiritual) character chiefly consists in the straightening out and unifying of the inner self."[3]

1. *The Varieties of Religious Experience*, William James, p. 228.

2. *Ibid.*, p. 229 Refers to Jonathan Edward's *Treatise on Religious Affections.*

3. Speaking on Arjuna's dejection on the battlefield of Kurukṣetra, Swami Chidbhavananda says:

"The Messengers of Light advocate this kind of distress as a prelude to spiritual enlightenment. Here it prepares Arjuna for yoga. Blessed are the distressed in heart; they shall be comforted in enlightenment. This is the law of life. Hence this distress of Arjuna is also called a System of Yoga (Arjuna-Viṣāda-Yoga — Yoga of Arjuna's Dejection)".

Introduction to the *Bhagavadgītā* p. 33.

There is sufficient evidence in the outpourings of her heart that she was on tenterhooks, mentally. The night of despair loomed large before her. She says:

14. Lalith-lalith **vadai bŏh vāy,**
    Tsĕta muhac pĕyiy māy,
    Roziy no pata lŏh-laṅgarac tshāy
    Niz-swarūp kyāh mŏṭhuy hāy.

ललिथ-ललिथ वदय बोह वाय
च्यत्ता मुहच प्ययिय माय
रोज़िय नो पत लोहलंगरच छाय
नि.ज स्वरूप क्याह मोठुय हाय ॥१४॥

I shall lament over your state, O Mind !
    softly and slowly,
Why have you got attached to the illusory world ?
Not a shadow of the worldly possessions will stand
    by you in the end.
Alas ! why have you forgotten your real, essential
    Self ?

It is an awful wail of frustration. Aspiration strikes against the wall of stark phenomenal world. Boring her way through was still a dream. To get involved in the earthly attachments, she knew, was to remain fettered down. The scriptures had taught her that she was a part and parcel of the Universal Spirit and to remain in a condition of separation from Him was agony.

It is likely that, on occasions, domestic preoccupations may have hampered her spiritual thoughts and lured her to attachment to things of the world. She seems to be shocked by her human weakness and reproaches herself for succumbing to mundane allurements. She was made of flesh and blood after all and physical considerations may not be ruled out. But it was not long before she gained the upper hand of her body and took note of her mistake. She realized that ultimately her kith and kin, and all the worldly possessions had very little to do with her salvation. The vakh makes one thing clear: her vacillation was momentary. Her digressions into the bylanes of life did not make her lose her way permanently, nor did she lose sight of her destination. She had not yet learnt how to preen her wings for the distant, upward flight. She was, of course, sad and she wailed and sobbed.

15. Hā Tsĕta kava chuy lŏgmut paramas,
Kava góy apazis pazyuk broṅt,
Dushibŏz vash kŏranakh par daramas
Yina gatshana zĕna-maranas kroṅt.

हा च्यत्ता कवु छुय लो_गमुत परमस
कवु गो_य अपुज़िस प.ज्युक ब्रोंत
दुशि-बो_ज़ वश को_रनख पर दर्मस
यिनु गछुनु ज्यनु मरनस क्रोंत ।।१५।।

O Mind ! why have you developed attachment for others ?
Why have you taken the unreal for the Real ?
Your lack of wisdom has ensnared you in a false-dharma.
You are getting involved in a never-ending cycle of birth and death.

The vakh is somewhat tricky. 'Paramas' may be a derivative of 'Parmātmā' equivalent to Īśvara — theistical God. She accuses her mind of developing liking for the faith of others. It may be understood as "why do you attach yourself to a *theistic* God ?" She castigates herself for mistaking the 'unreal' for the 'Real'. She confesses that the event of being overwhelmed by the faith of others had occurred owing to her 'dushibŏz'— perverse-understanding or lack of wisdom. She was convinced that the 'other-dharma' would not release her from the whirligig of birth and death.[1]

1. The pun on the word 'parmas' creates an ambiguity. 'Kava chuy logmut parmas' may also mean 'why have you got drunk with the wine of belief which does not help solve your problem ?' 'Parmas' may be broken up into 'par' and 'mas' — par for 'vŏpar' meaning 'alien' and 'mas' for 'wine' in Kashmiri. 'Mas lagun' is a Kashmiri idiom meaning 'to turn one's head' or 'getting overdrunk'.

Para-dharma may also mean consideration for the body, whereas sva-dharma may refer to spiritual realization.

This interpretation is supported by the second line of the vakh. 'Pŏz' — real, and 'apŏz' — unreal — are customarily used for 'the spirit' or soul and the body or worldly goods, respectively. Also, attachment to the body is said to lead to the cycle of birth and death.

Lalla appears to have been fully aware of the ensnaring dangers of 'rāga' or attachment to perishable worldly goods; she realizes full well that attachment leads to action which in turn leads to the fruit of action to be reaped in this life and thereafter. 'Kava gŏy apazis pazyuk broṅt ?' Why have you taken the false for the true ? The question haunts her. It was, as it were, running and making for a mirage to quench her thirst: 'par-dharma' was an illusion. As against this, sva-dharma led to her goal.[1] She had pinned her faith on 'yoga' — the ultimate unification with Parama-Śiva. That was the only means to the end of her aspiration for 'mokṣa'. So any other dharma or faith or way of life did not suit her objective. Rituals and oblations, as already noted, had ceased to bring her solace.

No dharma of institutional formalities and ritualism brought her the promise of union with the Lord. The Śaiva philosophy seems to have produced an indelible impress on her understanding of the Truth. The Lord was within and without us, all-pervading, immanent and transcendental, without beginning, middle or an end.[2] He was the Self in man. Realization of the Self was, therefore, the highest goal worthy of her aspiration. And scriptures said: 'yoga' or union of the microcosmic self with the Macrocosmic Self, which were in essence one and the same, is *possible*. *This*

1. *The Bhagavadgītā*. III, 35.

2. According to *Advaita Shaiva Philosophy of Kashmir*, "The Atman, that is the true and innermost Self in every being, is a changeless reality of the nature of a purely experiencing principle...." J. C. Chatterjee p. 43. (Research & Publication Deptt, Srinagar, Kashmir, 1962).

चैतन्यमात्मा ॥ ; *Śiva Sūtra*, I. 1.

"This Caitanya or Parama Śiva is the Reality which underlies, as its innermost and true self, not only every experiencing being but also everything else in the Universe, both separately, i.e., individually, as well as a totality, i.e. the universe as a whole. As the underlying reality in everything and being in the universe, Parama Śiva is one and the same in them all — undivided and unlimited by any of them, however much they may be separated either in time or in space. In other words, Parama Śiva is beyond the limits of time, space and form; and as such is Eternal and Infinite. Again, as the underlying reality in everything, He is all pervading; and at the same time, He is also transcending. That is to say, His nature has primarily a twofold aspect — an immanent aspect in which He pervades the universe, and a transcendental aspect in which He is beyond all Universal Manifestations." *Ibid.* pp. 44,45.

mystical union was the only way of escaping the grinding mill of birth after birth, she thought. Therefore, she seems to have come to the conclusion that no religion as understood and practised by common man, no dogmatic, hidebound faith, no way of life other than 'yoga practice' would suit her.

Hence, she reminds herself of the risk she was running by being caught in the meshes of Māyā, the world of unreal appearances. She is determined to get release from the law of cause and effect (Karma-bandhana), but she has not found how to achieve it. As yet she is groping in the dark and longs for a ray of light through a chink in the dark cave she is passing through. She is naturally sad and does not hide her discomfiture. She says:

16. Āyas vate gayas nā vate,
Suman svathimaṅz lūsum dŏh,
Candas vuchum ta hār na ate
(Harnāv na ate) . . . . . . (variant).
Nāva-tāras dima kyāh bŏh.

अायस वते गंयस ना वते
सुमन स्वथि मंज़ लूसुम दोह
चंदस वुछुम तु हार ना अते
नावु तारस दिमु क्याह बोह ।।१६।।

I came by the highway but did not return by the same,
In the middle of the long embankment and over the small bridge, I found the day coming to a close!
Searching my pocket I found not a penny.
Alas! what shall I pay the boatman to ferry me across?

A more delicate strain of despair may not be painted in a bolder imagery. The gateway of birth into this world as a human being is a blessing and a boon. It is in the evolved human form alone that the Spirit can aspire for upward flight and attempt the realization of the Self.[1] Lalla had, accordingly, the intensely burning desire to make the most of her earthly days, as a sentient being endowed with spiritual aspiration. She was trying her best to find the highroad of salvation, but so far no such

1. Kena-Up. 2.5.

road was visible. She was trudging along an unfrequented embankment broken by a stream which cut across it and over which stood not even a rickety, ramshackle wooden bridge. Time was on wings and she was no nearer the highway leading back *Home*. Despair verged on desperation when she found that she had no means to cross the stream by the dike. She had not got even a penny to pay the boatman to ferry her across.

In the mystical parlance, it was a bleak prospect. Human life is not such a long affair, after all. The dusk appeared to be stealing in and the dark night sweeping agallop over the vista of her hopes. She had not as yet earned a penny-worth[1] of spiritual wages to pay to the boatman to carry her across the river of existence, so that she might fulfil her ambition of reaching her destination where the individual soul gets merged with the Universal Soul. The right road to spiritual perfection was yet to be found out. Lalla-ded had reason to get unnerved. She wails in metaphors. Her spiritual barque is in the doldrums. She knows only too well that human life is the only spring-board for the leap to the height of spiritual realization. She longs for a favourable wind of enlightenment to lead her on to the highroad of mystical perfection. This ocean of existence is to be crossed and the ferryman[2] is the Preceptor who demands

1. The variant 'Hara nāv na ate', that she had not even learnt to chant the name of 'Śiva' or 'Hara', does not suit the verse as a whole. We have already gone through enough material to show that she was moving on the path. It is unimaginable that she did not repeat the Lord's name. Besides, it would be an utterly unsuitable combination to put together pocket and name of the Lord. Further, 'hār' or a 'cowry' — used for a small coin, the unit of business transaction in Kashmir in olden days — fits in well with the payment to a boatman for ferrying across. Also 'Hara nāv na ate' jars on the metre of the vakh.

2. One is reminded of Charon of the Greek Mythology conveying souls across the Styx to Hades.

Sir Grierson's comment:—"But she did not avail herself of the opportunity, and so, when she died, she left the highway of salvation, and was compelled to be born and reborn", is not tenable. Sir Grierson has not grasped the vakh, or it has been misinterpreted to him. His note states that Lalla died without achieving her spiritual end, which is corroborated neither by tradition nor by the text of her poetry. On the contrary, the present work maintains and *proves* that she was a 'yogini' who reached in lifetime

payment, and the payment is not accepted in terms of money but in terms of the aspirant's own cultivated and developed spiritual calibre to receive help. Ruskin says about master-minds, in the field of books, that they do not assist and help by way of charity. Lalla says the same thing regarding the high-brows of mystical knowledge. They measure and gauge the aspirant's capacity to receive. One's desire alone does not carry one far. One must deserve to hold their helping hand. Lalla is duly humble and unassuming about her own deserts. She is despondent because she has not developed in herself a *'cowry'* worth of spiritual merit to deserve being ferried across to the definite and sure road leading to salvation.

'Suman' may be read as Sva-man.[1] 'Sum' is the crazy bridge, across a stream. 'Sva-man' would mean 'of one's own mind.' Then the second line may be interpreted as: her day came to a close on the embankment of her own mind. She was trudging on the spiritual embankment of her own mind, and she found that night was falling fast. She had a mistrust that she would not be ferried across the river of existence and brought to the other bank — the bank of release from birth and death.

This vakh confirms the thesis that she was in a state of mental agony; for, in spite of her ardent desire, she feared this life of hers was running to waste, as the days rolled by. The state of her own helplessness could, perhaps, not be voiced in more candid feeling and apter language. She sings in parables, but only a little effort of sympathy unveils her bruised heart.

The same sentiment of despair is evident from the following vakh:

17. Hacivi härinji pĕtsiv-kān gom
Abakh Chān pyom yath rāzdhāne;
Maṅzbāg bāzaras kulfa-rŏst vān gom
Tirtha - rŏst pān gom kus māli zāne?

the acme of spiritual evolution and became jivanmukta i.e. freed from bondage while she lived her apportioned earthly days.

Grierson's references to the Vaitariṇī stream and the ferryman there, etc. seem to have been built on the *basic error that this vakh refers to Lalla's death.*

1. Since Lalla-vakhs have been passed on by word of mouth till recently, it is not easy to come upon the text as she meant it to be.

हृचिवि हांरिजि प्यंचिव कान गोम
अबख छान प्योम यथ रा.जुदाने
मंजबाग बाजुरस कुल्फु रो_स्त वान गोम
तिर्थं-रो_स्त पान गोम कुस मालि जाने ॥१७॥

Alas! My wooden bow has but arrows of weeds,
The palace (of my mind) has been entrusted to a witless carpenter;
My spiritual economy is shattered, like that of a shop without lock and key in a busy street;
Pilgrimages have I had none ! Who can understand my plight?

By any standards, this is quite an unenviable position for a devout aspirant and a seeker. She bemoans her lot, for nobody around her could fathom her pitiable condition. Physical ailment draws sympathy, but spiritual pangs may remain unheard.

Lalla was acutely conscious of her impelling spiritual urge, and she was conscious too of the circumstances in which destiny had placed her. Her spiritual stamina is compared to a strongly built wooden bow, but the arrows, with which to kill the enemies,[1] were pithless weeds. With such darts,[2] as have neither sap nor substance, in her quiver, she felt rather shaky in her shoes. Her body was like a palace in which dwelt the Royal Soul, but for its spiritual construction she had to depend on a witless carpenter. For the aspirant, physical fitness is a *sine qua non* for fulfilment of spiritual aspiration. Her spiritual economy was in shambles, and her body had not even the benefit of holy baths,

1. The enemies on the mystical path are said to be :

(i) The five intellectual functions of Citta, the mental organism, viz., pramāṇa, viparyaya, vikalpa, nidrā and smṛti.

(ii) The mind is also involved in five afflictions (क्लेश) — the Kleśas — viz, avidyā, asmitā, rāga, dveṣa and abhiniveśa. The 'Kleśas' move the subject of thought constantly to works — 'Karma' — from which arise 'saṁskāras', and 'vāsanās' or mental predispositions, moving him to corresponding future works.

2. She may have been making attempts to rouse the *Kuṇḍalinī* but without success.

Author at Lalla-Trag
The Miracle Pond at Pampore

[p. 39

the common man's way of purification of the soul. She is at a loss to understand what to do with herself, with all her seething aspiration for spiritual success. Her mood of wretchedness was becoming poignant because none could have an inkling of her suffering. Here is the agony which passeth show.

Maybe the 'arrows' refer to some 'Mantras' which she chanted, but she was dismayed because it did not help her achieve her goal. '*The witless Carpenter*' may be her own intellect circumscribed by limitations of time and space: and dissecting intellect is a poor thing, wholly useless in obtaining spiritual light. Or the phrase may have a reference to some person whom she looked upto for guidance. Maybe it is an acerbitic hint at the Guru who did not yet come forward to pull her out of her despondency.

Whatever the reference, the vakh boils down to a note of gnawing despair. The next few vakhs dwell on the same theme. She says :

18. Yi kyāh äsith yi kyuth raṅg gom,
Caṅg gom tsaṭith hudhudne digai:.
Sārinay padan kunuy vakhun pyom :
Lali mĕ trāg[1] gom, laga kami shāṭhai.

यि क्याह् ग्रा॑सिथ यि क्युय रंग गोम
चंग गोम च॑टिथ हुवहुव ने दिगय
सारिनय पदन कुनुय वखुन प्योम
ललि म्यं त्राग गोम लगु कमि शाठय ॥१८॥

1. Trāg means a large hole. There is a large pond called Lalla-Trāg at Pampore. Though the source of the water is not known, the pond is filled with water all the year round. The devotees of Lalla-ded regard the pond as a sacred place, to this day. Legend has it that one day her mother-in-law complained that Lalla had not fetched enough water from the river, the moment the latter arrived with a pail of water. Upon this, Lalla performed a miracle. She filled all the available vessels in the house out of that pail, and spilt the rest out of the window into a ditch at the back of the house. That is the genesis of the Lalla-Trāg, they say.

In spite of being different, what a dye have I been dyed in!
Adverse winds are tearing holes in me, as does the hoopoe peck holes in the ground;
All my verses have the same burden (of despair).
A large hole has been dug in Lalla's heart : I know not the sandy shoal on which my bark may wreck.

She has an innate conviction that she was born different. With instinctive optimism, she had chosen the course of her life. But the 'original' rosiness of instinctive optimism had changed into the pallor of pessimism. Adverse winds were tearing off the sails of the vessel of her spirit, and she was afraid lest she should get wrecked on a sandy shoal. The burden of her song had become the wail of despair and she was all but drowned in the veritable *Slough of Despond.*

One can read temporal meaning in this vakh. She was born a 'child of light' and she had 'intimations of her immortality' fresh and green in her mind. She had selected the spiritual path for her own redemption. But she was misunderstood. She was even scandalized by her mother-in-law, who incited her son to spy on his wife. This was, doubtless, an outrageous situation for Lalla. 'Yi kyāh rang gom' can easily be interpreted in this context. She was painted in the darkest colours and she felt as it were holes being bored into her heart.

The cry of helplessness is raised in yet another verse. She says :

19. Āyas kami dīsha ta kami vate,
Gatsha kami děsha kava zāna vath;
Antidāy lagimai tate,
Chanis phŏkas kāṅch (kaṅh) ti no sath.

आयस कमि दीशु तु कमि वत्ते
ग़छु कमि दशि कवु ज़ानु वथ
अन्तिदाय लगिमय तत्ते
छंनिस फोकस कांह ति नो सथ ॥१६॥

From what country did I come and by what road?
To what quarter shall I go? How shall I know the road?

How I wish I were to receive right guidance at long last so as to put me on the right path !
For there is no substance in an empty breath.

About the *descent*[1] of the self, she had learnt all that was needed and had understood how the manifest universe, and for that matter Lalla herself as an individual, had come to be. "Indeed, the *Universe* with all its infinite variety of objects, and means of experience is nothing but a manifestation of the immanent aspect of Parama Śiva Himself. It has no other basis or ingredient in it."[2]

1. It needs a little care to make out the words *descent* and *ascent* used in this text. Śaivaism does not postulate any process of climbing down or climbing up as such. The words have been used metaphorically to denote a mystical state in which the concepts of time and space are not involved. The *climb* is here used to describe an otherwise indescribable state of consciousness of unity. As the consciousness of *unity* recedes and becomes dimmer, the self is *descending* "Involution" and, conversely, as it approaches the Fountain-head of Life and becomes brighter and clearer, the self is *ascending* "Evolution".

2. J.C. Chatterjee. *K. Sh.* p. 45.

Also cf. श्रीमत्परमशिवस्य पुन: विश्वोत्तीर्ण-विश्वात्मक-परमानन्दमयप्रकाशैक-घनस्य.. अखिलम् अभेदेनैव स्फुरति; न तु वस्तुत: अन्यत् किञ्चित् ग्राह्यं ग्राहकं वा, अपि तु श्रीपरमशिवभट्टारक एव इत्थं नानावैचित्र्यसहस्रै: स्फुरतीति अभिहितप्रायम् ॥

Pratyabhijñāhṛdayam. p. 28.

चिदेव भगवती ... तत्तदनन्त जगदात्मना स्फुरतीत्येतावत् परमार्थोऽयं कार्यकारणभाव: ॥

Ibid., p. 3.

"And again, the entire universe so constituted, from Śiva to the earth, flashes in identity with the blissful Parama Śiva. (The latter) transcends and is the universe at one and the same time, and consists of the highest bliss and nothing but light. (In regard to the universe that flashes up, it is) truly no other (than the one mentioned above), be it object or subject. Nevertheless, the magnificent *Paramaśiva bhaṭṭāraka* manifests himself in just this manner in thousands of forms of a heterogenous multiplicity.

Tr. by F. Leidecker. p. 29.

"Only Cit it is, the exalted One, qualified by its luminous absoluteness, which flashes in the real essence of the unlimited world then in existence. These words convey that this highest comprehensive reality is effect and cause (at one and the same time)" *Ibid.*, p. 22.

She had studied Śaivaism and learnt that through His immanent aspect, — Śakti, functioning by her five modes, viz., Cit Śakti, Ānanda Śakti, Icchā Śakti, Jñāna Śakti and Kriyā Śakti —, the infinite variety of objects comes into being. But that makes one aspect of knowledge at the best, and only a theoretical aspect upon that. What was more pertinent and meaningful to her objective was the route directing her 'ascent' up to Parama Śiva. The practical aspect mattered most with her. She was at sea because she lacked practical guidance. And this she bemoans. She had known the path by which she had come, but she did not know the road which leads one Home. Physical breath is an empty thing and cannot be relied upon to stay with us for ever. Life is short and the demand of a solution to her problem was pressing. She was naturally upset. Human life, as already said, is a means to an end, and which direction she should take to achieve the end, she is at a loss to understand.

However, notwithstanding the dark clouds, the silver lining is visible. The upward progress of her self was not retarded. Surely her conscious self was growingly functioning on a higher plane. She had ceased to discriminate between one individual and another, between herself and others. Śiva-Śakti tattvas being basic to all, the variety was superficial. The dark night of the aspirant was beginning to be the precursor of the dawn of Hope. She says :

20. Nāthā ! na pān na par zonum,
Sadai būdum yi kwa dih ;
(or) (Sadai būdum yiko dih);
Tsa bŏh, bŏh tsa myul nā zonum,
Tsa kus bŏh kwasa chum saṅdīh.

नाथा ! न पान न पर ज़ोनुम
सदै बूदुम यि क्व दीह
.चु बो_ह बो_ह .चु म्युल ना ज़ोनुम
.चु कुस बो_ क्वसु छु सन्दीह ।।२०।।

O Master ! I never differentiated between myself and others ;

Always did I mortify this unreal[1] body ;
Alt. (Always did I realize that all bodies were the same)
Thou art I, and I Thou; but I have not learnt how to merge
the two.
Who art Thou and who am I ? In a state of doubtful
(non-recognition) am I.

Grierson renders the vakh as follows :

Lord ! I have not known myself or other than myself,
Continually have I mortified this vile body.
That thou art I, that I am Thou, that these are joined in
one I knew not.
It is doubt to say, 'who am I ?' and 'who art thou' ?

Grierson's comments are :

"Lalla declares that in her ignorance she has not known the true relation of herself to others. She still clung to the conception of her personal identity, and was ignorant of the real nature of her self, as only one manifestation of the Supreme. She has worn her body out by attempting to gain salvation by attending to her duties, not recognizing that these lead only to further transmigrations and are all in vain. The only hope of salvation is the recognition of the identity of her self with the Supreme. To wonder who I am, and who He is, i.e. to doubt this identity is indeed the fatal doubt of doubts."

Sir Grierson has taken the vakh in isolation; his interpretation is, *consequently*, faulty. The body of verse which precedes this vakh adequately supports the view that she had recognised the relationship of identity between her own self and the Self-essence present in others. But what troubled her was that she had not realized the Self ; she had not '*experienced*' It, — either as her self or the self of others. She uses the word 'kva' with 'dih'. 'Kva'[2] does not mean 'vile', as translated by Grierson, for

1. Unreal in the sense of mortal as opposed to immortal 'self'.

2. क्व is a prefix like स्व, which is its opposite. Lalla uses स्व आत्म in verse 72, which is opposite in meaning to क्व दिह। 'Ātmā' is real while 'body' is unreal.

that may connote moral depravity. In fact 'Kva-dih' should be rendered as the body which is not the *essence*. The body being mortal is unimportant for its own sake. She admits that she had always unnecessarily mortified the body with fasts and penance. Though she had learnt theoretically about the oneness of her self with the Universal Self, yet she had not had a glimpse of this Unity as a matter of experience. She was tormented by the doubt whether she should ever be able to experience and realize the Self.

That the theoretical knowledge of Advaita Philosophy had taken firm roots in the mind of Lalla is amply supported by the following vakh. She says :

21. Yimay shĕ tsĕ timay shĕ mĕ,
Shyāmagala tsĕ byõn tāṭhis,
Yŏhai bĕnabhīd tsĕ ta mĕ
Tsa shĕn svāmī bŏh shĕyi mashis.

इमय श्यं .च्य तिमय श्यं म्यं
श्यामुगला .च्यं ब्यो_न तांठिस
युहो_य ब्यनु-बीद .च्यं तु म्यं
.चु श्यन स्वामी बो ह् शंयि मंशिस ॥२१॥

The very six that Thou hast are possessed by me too.
O God of the azure throat ! in a state of separation,
I am sorely miserable.
The only difference, (though not the essential difference),
lies in the fact,
Thou art master of the six, while I forgot myself the six.

Lalla's misery is entirely due to her thought of separation from her Lord. This vakh tells us what ails her. She discloses in unambiguous words that she is pining for the union with the Absolute. This is a corollary to her conviction that man's self and the Ultimate Reality are one. One cannot but come to the conclusion that her understanding of the spiritual mystery had been nurtured and developed by scriptural study, close and profound, and that she had no doubt left in her mind that the self in the human microcosm and the Self of the Universal macrocosm were one and the same. But the fact that she had not learnt how to experience the bliss of oneness of Self, in a mystically conscious state, made it hell of a life for her. The study of scriptures had educated her about the divine attributes of Parama Śiva, viz., (1) Omniscience (Sarvajñatā), (2) Self-satisfaction and contentment (Tṛpti), (3) Perceptual knowledge from eternity (Anādibodha), (4) Absolute Freedom (Svatantratā), (5) Irreducible Potency (Nityamalupta Śakti), and (6) Omnipotence (Ananta Śakti).

In view of the limitations of the Jīva (paśu), she knew as surely her own position. In the state of manifestation of the Lord, she was the inheritor of the six hindrances (Kañcukas). "As to the souls themselves, they are nothing other than Śiva who, in virtue of his sovereign will, suffers limitation."[1] But she recognises the essential unity of the 'Pati' and 'Paśu' — the transcendental Lord and his manifested form. She is worried that her individual mind has not learnt how to break off the chains of six 'limitations'[2] which thwart the process of union. It makes her sad because she is very much aware of the power of the limitations through which she has to fight her way up to Self-realization.

The first line of the vakh may also be interpreted so as to show that Lalla recognized the essential identity between (Jīvātmā) the individual self and (Paramātmā) the Divine Self ; that the individual self had the attributes of Paramaśiva, as the latent potentiality, and that the Jīva suffered because of his ignorance

1. *Pratyabhijñahṛdyam* tr. by K. F. Leidecker: Introduction, p. 14.
2. "The six principles of subjective limitation are :
   (i) Kāla or limitation in regard to duration of presence and simultaneity of Experience — leading to the necessity of having experiences for limited periods and in succession;
   (ii) *Niyati* or limitation in regard to presence, as in space ..
   (iii) Rāga or limitation in regard to interest . .
   (iv) Vidyā or limited knowledge or limited sphere of cognition.
   (v) Kalā or the power of limited creation.
   (vi) Māyā or the generally limiting, self forgetting and differentiating power—the force of Obscuration".

   The six Kañcukas—*K. Sh.*, J. C. Chatterjee. pp. 77-85.

and separation. Paramaśiva as Absolute Self-luminous Consciousness was (svatantra) free[1] and of sovereign will; hence the master of the six attributes. The Jīva, on the other hand, by virtue of his *descent* into the manifested state had automatically forgotten his essence owing to the six attributes.

1. चितिः स्वतन्त्रा विश्वसिद्धिहेतुः ।

Pratyabhijñāhṛdayam 1.

"The absolute citi is the cause when the universe is in the process of becoming perfected." Transl. by Leidecker. p. 20.

7

THE DAWN OF HOPE

Whatever the interpretation, a salutary sign draws our attention. Doubt, surely, is a positive psychological state and, more often than not, leads to redoubled efforts towards dissipation of doubt and expulsion of fears. The darkest cloud has a silver lining and the saffron streaks of light follow the pre-dawn gloom. The cognizance of the hurdles is a sign of sanguineness. The Dark Night of Despair must, of necessity, yield place to radiant Hope.

From the Northern magnetic pole, Aurora Borealis was dispelling fast the gloom and dyeing the firmament of her consciousness with sober yet fascinating colours. The horizon of her optimism was broadening out and faith nourished her mind and let it grow large and sound. She placed herself, lock, stock and barrel, into *His* hands. Unquestioning resignation to His will,[1] the mystics hold, is indeed a step towards the discovery of the right and straight road. She says :

1. बहूनां जन्मनामन्ते ज्ञानवान्मां प्रपद्यते ।
वासुदेवः सर्वमिति स महात्मा सुदुर्लभः ।।

Bhagavadgītā, VII. 19.

"At the end of many births, the man of wisdom takes refuge in Me, realizing that Vāsudeva is all that is. Rare indeed is that great soul." Also cf. *Ibid*,, VII.29.

22. Tsal tsĕtā vŏṅdas bhayi mo bar
Con tsiṅth karān pāna Anād,
Tsĕ kawa zananiya khyŏd hari kar
Kīval tasuṅduy tāruk nād.

चल च्यत्ता व्वन्दस बयि मो बर
चोन च्यन्त करान पानु अनाद
च्यं कशु ज़नुनीय क्ष्यो_द हरि कर
कीवल तसुन्दुय तारुक नाद ॥२२॥

O fickle mind ! Do not harbour fears,
The Beginningless Himself worries for you;
How can you know when He will satisfy your (spiritual) hunger ?
You have only to wait for His divine call to ferry you across.

She consoles and encourages her heart not to give way to fear and despondence. Her unshakable faith in the benignity of the Lord succours her out of the slough. All that remained for her to do was to be patient and wait for the Divine call.

(The last line of the vakh has also been rendered as: "She should only repeat 'Oṃ' — the sacred syllable — which has the potency to ferry the aspirant across the ocean of life.")

The vakh shows that her mind had not yet got entirely rid of its basic quality of restlessness. She had not acquired complete concentration, the stage of perfect 'dhāraṇā' and 'dhyāna'. She had had spasms of fear of spiritual failure. Nevertheless, her immeasurable faith in the Lord acted as a shield against the thrusts of despair. *Hope and faith* constituted the sheet-anchor of her progressive journey upwards. She was, with all her wits about her, taking stock of her position and laying out a planned strategy to defeat the enemy — the fickle mind. She says:

23. Rut ta krut soruy pazĕm
Kanan na bozun, achin na bāva,
Oruk dapun yĕli vŏṅdi vuzĕm
Ratandīp prazalĕm varzani vāva.

रुत तु क्रुत सोरुय पज़्यम
कनन न बो.ज़ुन अछिन न बाव
ओरुक वपुन यलि ह्वन्दि वुज़्यम
रत्नदीप प्र.ज़ल्यम वरज़ुनि वाव ॥२३॥

Fair or foul must I put up with,
Deaf to external sounds and blind to external sights;
When the Divine call awakens my soul
The candle will blaze up in the midst of a hurricane !

This vakh has a veiled, indirect suggestion implicit in it. She looks forward to the Divine 'Anugraha' or grace. Sooner or later He would give her the clarion call : 'Awake and arise ! Thou soul in bondage'. Then the candle of Light that she was in essence would blaze up and shine forth in spite of the stormy gusts of circumstantial difficulties and personal limitations. Her present flutter of fear and doubt would calm down and vanish.

Meanwhile, she must act upon the 'Sādhanā' or the means to that end. She must prepare herself to receive the 'Grace'. She was aware of the fact that the five factors constituting the materiality of the sensible world — the five Bhūtas of Pṛthvī (earth), Āpa (water), Agni (fire), Vāyu (air) and Ākāśa (vacuity) — which veiled and obscured the Reality should not stand in her way. Furthermore, she appears to have known that this could be achieved by bringing under the five Jñānendriyas or capacities for sense-perception, such as the eyes, ears, the organs of smell and touch and taste. Therefore, she should muster up all her nerves to put up with everything adverse to her purpose; she should train her capacities for sense-perception so that these were not affected by the material inanities which might lead her astray from the path she had chosen for herself. And having achieved this, she must await the Divine Call. She seems to have had premonitions, as it were, that sooner or later she would hear the call within. *Hope* may not be clothed in more explicit language.

Lalla was moving up the climb with slow but steady steps. She does not adduce any logical reason for her hopefulness. But we do have a glimpse of her brightening mental horizon.

8

THE GURU GIVES THE WORD

A genuine yogi is not supposed to believe in passivity and escapism. Sādhanā and perseverance are fundamental to spiritual accomplishment; but all action, whether on the gross material plane or the subtle plane of consciousness, presumes not only direction but also the definite help of a worthy preceptor. The need of a Guru, the spiritual guide, is stressed in the Upaniṣads as well as other scriptures. "Those who wish to go farther, and to put into actual process this yoga, must first satisfy themselves of the value and suitability of this yoga and then learn directly of a *Guru* who has himself been through it. His experience alone will say whether the aspirant is capable of success. It is said that of those who attempt it, one out of a thousand may have success. If the latter enters upon the path, the Guru alone can save him from attendant risks, moulding and guiding the practice as he will according to the particular capacities and needs of his disciple."[1] "That art Thou" is easier said than realized. The tortuous road to His Abode cannot be taken safely and the destination arrived at, without the blessings and practical assistance of a guide, preceptor and mentor who is himself an adept in the occult science of mysticism. He should be a siddha — an accomplished yogi.[2] By common consent it is assumed that the Lord Himself responds to the self-consuming, intense desire of the aspirant and hammers the white-hot element of hope into shape. The scriptures do not lack

1. *The Serpent Power*—Woodroffe. pp. 29-30.
2. Kaṭh-Up. 1.2. 7, 8.

references to individuals to whom the Lord extended His helping hand, particularly in situations of dire despondence. He has His agents and instruments in human flesh and blood who carry out the Lord's behests. Unless He ordains it, you cannot find the right Guru. Ultimately the Lord is the Guru *par excellence.*[1]

Siddha Śrīkaṇṭha, presumably a scholar of Śaivaism and a realized soul, must have all along been keenly watching her progress from close quarters, and she had had the benefit of his advice and guidance already from the beginning. His knowledge of the esoteric art of yoga must have been thorough and practical. The mystical perfection which his pupil attained is evidence of the Guru's powers. It is not unlikely that he had been magnetically drawn towards Lalla by her inborn mystical potential. He had, perhaps, behind the scenes, taken it upon himself to handle the rudder of her spiritual boat from time to time. He must have been observing the ups and downs in the curves of her mind and watching her varying moods of depression and hopefulness.

It is equally probable that there was a complete rapport between Lalla and her guru. She could not but have understood that without him she could not make much headway. She had been burnishing her faculties with self-control and self-discipline. Hers was a temper not to be cooled down by the icy winds of despair. Day in, day out she continued preparing herself for the Divine Grace. "True knowledge of Reality exists in Reality and is not built up by the human brain. And this basic or original knowledge is obtainable by men only through revelation, which means that it is self-manifest. That which exists alone can be revealed, and the revelation takes place only when *some spiritual genius makes himself fit to receive it,* as the result

1. गुरुरादिरनादिश्च गुरुः परमदैवतम् ।
गुरोः परतरं नास्ति तस्मै श्री गुरवे नमः ॥

—*Viśvasāra Tantra*

"The Guru is the beginning of the Universe, yet He Himself is without a beginning; the Guru is the highest deity; there is none higher than the Guru. Salutations to that Guru !"

of the development of the proper faculty or faculties."[1] And "for the development of proper faculty or faculties" one has to sit at the feet of a 'Godman'.[2] "Each soul gains in spiritual grace in proportion to her receptivity. The more a person develops this receptivity, the more he experiences grace and spiritual benefit. Gifted with a limitless spiritual wealth, he (the godman) generously bestows it on all who aspire for it."[3] Whether it comes 'only through revelation' is questionable. The thing which leaves no room for doubt is that the recipient must prove worthy of knowledge, of the mystical trust reposed in him. "Seek that enlightenment by prostrating, by questions and by service; the wise, the seers into the Truth will instruct you in that knowledge."[4] "If the aspirant is earnest about spiritual enlightenment, the Lord sees to it that he comes in contact with an enlightened one. Seek and the light is sent to you."[5]

It is, therefore, probable that the yoginī must have, with due veneration, prostrated herself at the feet of her guru and the latter, recognising his pupil's deserts and her great urge for being instructed, took her on his hands. What discourses may have followed nobody knows. The reference to her dialogues with her guru is rather scanty. But, surely, she does acknowledge the debt of gratitude to her guru, though, as is natural, his recipe at first caused confusion and alarm to her. She says:

> 24. Nābadi bāras aṭah-gaṅḍ ḍyŏl gom,
> Diha-kān hŏl gom hyaka kiho;
> Gwara sund vanun rāvan-tyŏl[6] pĕom,
> Pahali-rŏst khyŏl gom hyaka kiho.

1. *The Cultural Heritage of India*, Vol. IV. edited by Haridas Bhattacharyya, M.A., B.L., P.R.S. Darśansagar.
2. *Godman* by Shri Kirpal Singh — Ruhani Satsang, Sawan Ashram, Delhi-7.
3. *Ibid.*, p. 4.
4. *Bhagavad Gītā*, IV, 34.
5. Sri Ramakrishna Paramahamsa.
6. 'Ravantyol': acute grief as of a young lady who suddenly becomes a widow.

नावुद्य बा:रस अटुगंड ड्योल गोम
दिहु-कान होल गोम ह्यकु क्यहो
ग्वरु सुन्द वनुन रावन-त्योल प्योम
पहलि रोस्त ख्योल गोम ह्यकु क्यहो ॥२४॥

The knot of the porter's sling helping me carry the load of sugar-candy has come loose;
My backbone is bent; how can I bear this too heavy a burden ?
The instruction of the guru has put me to agony, as it were I had lost some cherished object;
My flock has lost its shepherd, how can I bear the burden?

She had been carrying a burden of sweet dreams of spiritual illusions. Suddenly the guru's mystical precept gave her a jolt and the knot of her porter's sling of the mind came loose. It galled her tender shoulders and she was afraid she could carry the load no further. The guru's word, instead of working as a soothing balm, suddenly made her miserable. She was in confusion as if she had lost control of herself and her flock of sense-organs, sense perceptions, vaso-motor system etc., seemed to have lost their shepherd, the mind. The guru appears to have disturbed her balance of thought by some esoteric suggestion which shattered the sweet dream-world she was hitherto living in. Perhaps some hint of True knowledge was thrown at her; perhaps she was made to feel the depth of the waters in which she stood; perhaps she was given a foretaste of her own mystical potentiality, the same way as was received by Swami Vivekananda from his guru, Shri Ramakrishna. Be that as it may, Lalla appears to have become uneasy and out of sorts. The old load appears to her unworthy of being carried and the new load is in no way lighter. Mentally she is in disarray, and perplexed how she should compose herself and bear the new burden — the burden of practical yoga. "Strait is the gate, and narrow the way which leadeth unto life, and few there be that find it."[1]

1. Mathew, 7 : 7.

But Lalla's guru was fully acquainted with the spiritual strength and the nerve-fibre of his pupil, for he must have reasonably well entered the recesses of her heart and gauged her capacity to bear the strain of yogic practice. Despite the odds, her own deep-rooted appetite of the soul could not but impel her to grab at the precept. Her faith in her guru was firm as a rock. She had to follow the beacon-light to wheresoever it led and her spiritual equilibrium stood by her. She says:

> 25. Rājas boji yami kartal tyäji.[1]
> Swargas bäji chiy taph tay dān;
> Sahazas boji yami gwarakath pāji
> Pāpa-pwañi boji chuy pananuy pān.

> राजस बोज यम्य करतल त्यांज
> स्वर्गस बांज छिय तफ़ तय दान
> सहज़स बोज यम्य ग्वरु-कथ पांज
> पापु-प्वण्यु बोज छुय पनुनुय पान ॥२५॥

One who abandons the sword (gives up oppression) enjoys the fruit of a kingdom.
The enjoyment of heavenly bliss rests on ascetic self-discipline and charity;
Truth is enjoyed by one who acts upon the precept of his Guru.
And the fruit of actions, good and evil, needs must be borne by one's own self.

This verse leaves us in no doubt that Lalla knew only too well that the bedrock of yogic success was the instruction of the guru which had to be submitted to and carried out, in spite of the hazardous, thorny beginning. The only hope of ultimate release was the realization of the Self. She came to understand, without any second thoughts, that this was possible only with the sympathetic assistance and guidance of the Guru. "By transmitting his own life-impulse, the 'Sadguru' enlivens the spirit

1. 'Tyāji' derived from त्यजन to give up.

lying helplessly shrivelled in the body under the dead weight of mind and matter."[1] But the wisemen, as John Ruskin says, do not impart their wisdom by way of charity. They do not stoop to your level; you must aspire to their level: you must have a burning desire and capacity to bear the brunt of it. Ruskin speaks of the intellectual highbrows. But the same holds good in the case of the masters of esoteric knowledge. They would not expose their heart at once; not until they are fully convinced that the aspirant's will to learn is steadfast and that the aspirant has the requisite stamina.

It may not be a wild surmise that she too had gauged and measured her guru. She knew that Śrī Śrīkaṇṭha was a Siddha — a realised soul. She must have had a hard time of it extracting guidance from him; not because he would not like to place it at her disposal, but that he would surely ascertain first the depth of her longing and her strength to stand the test, before consigning to her charge the precious jewel — the secret of mystical practice. She says:

26. Gwaras pritshom sāsi late,
Yas na kĕṅh vanān tas kyāh nāv;
Pritshān pritshān thacis ta lūsas,
Kĕṅh nasa nishi kyāhtām drāv.

ग्वरस पृछ़ोम सासि लटे
यस नु कॆह् वनान तस क्याह् नाव
पृछ़ान पृछ़ान थचिस तु लूसुस
कॆंह्नस निशि क्याह्ताम द्राव ॥२६॥

A thousand times I asked my guru,
'The name of the One who is known by No-thing',
Tired and exhausted was I, asking time and again:
Out of Nothing emerged Something, bewildering and great!

Underlying this vakh is the fact that the yogeśvarī had studied, at the feet of her guru, the Upanisads. She was fully

1. *Godman*. p. 29.

conversant with the Vedāntic Philosophy, in which the Brahman is described by negatives. *Śaunaka*, the great householder, approached Aṅgiras[1] respectfully and asked: "Sir, what is that through which, if it is known, everything else becomes known?" He said to him, "Two kinds of knowledge must be known, this is what all who know Brahman tell us, the higher and the lower knowledge ... but the higher knowledge is that by which the Indestructible Brahman is apprehended. That which cannot be seen, nor seized, which has no family and no caste (which is without origin and without qualities), no eyes nor ears, no hands, nor feet, the eternal ... that it is which the wise regard as the source of all beings."[2]

Yājñavalkya said: ... "That Self (Ātman) is to be described by *No, No*! He is incomprehensible, for he cannot be (is not) comprehended; he is imperishable, for he cannot perish; he is unattached, for he does not attach himself; unfettered, he does not suffer, he does not fail."[3] The last line of this vakh compares with: "From him who perceives all and who knows all, whose brooding (penance) consists of knowledge, from Him (the highest Brahman) is born that Brahman (Hiraṇygarbha), name, form and matter (food)."[4] And again "verily in the beginning this was Brahman, that Brahman knew (its) self only, saying, 'I am Brahman'. From it all this sprang."[5]

The description by negative adjuncts, 'He is not this, He is not this,' did not satisfy her. She wanted to know the Lord by a positive image of Him. Mental concentration presumes some physical, conceptual, or ideational hallowed name or form. Accordingly, she did not get tired of pestering the Guru with this question: "Yas na kĕṅh vanān tas kyāh nāv?", much the same

1. The line of gurus is accepted in Upaniṣads. Brahmā was the first of the Devas. He told the Knowledge of Brahman, the foundation of all knowledge, to his eldest son Atharva. Atharva told to Aṅgiras; he told it to Satyavāha Bharadvāja who told it in succession to Aṅgiras.
2. Muṇḍaka-Upaniṣad. I. 1, 3, 4, 6. (Max Müller : pp. 27, 28).
3. Bṛhad-Up. III. 9. 26. Translated by F. Max Müller, pp. 148-49.
4. Muṇḍaka-Up. I. 1, 9. p. 29.
5. Bṛhad-Up. I. 4. 9.

way as Ānanda pestered the Buddha with questions. The Guru appreciates and encourages an honest enquirer, a disciple who wants to **learn.**[1] Such questions may be laid down as mere curiosity. But the thirst for true knowledge, in a genuine disciple, "will not let him be." Like quick-lime, this fire must be slaked and cooled, or it will burn one's hand. She was not a dabbler in mysticism, nor an amateur indulging herself. The sage did, at last, make her realize the immanence of the world: "Keṅh-nasa nishi kyāhtām drāv" — out of Nothing came into being everything. That was the sum and substance of knowledge. "The One manifests Himself as the many!"

At last her Guru was able to lay the ghost of Lalla's doubts without further ado. "Śiva is the Reality inherent in all, and is not one among many deities, or a decorated image, which is only a help to the uninitiated."[2] She learnt that Śiva and Śakti are not two separate realities but two conceptual aspects of the same Absolute Reality, Parā Samvid (the Supreme Experiencer), Parama Śiva, or Parameśvara.[3] The whole apparent universe is but the shining forth of the Absolute.[4] There was no duality, no separateness and, therefore, nothing to provide ground for doubt and contention. Lalla was satisfied that ontologically it was of little import by what name we may call Him. To *realise* Him was the thing.

Henceforth, Lalla got involved directly in 'yoga'—the practical aspect of mystical knowledge; and for this, more than for the theoretical hairsplitting, she had to depend on her guru.

How long it took her to get initiated into the mysteries of the sacred lore, and how long she subjected herself, body and mind, quietly and secretly to the rigours of practical technique of this esoteric science, we cannot know. We have no source to tap in this behalf. The body of her vakhs is quite silent on this point.

1. *Kaṭha* Up. I. 2. 9.
2. *Bhāskarī* I, p. 395. *Śiva-sūtra Vārttika* by Bhāskara
3. *Parātriṁśikā-vivaraṇa*—Abhinavagupta.
4. तत्र आभासरूपा एव जडचेतनपदार्थाः ।
Pratyabhijñavimarśinī III. I. (i), Abhinavagupta.

It may have taken her quite some time before her guru found her fit and ready to receive the 'Word'. As has already been said, Lalla does not seem to have been completely a novice in the art. What with her saṁskāras and predilections and what with her extraordinary zeal to dive into the waters of mystical knowledge, we may well guess that for her the yogic practices may not have been as much of an uphill task as it might be for a person soiled with the splash of past actions, base and unwholesome, and engrossed in the acquisition of earthly riches. The assumption has been that she was born with a predisposition for a mystical enterprise. We may, therefore, safely say that yogic exercises were taken up naturally. She must have felt like swimming in her own element. It is likely that the maturing process had been developing unconsciously and even consciously. Imperceptibly, the seed had taken its nourishment underground; and unknown to her and to others around her, it was getting ready for sprouting. She was waiting for the guru's Word. And when the *Word* came, lo and behold !, it worked as a magic spell. Perhaps the wand of Moses could not produce effects more instantaneous and more amazing. She says :

27. Gwaran vŏnanam kunuy vatsun,
Nĕbra dŏpanam aṅdaray atsun;
Suy gav Lali mĕ vākh ta vatsun,
Tavay mĕ hyŏtum naṅgay natsun.

ग्वरन वो_नुनम कुनुय व.चुन
न्यबुर् दो_पुनम अन्दुरुय अ.चुन
सुय गव ललि म्यँ वाख तु व.चुन
तवय म्यँ ह्यो_तुम नंगय न.चुन ॥२७॥

The Guru gave me only one Word :
Enter into thyself from the outer world.
The guru's precept came to me as God's word,
That 's why I started dancing nude.

The guru told her in a nutshell that she must relinquish the outer world and take refuge in the sanctuary of her own self[1].

1· Cf. *Katha* Up. II. 1.1

The word of the guru cast a spell on her. It brought about a complete spiritual metamorphosis. Joy welled up in her mind and caution of public exposure was cast to the winds. Lalla had carried on her domestic duties so far side by side with her religious obligations without a demur. The spiritual practices, like breath-control and mental concentration etc., were done by herself, away from the gaze of the other members of the family, and quite apart from the public view. Life had been running its uneventful course, and ostensibly she had been floating along the current. It is not beyond the bounds of reasonable conjecture that thus far she had led a life like any other housewife in the village—sweeping and daubbing with yellow clay the mud plastered floors and walls, scrubbing the cooking utensils, laundering, drawing water, and attending to a hundred minor odd jobs of home. Appearances had been kept up in spite of her 'Other worldliness'. Nobody had perhaps the slightest inkling of what was brewing within her. For all intents and purposes, she was taken for an ordinary woman attending to her round of household duties.

But deep down her soul, a spiritual volcano had been gathering momentum. The word of the guru, that time was ripe for her to abandon the thoughts of the external world and to dedicate her energies, wholly and solely, to the yogic practice — concentrating her powers on the Self within her —, acted as the igniting fuse to the dynamite of her pent up and suppressed resolve. The dynamite burst, with a devastating effect on her natural shyness and reserve. She felt, as it were, in an *essential* vertigo. Even if she were exposed she did not mind. The cover of public disapprobation was torn to smithereens. The guru's Word worked as a talisman upon her. She was filled with joy that at least she was launched on the springtide of self realization. They may jeer or jibe at her, for aught she cared. Her heart danced with joy, regardless of what others would say. She cast to the four winds her reserve and demureness because she was determined to follow the path chalked out for her by Destiny. She exhibited her pleasure in her spiritual pursuit, probably in the presence of everybody in the household to their shock and chagrin, perhaps. For her the barriers of social taboos fell at long last. This world suddenly became one vast dancing stage.

It is not easy, one would say possible, to reconcile her sanity

Note : "Naṅgay Natsun" has been taken literally by some translators of Lalla-vakhs. Fanciful stories of her dancing nude have been woven around it. They say that this yoginī is called Lalla because 'lal' in Kashmiri means a loose, hanging abdomen : as she danced and ran up and down the streets, the loose abdomen came so low as to cover her female parts.

They also say that on hearing the mystic Word from her Guru, she tore off her clothes and started dancing naked.

Another story goes that it was the time when Śri Soma Bhaṭ, her husband, discovered that Lalla rode the Divine Lion in the early hours of the morning to make her journey to the holy cave of Śiva (Harshishwar) in the mountain, and snatching his opportunity, he held the tail of the animal. Consequently, he was badly wounded. Hanging by the tail of the animal, he had been dragged up and down the mountain. Next day he breathed his last. For Lalla, the family bond had broken finally. She tore off her clothes and wandered about quite naked.

The folk-tales tell us about her nude wanderings to the end of her days. Asked why she danced shamelessly, she is said to have retorted that there was no 'man' about; till one day, in the course of wanderings she saw from a distance, Sayyed Mir Ali Hamdani, popularly known Shahi Hamdan Saheb, one of the patron saints of Kashmiri Muslims. Suddenly she cried : 'I have seen a man !' She ran down the street to hide her nakedness and shame. When a grocer refused to give her shelter, she jumped into the burning oven of a baker who closed the lid out of fear of being apprehended for murder. But the poor baker was amazed, almost to the loss of his wits, when she came out of the lower opening of the oven, wearing celestial garments of emerald green, and greeted the Muslim saint who had followed this 'lightning' on earth.

From the last tale, three things emerge, viz. (1) that Lalla was a saint of a very high order, (2) Shahi Hamdan Saheb recognised her spiritual status, (3) it dates her life, and (4) it gives us an idea of the amount of reverence with which the people of Kashmir, Hindus and Muslims alike, look upon her.

Grierson :

"The dance, called Tāṇḍava, of the naked devotee is supposed to be a copy of the dance of Śiva, typifying the course of the cosmos under God's rule. It implies that the devotee has wholly surrendered the world, and become united with Śiva."—*Lalla-Vākyāni.*

Grierson's version that Lalla wandered about in a nude condition of her body, does not hold water on close examination. His annotation that Lalla conducted a *Tāṇḍava Nṛtya,* the dance of Śiva, is a far fetched and inappropriate analogy.

and sobriety which oozes from every pore of the body of her outpourings with a rash, insane act of wandering about in a naked condition,[1] as she is said to have done. To speak nothing of her nudity, one hesitates considering her as a 'wandering and roaming' mendicant—, a 'mastāna', or God-mad person fallen from the path, as Mehar Baba would categorize such a one. Wanderring semi-nude, or completely nude, God-mad persons are lost to the world in general and to human society in particular. There is an extremely thin partition keeping them apart from lunatics. Not unoften, their mouths are either sealed or they vociferate, bursting into spurts of foul language and abuses. There is coherence neither in their thought nor in their speech. Such wandering nudes do not reply a straight question in a straight, logical way: "I wander nude because I see no 'man' about". The question and the answer appear to be a fib, projected by a devotee's mind. Lalla's coherent, sane and exalted poetry, loaded with supreme knowledge and couched in language chaste and polished, scintillating and glistening with ornaments of poetic art — simile and metaphor, parable and allegory, and images so graphic and life-like — is not the work of a God-mad person. The *internal evidence* does not at all lend support to the view that she left hearth and home on a sudden and ran down the streets with all the feminine shame exposed. The superb mystical poetry of Lalla, perfect in content and form, at places consciously chiselled and beautified, is not the achievement of a person as she is described to be. And in Lalla's time, as in our own, nakedness of body could mean nothing short of lunacy. There is not the remotest likelihood of her poetry being the creative art of a lunatic.

Besides, a person whose brain comes unscrewed cannot imaginably concentrate on the complex mental and spiritual processes of self-realization. Lalla's vakhs strongly and irrefutably support the view that she subjected herself to rigorous practice of breath control and other 'sādhanās', essential for a yogi to go through. Of necessity, solitude and reasonably stationary life are the demands of the discipline— 'yogābhyāsa'. Breath control;

1. Cf. this vakh with vakh No. 81. She does not preach nakedness of the body.

awakening of the Kuṇḍalinī; concentration on the Primal Anāhata Dhvani; progress through the different 'cakras' or plexi—the centres and planes of consciousness as laid down in the Tantras—getting absorbed in the highest cerebral centre—the Sahasrāra; and realizing the unity of the microcosmic void with the Macrocosmic Void; all these are not the yogic feats performed by a nude, insane wanderer. A mad person does not give a reason for tearing off his or her clothes and for dancing nude. She says : 'Tavay me hyŏtum naṅgay natsun'[1] '*Therefore*, have I started dancing nude.' The first word of the line is intriguing.

Hence, one can safely conclude that 'dancing nude' is a metaphorical way of saying that her joy knew no bounds, on obtaining the 'key' to the treasures of mystical knowledge. The Guru had at last come forward with a practical suggestion, nay a practical solution of her problem. So the bells rang, not only within her but without her too. She did not care a hoot whosoever heard them, for they were the bells of uncontrollable joy. She was not afraid of getting exposed. She had to renounce the outer world and she went into raptures.

Why the yogeśvarī is called "Lalla' is a simple case of Sanskrit etymology. 'Lal' is a Kashmiri derivative of Sanskrit 'lālasā', meaning 'eager desire', 'to long for', 'to seek', 'to obtain'. She was called "Lalla' or Lalla-ded because she was a seeker

1. 'Naṅga gatshun' is a Kashmiri idiom equivalent to *getting exposed*, and the stage was reached when Lalla was prepared for being exposed.

2. Shri Chaman Lal Sapru has pointed out that 'naṅgay natsun' is a misreading for 'Nŏṅguy natsun'. He quotes late Master Pandit Shanker Kaul, the first Headmaster of C. M. S. Tyndale Biscoe School, Srinagar, who was a known scholar of Kashmir Shaiva philosophy, as saying that it was not 'naṅgay' but 'nŏṅguy', and the text of Lalla's verse ought to be emended accordingly. He contends that it was utter falsehood that Lalla wandered about without apparel. 'Naṅgay' was a distortion of 'nŏṅguy' which was the name of a flower found on the high altitudes of Kashmir. A great hiker as the Masterji had been, he had seen the flower and handled it. When its stem was pressed between the thumb and the forefinger it would rise up and dance. Therefore; he affirmed that 'nŏṅguy natsun' in Lalla's verse indicated the flow of joy into the heart of the yoginī, the moment she heard the Guru's Word.

—*Kashur Samachar*, spl. issue, January, 1971.

after the Truth, and in her life-time on this earth had attained yoga. This is amply corroborated by *internal evidence* of the vakhs. In verse 37 of this book, she tells us that she was called Lalla because she sought the Truth and completely surrendered herself to the Lord's will. Verses 32, and 35 also support this view. In fact, the whole text stands for the definition of 'Lalla' given above. Also cf. vv. 44, 1.

1. A Sanskrit-English Dictionary: Sir Monier Monier-Williams (1974) p. 900.

Sanskrit Dictionary by Horace Hayman Wilson (1819).

Note : "Initiation by 'Śaktipāta Dikṣā' at the hands of a Siddha Guru is said to be essential for an aspirant. Śaktipāta or initial transmission of Śakti by sight, touch, mantra or simply by the will power of the master acts so as to awaken the dormant power of Kuṇḍalinī in the aspirant."

—*Devātma Shakti*. Swami Vishnu Tirth Ji Maharaj.

9

THE MILL OF YOGIC PRACTICE

The die was cast. The caterpillar got to weaving its cocoon around itself to emerge with the perfected, variegated wings of the butterfly. As Lalla-ded went on with the discipline, she experienced ever new phenomena of the spirit and she could not help singing. It cannot be stressed too often that her spiritual soil was rich and fertile. There was no dry rot from which she suffered within. All along she had been on the path. When the steering wheel was set and the gear put in position, the march forward gathered an amazing speed. Yoga practice came natural to her. She was poised for the rigours of the discipline and she submitted herself to it with a willing, cheerful heart.

> "In the beginning was the Word
> And that Word was with God
> and the Word was God.
> The same was in the beginning with God.
> All things were made by it
> and without it was not anything made
> that was made."[1]

1. St John. The Gospel.

Lalla received the *Word* from her Guru and concentrated on it with all her might and main. She says :

28. Akuy Omkār yus nābhi dhare,
Kumbhai Brahmāṇḍas sum gare;
Akh suy manthr tsĕtas kare,
Tas sās manthr kyāh kare.

अकुय ऊँकार युस नाबि दरे
क्वबुय ब्रह्माण्डस सुम गरे
अख सुय मन्त्र च्यतस करे
तस सास मन्त्र क्याह् करे ।।२८।।

One who fixes up only one Word—Ōṁkar—at the navel
And with the exercise of retained breath, makes a bridge
(in one span from the navel) upto the Brahmāṇḍ,
And cons only that (Ōṁkār) mantra,
A thousand mantras have no use for him.

On the threshold of yoga exercise, the first step is that of concentration. "The first Bīja of the Vedas, — Ōṃ or the Praṇava—, which is the abode of the most excellent Śakti"[1] is to be meditated upon, at the region of the navel (The Maṇipūra Cakra).[2]

About the efficacy of concentration upon repeating the Bīja-mantra, the Upaniṣad says :

"Naciketa said: 'That which thou seest as neither this nor that, as neither effect nor cause, as neither past nor future tell me that.'

1. वेदानामादिबीजम् verse 33. —*Ṣaṭ-cakra-nirūpaṇa* refers to Ājñā cakra between the eyebrows. Woodroffe pp. 445-46.

[For detailed description and explantion of "Auṃ", refer to *The Grandeur of Gayatri* by Swami Prem Bikshu, Chap.— The Glory of the Name Aum, pages 44-52.]

2. "Above the Svādhiṣṭhāna, and at the root of the navel, is the shining lotus of ten petals, of the colour of heavy-laden rain-clouds. Within it are the letters Da to Pha, of the colour of the blue lotus with the Nāda and Bindu above them. Meditate there on the region of Fire . . . . ."

Ibid. verse 19. p. 411.

Yama said : 'That word (or place) which all the Vedas record, which all penances proclaim, which men desire when they live as religious students, that word I tell thee briefly, it is Oṃ.

'That (imperishable) syllable means Brahman, that syllable means the highest Brahman; he who knows that syllable, whatever he desires, is his.'[1]"

Lalla was initiated into this yogic practice to give her a go. She had had the theoretical knowledge of the usefulness of chanting this Bīja-mantra. She may even have been taught the technique of breath-control (prāṇāyāma). Holding the breath (Kumbhaka)[2] she may have successfully awakened the 'Kuṇḍalinī. But raising it through the Suṣumnā nāḍī[3] to the uppermost cakra, as it were building a spanless bridge of the Divine Light between Maṇipūra and Sahasrāra, was the crux of the mystical effort. She says that whosoever could achieve that would get merged and dissolved into the macrocosmic Self and thus attain perfection. We can infer that the Yogeśvarī had learnt the importance of meditating on Oṃkar at the region of the navel.

The guru had found her (as a sādhaka) competent (adhikāri) to receive the Word. Directly she engaged herself with the yogic practice. "The yogis say that the piercing of the 'Brahmagranthi', or knot, sometimes involves considerable pain, physical disorder, and even disease, as is not unlikely to follow from concentration on such a centre as the navel (Nābhipadma)".[4] Lalleśvarī, too, does not make light of the task. In her teachings, reference to which is made later on, she repeatedly warns that "Śiva is

1. *Kaṭh.* Up. (Tr. Max Müller). I-2-14 to 16. Also cf. *Bh. Gītā.* VIII. 12, 13.

गिरामस्म्येकमक्षरम् । *Ibid.* chap. X. 25

(Of utterances I am the monosyllable Oṃ). "Oṃ is also called Praṇava and is a name of God. *Atharva-śikhopaniṣad* says that Praṇava is so called because through its repetition it makes all the prāṇas bow down unto Paramātman who is the soul of all souls. प्राणान्सर्वान् प्रणामयतीत्येतस्मात् प्रणवः ।

It is so because the pronunciation of Oṃ generates currents of Prāṇa to flow up the Suṣumnā to Sahasrāra, where they merge into Paramātma."

Devātma Shakti by Vishnu Tirth, p. 94.

2. Kāki-Mudrā : "Śruti says that when Vāyu is drawn in by this mudrā and stopped by Kumbhaka, steadiness of mind is produced."

Woodroffe. p. 453-footnote.

3. Brahma-sūtra or the Nāḍī Citriṇī is said to be within the Suṣumnā.

4. *The Serpent Power.* Introduction, p. 13.

difficult to attain, take heed."[1] All the same she walks on the path, despite the dangers.

"The yogi is deemed superior to ascetics, superior to men of knowledge even: he is also superior to ritualists. Therefore, be thou a yogi, Arjuna".[2] Therefore, vigorous practice, single-minded meditation, patience and perseverance were employed for attainment of yoga.

To Lalla, yoga was as stiff and severe and, at first, as unyielding as to any other novice. She says :

1. Cf. *Katha Upaniṣad.* I. 3. 14.

Note : (A) This verse involves four factors : (a) Breath-control; (b) The Maṇipūra-cakra at the navel; (c) Oṁkār; and (d) Concentration.

Breath-control (Prāṇāyāma) has three phases : (i) inhalation पूरक (ij) stoppage of inhaled breath (कुम्भक), and (iii) exhalation (रेचक).

For Maṇipūra-cakra and other details reference may be made to the *Ṣaṭ-cakra-nirūpaṇa* by Woodroffe. The Cakras are named. (a) Mūlādhāra (b) Svādhiṣṭhāna (c) Maṇipūra (d) Anāhata (e) Viśuddha (f) Ājña, and (g) Sahasrāra.

(B) *Brahmāṇḍa or Sahasrāra* :

"Above all these in the vacant space (Parama-vyōma) where is Śaṅkhini Nāḍī, and below Visarga is the lotus of a thousand petals. This Lotus, lustrous and whiter than the full Moon, has its head turned downward. It charms . . ., and it is the absolute bliss. 'Within it (Sahasrāra) is the full Moon, without the marks of the hare, resplendent as in a clear sky . . . Inside it (Candra-Maṇḍala), constantly shining like lightning is the triangle and inside this again, shines the Great Void which is served in secret by all the Suras'. 'Well concealed, and attainable only by great effort, is that subtle Bindu (Śūnya) which is the chief root of liberation and which manifests the pure Nirvāṇa-Kalā with Amā-Kalā. Here is the Deva who is known to all as Parama-Śiva. He is the Brahman and the Ātman' of all beings. In Him are united both Rasa and Virasa, and He is the Sun which destroys the darkness of nescience and delusion"— Ajñāna and Moha.

The Amā-Kalā is the nectar dropping digit of the Moon. *Ṣaṭ-cakra-nirūpaṇa.* verses 40, 41, 43.—Woodroffe.

Reference also may be made to "*A word of Lalla, The Prophetess*" by Sir Richard Temple pp. 156-158 and *Lallā Vākyāni* by Grierson and Dr. Barnett, pp. 12-15.

(C) For detailed explanation of the six cakras, reference may be made to Commentary on Śloka 21. *Saundaryalaharī* by Shri 108 Swami Vishnutirth ji Maharaj. pp. 149-165.

2 *The Bhagavadgītā.* VI. 46.

29. Zānaha nāḍidal raṭith,
Tsaṭith vaṭith kuṭith kalīsh;
Zānaha ada astah rasāyan gaṭith,
Shivchuy krūṭh ta tsen vŏpadīsh.

ज़ानुहा नाडिदल रैटिथ
च़टिथ वटिथ कुटिथ क्लीश
ज़ानुहा अदु असतु रसायन गटिथ
शिव छुय क्रूठ तु .चेन व्वपुदीश ॥२६॥

How I wish I were to know how to bring my Nāḍīs into my grip,
Tearing into shreds, collecting and pulverizing the Kleśas
Then would I learn, by and by, how to pound and prepare the (mystic) potion (of yoga) :
Śiva is difficult (to attain), and this is the lesson thou (the aspirant) shouldst bear in mind.

It was not just a walk over from the gross, temporal state of mind to the subtle, spiritual state. The complex system of Nāḍīs — as enunciated in the yogic discipline — posed a challenge to her. To manage and control these vital nerves on the supra-mental plane for practice in yoga was more than a Herculean feat. She wished she were equal to the task. The trilineal nerves —Iḍā, Piṅgalā and Suṣumnā—do not lend themselves to physical tongs and pincers, and the middle one, Suṣumnā, makes the passage for the Kuṇḍalinī to come up. Opening into the bulb (Kanda) of the Nābhipadma, this nerve is said by the yogis to be illusive and hard to grasp. Since yogic practice is difficult to describe in our common language which is but the vehicle of ordinary worldly experiences, Lalla seems constrained to use metaphorical language. Admitting that she had to grapple with the subtle nāḍīs, which played the will-o'

1. Nāḍīdal—The bunch of Nāḍīs. *Ṣaṭ-cakra-nirūpaṇa* describes the nāḍīs or 'Channels of energy' : Verse 1. Page 362. "In the space outside the Meru (The spinal column), placed on the left and the right, are the two Śirās, Śasi and Mihira. The Nāḍī Suṣumnā, whose substance is the threefold Guṇas, is in the middle. She is the form of Moon, Sun and fire (Citriṇī,

the wisp with her, she takes the apothecary's paraphernalia, pestle and mortar in particular, as her aids for graphic expression. The whole bunch of mystical vessels, not of course corresponding to our organic blood vessels, is to be brought into one's grip. The Kleśas are not merely abstract moral evils and subtle metaphysical difficulties. They are veritable chains and ropes which needs must be torn asunder, and carded into minute shreds; the broken threads are to be gathered and wound up; and the afflictions are to be powdered in the mortar of the mind with the pestle of the will. The (rasāyana) potion with its efficacy of curing spiritual ailments is to be compounded. It is to be swallowed so as to convert the dross of fleshly consciousness into the gold of spiritual consciousness. The metaphor of mystical alchemy used is superb. When the song of the subtle suffering has been sung, the finale is led in by a simple advice, almost in a whisper : "Śiva is difficult to attain !"

It is not a warning issuing out of defeat and dejection, much less is it an acceptance of surrender. She does not "betray a timidity of spirit" since she has resolved "to ascend to the height of spiritual realization."[1]

Lalla was seized of the problem facing her. It is said by the yogis that 'Kleśas' display their disturbing prowess most at the Maṇipūra centre. Once the nāḍīs have been controlled and "Nāda and Bindu" fixed upon, and Kuṇḍalinī awakened and raised above the Maṇipūra to the Anāhata Cakra, the yogi's citavṛttis are at rest. But the beginner has still to cope with the

Vajriṇī and Suṣumnā) : Her body, a string of blooming Dhatura flowers, extends from the middle of the Kanda to the Head, and the vajra inside Her extends, shining from the Meḍhra to the Head."

"The Iḍā is placed on the left, and the Piṅgalā on the right of the Meru". cf. *The Bhūta-Shuddhi Tantra* and *The Sammohana-Tantra*. "These two go straight up, alternating from left to right and right to left, and having thus gone round all the lotuses (cakras), these auspicious ones proceed to the nostrils."

For details see Description of the six centres, *The Serpent Power*—Woodroffe. pp. 362-373. First three verses and the commentary thereon.

There are 72000 Nāḍīs emanating from the Kanda or Bulb.

"The plexuses or cakras are connected by energy-currents called 'nādis' . . . The yogic nāḍīs are neither the veins nor the arteries nor the nerves . . . 'Nāḍī' is commonly understood as nerve, but in fact it is astral and not physical". *Devātma Shakti*. p. 157.

1. Cf. *Hindu Mysticism*—M. Sircar. p. 176.

mind, mobile as quicksilver and devouring as quicksand. The psychological laws of association take their natural course; thoughts and images you are least interested in stalk you, occupying the field of consciousness and dislocating the thoughts and images you are most desirous of attending to. Lalla, as a normal human being, was no exception to the persistent incursions of the restless processes of mind. She says :

30. Tsĕta turg gagna bramavon,
Nimishi aki tshanḍi yūzan[1] lach;
Yĕmina vagi yih raṭith zon
Prān-Apān phuṭaranas pakhach.

Alt. (Tsĕtani vagi bŏdhi raṭith zon
Prān-Apān **sandārith** pakhach.)

.च्यतु तुर्ग गगनु भ्रमुवोन
निमिशि अकि छन्डि यूज़नु लछ
यॅम्य नु वगि यि रॅटिथ ज़ोन
प्राण-अपान फुटुरुनस पखुच ॥ ॥३०॥

Alt. { .च्यतुनि वगि ब्वदि रॅटिथ ज़ोन
प्राण-अपान सन्दारिथ पखुच ॥ }

The steed of the mind (citta) roams the sky,
Covering a hundred thousand miles, in a jiffy !
One, who does not know how to hold it by the reins,
May be beaten to death by Prān-Apān (the exercise of Prāṇāyām).

Alt.

(Sitting in the right yogic posture, controlling one's breath, one's intelligence alone can manage the reins of the mind).

The first and foremost task for her was to bring under control

1. Yūzan= ̂ Kos

her roving mind (citta).[1] What effort it must have involved, what chastisement the unruly mind must have received, and

1. (a) चितिरेव चेतनपदादवरूढा चेत्यसंकोचिनी चित्तम् ॥

Pratybhijnāhṛdayam—Sūtra 5. Kṣemarāja.

"Citta is only citi descended from the stage of cetanā and passed into a condition of limitation due to the object of perception."

Tr. by Leidecker

(b) चितिः स्वतन्त्रा विश्वसिद्धिहेतुः ॥

Ibid. Sū I.

Citta is to be differentiated from 'citi'—the cause when the Universe is in the process of becoming perfect

Citi also called Caitanya and Parā Samvit, is equivalent to the Supreme Experiencer or Parama Śiva.

(c) "Citta" as referred to in this verse is the powerful अन्तः करण mind (मनस्)—"the ever moving or the ever flowing one". "Manas... is a state of activity—it being busily engaged in building up images, as fast as the senses supply the manifold of the external Universe."

Kashmir Shaivism, J.C. Chatterjee p. 115.

(d) Also *Bhagavadgītā* –VI. 34.

(e) "Thus it is, that Manas is intensely active and restless, as it moves constantly, on the one hand from senses to the Ahaṅkāra to which it 'hands over' the sense-manifold after it has been transferred into images to be presently endowed with other elements by the Ahaṅkāra itself from its own store-house. It is a *Kinetic State*."

Kash. Sh. p. 117.

(f) "But, although blind and moving and working in the dark, still Manas is an experience of groping, of *seeking* however *unintelligently*. It is, therefore, the seat of 'desires'. Indeed Manas is 'desire' incarnate."

Ibid p. 119.

(g) यदा प्रार्थयते किंचित् तदा भवति सा मनः ॥ *Mahābhārata*.

Buddhi, Ahaṅkāra and Manas work together in man as the three powerful Antaḥkaraṇas. In Buddhi Sattvaguṇa predominates ; in Ahaṅkāra, Rajas; and in Manas and the Indriyas and their objects, Tamas.

(h) "Citta in its special sense is that faculty (Vṛtti) by which the Mind first recalls to memory (smaraṇam) that of which there has been previously Anubhava or Pratyakṣa Jñāna—i.e. immediate cognition."

The Serpent Power. Woodroffe p.74.

(i) 'Cinta' derives from Citta. चेतयत्यनेनेति चित्तम् ॥

Sāṅkhyapravacanasūtra II. 47.

"According to Vedānta, Buddhi determines but once only, and the further recall and thought upon the mental object so determined is the faculty of the separate mental category called Citta."

S. P. p. 75.

"To sum the functions of the subtle body : the sense-objects (Bhūta, derived from Tanmātra) affect the senses (Indriyas) and are perceived by Manas, are referred to the self by Ahaṅkāra, and are determined by Buddhi." *Ibid.* p. 75.

"The Jīva lives in his subtle or mental body alone when in the dreaming (Svapna) state. For the outside world of objects (Mahā-bhūta) is then shut out and the consciousness wanders in the world of ideas. The subtle body is imperishable until Liberation is attained . . . Mind in the subtle body bears saṁskāras which are the result of past actions . . " *Ibid.* p. 76.

Prāṇa-Apāna

(a) "Different from this (food), which consists of the essence of food, is the other, the inner-Self, which consists of breath. The former is filled by this. It also has the shape of man. Like the human shape of the former is the human shape of the latter, prāna (up-breathing) is its head, vyāna (back-breathing) is its right arm. Apâna (down-breathing) is its left arm. Ether is its trunk. The earth the seat (the support)."

Taitt-Up. II. 2.

(b) "The Devas breathe after breath (Prāṇa), so do men and cattle. Breath is the life of beings, therefore it is called Sarvāyuṣa (all-enlivening). They who worship breath as Brahman, obtain the full life. For breath is the life of all beings, and therefore it is called Sarvâyuṣa. The embodied Self of this (consisting of breath) is the same as that of the former (consisting of food)."

Taitt-Up. II. 3. Tr. F. Max Müller.

Prāṇa as Mahāprāṇa means the *elan vital* of the universe

(c) "The Lord of Creation (Prajāpati), verily was desirous of creatures (off-spring, prajā). He performed austerities. Having performed austerities, he produced a pair, matter (Raye) and life (prāṇa), thinking: these two will make creatures for me in manifold ways."

Praśna Up. quoted by M. Sircar.

(d) "Prāṇa is the fourth part of Brahman. It shines and glows with vāyu as its light......"

The Chāndogya-Up. III. 18, 4.

(e) Again in iv, 30: "Brahman is prāṇa, Brahman is joy."
In Kauṣītaki Up., Indra says:
"I am the breathing spirit (Prāṇa), the intelligent self (Prajñātman), Āyu (life) is Prāṇa. Prāṇa is verily Āyu, Prāṇa is in the body, so long is life......."

Prāṇa refers to cosmic energy.

(f) *Hindu Mysticism.* pp. 137-141.

(g) Again: "The gross and subtle bodies .... are vitalized and held together as an organism by prāṇa which is evolved from the active energy (Kriyā Śakti) of the Liṅga śarīra. Prāṇa, or the vital principle, is the special relation of the Ātman wtih a certain form of matter which by this relation the Ātman organizes and builds up as a means of having experience. This special relation constitutes the individual prāṇa in the individual body.

The cosmic all-pervading prāṇa is not prāṇa in this gross sense, but *is a name for Brahman* as the author of the individual prāṇa. The individual prāṇa is limited to the particular body which it vitalizes and is a manifestation in all breathing creatures (prāṇi) of the creative and sustaining activity of the Brahman who is represented in individual bodies by the Devī Kuṇḍalinī."

The Serpent Power—Woodroffe. p. 85.

(h) Also, cf. *Devatma Shakti* pp. 54-69.

what iron will she must have had to employ, is left unsaid. But one thing is made very clear by this verse: an aspirant who does not learn the art of controlling the steed of his restless mind before entering upon the yogic sādhanā, and before taking to the exercise of breath-control, is surely jeopardizing his body. "The Mystic is the Truth-seer, not in the sense of enjoying ecstatic intoxication—that, no doubt, is his peculiar claim and privilege—but in the sense of an adventurous experimentalist who claims to see the exact constitution of the human fabric, the instincts, the vital urges, the impulses, the ideas, in their intricate blending and complete unison."[1] So her warning to the sādhakas is opportune and valuable. We may conclude from this vakh, by implication, that she had overcome the restlessness of her mind. This is also borne out by the later stages of success she achieved in yoga.

Lalla neither fights shy of expressing and revealing her difficulties, nor does she leave us in suspense as to what steps she took to surmount them. She gives a neat exposition of her method. She says:

31. Dihaci lari dāri-bar trŏprim,
Prāna-tsūr **rŏṭum** ta dyutmas daṃ;
Hradayici kūṭhari aṅdar gŏṅduṃ,
Ōmaki cobuka tulimas baṃ.

दिहिचि लरि दारि-बर त्रोपुरिम
प्राणु-.चूर रोटुम तु द्युतुमस दम
हृदयिचि कूठरि अन्दर गोंडुम
वोंमुकि चोबुक तुलिमस बम ॥३१॥

1. *Hindu Mysticism*, M. Sircar.

Closing fast the windows and doors of the house of my body,
I caught hold of the thief, Prāṇa, and barred him in;
Tying him hand and foot inside the closet of my heart,
I lashed him hard with the whip of Ōṃ.

Rigid discipline of a Sādhaka has been couched in compact, delightful verse. Personification and metaphor could not, perhaps, be put to an apter use in poetry. The human body is a house and the sense-organs are the doors and windows. Will is the dominating power of the aspirant. Lalla shut all the apertures, and the external world of sense was completely left out and ignored. Her preceptor had enjoined on her to shut the world of sense out. She had learnt from the śāstras that Śiva was in us as much as outside us.[1] She had been told to enter into her Self. And she did not need to be told twice. Having controlled her indriyas and Manas, the next thing was to attack Prāṇa.[2] Prāṇa is personified as a thief, who makes off with our life, if he is not engaged usefully. The vital principle of life is to be imprisoned, broken in and harnessed to the cart of life; his movements being regulated to the will of the driver—the individual self. Faultlessly, Lalla constructs the image of breaking in of a cart-horse. Her whip is the sacred syllable, Oṃ,[3] which she had received from the guru.

1. *Muṇḍaka-Upaniṣad.* III.4.10.

"He is both without and within....", "...He is indeed the inner Self of all things", "...he who knows this hidden in the cave (of the heart), he, O friend, scatters the knot of ignorance here on this earth."

Translation by Max Müller.

"Verily in the beginning this was Brahman...... Therefore, now also he who thus knows that he is Brahman, becomes all this, and even the Devas cannot prevent it, for he himself is their Self."

Bṛhad. Up. I. 4-10.

2. *Taittirīya Up.* 5.3. Also *Bṛhad. Up.* I. I.

3. गुणसाधारण्य श्रुतेश्च ॥

So the sense perceptions from the outer world were ignored, the mind was put at rest, and the movement of Prāṇa was regulated by a hard training of concentration and meditation on Oṃ.

Lalla seems to have become dead to her social surroundings. She seems to have crossed several stages, in the Aṣṭāṅga;—the stages of Yama, Niyama, Āsana, Prāṇāyāma, Pratyāhāra and Dhāraṇā—and had reached the stage of acute 'Dhyāna' without the least distraction. Her faith supported her, and cut her physical and mental exhaustion fine. This is a great example of faith bolstered up by optimism. She says:

32. Lala bŏh lūsas tshāṅḍān ta gwārān
Hal mĕ kŏrmas rasanishiti;
Vuchun hyŏtmas ***tāri*** dīṅṭhmas baran,
Mĕti kal gañeyam zi zogmas tati.

लल बो ह लूसुस छाँडान तु गारान
हाल म्यं को रमस रसुनिशतिय
वुछुन ह्यो तुमस तांयं डींठिमस बरन
म्यंति कल गनेयम जि़ ज़ोगमस तंतिय ॥३२॥

I, Lalla (a seeker), was tired with searching and waiting (for Him),
I pursued Him close, slowly and steadily;
I tried to have a glimpse of Him, but found his doors bolted and barred,
But my longing deepened, and I lay in wait for Him there (within myself).

She had been seeking her Lord for nobody knows how long. Physical and mental exhaustion was inevitable. But she would not allow the Self to elude her. She pursued her objective, trying to become conscious of the Self. The closet of Self was strongly

"And from the Śruti declaring the syllable Oṃ which is a common feature (of the Udgītha Vidyā), to be common to all the Vedas."
Brahma Sūtra III. 30. 64. (Com. by Swami Vireshwarananda)
Also "through *this* (Ōṃ) does the Vedic vidyā proceed." *Ch. Up.* I.1.9

bolted. The stubbornness of self to remain hidden and veiled sharpened her appetite all the more and she waited for the Beloved, as it were, outside his door !

The verse shows the dauntless spirit of Lalla in her pursuit of the Self. With a redoubled zeal she went on with the yogic practice. She says :

33. Damāh dam kŏrmas damanhāle,
Prazalyom däph ta naňeyam zāth;
Andrium Prakāsh nĕbar tshŏṭum,
Gaṭi rŏṭum ta karmas thaph.

दमाह् दम को्रमस दमनह्ाले
प्र.जुल्योम दूफ तु नन्येयम ज्ञाथ
अन्दुर्युम प्रकाश न्यबर छो़ुम
गटि रो्टुम तु क्रमस थफ ॥३३।

For a moment I suppressed the bellows of respiration,
Lo and behold ! The Lamp lit up brightly and I realized my Self !
The light within me sparkled out;
In the encompassing darkness, I seized at It (the bright gem of Self) and gripped It tightly.

The direct apprehension of Self was achieved.[1] During her long drawn practice of breath-control, when the external world had ceased to be for her, when the Indriyas and the Antaḥkaranas had come to rest, a moment came when suddenly she stood face to face with the dazzling light of the Lamp,[2] the Ātman.

1. "It is an experience of the Yogi by which he acquires knowledge of the true nature of his own self (विमर्श)."

Kṣemarāja, *Sh. SV.* 116,14. quoted by Leidecker.

2. तदुत्तीर्णशिवभट्टारकस्य प्रकाशैकवपुषः प्रकाशकरूपा एव भावाः

Pratybhijñāhradyam. Com. by Kṣemaraja. Sūtra-3.

Also: "The person not larger than a thumb, the inner Self, is always settled in the heart of men. Let a man draw that Self forth from his body with steadiness, as one draws the pith from a reed. Let him know that Self as the *Bright*, as *Immortal*; yes, as the Bright, as the immortal."

Kaṭha Up. II. 3.17. Also *Śvet. Up.* III.13.

She became conscious of the nature of the Self. It shone too bright to be contained within her fleshly frame. In other words, the all-prevading Śiva was realised as a luminous flame within and without. Hitherto it had been a world of darkness in which she had been groping. In the midst of the Tamas of ignorance, the Lamp of Self, dissipating all darkness, suddenly blazed up. The knowledge of Self dawned upon her, not figuratively but literally. The thought of duality[1]—of 'I' (Ahantā) and 'this' (Idantā)—and separateness disappeared once for ever. She discovered the essence of the individual self as nothing other than the effulgent Cosmic Self.[2]

It is not a condition of a psychic vision or a transitory hallucination. She had been exerting all her powers towards the realization of this goal. The adepts in yoga affirm this condition : the scriptures dealing with the yogic culture, and above all her guru had promised her that realization of the Self was possible. She had conducted intensive penance; and the meditation on the sacred syllable, Oṃ, bore fruit. She succeeded in apprehending her Self. as a brightly shining Lamp within her, and the light splashed out. About Parama Śiva it is said that He is self-luminous.[3] Parama

1. तन्नाना अनुरूपग्राह्यग्राहकभेदात् ॥

Pratybhijñāhṛdayam, Sūtra 3.

2. "A mortal who has heard this and embraced it, who has separated from it all qualities, and has thus reached the subtle Being, rejoices, because he has obtained what is a cause for rejoicing. The house (of Brahman) is open, I believe, O Naciketa, said Yama". *Kaṭha-Up.* 1.2.13.

3. स्वयं प्रकाशः ॥

Note:

(i) In passing, we may revert to the question whether Lalla wandered about nude. Sanity would brush aside the tradition on studying this vakh closely. The sublime content of this mystical verse giving a vivid picture of the Self does not even distantly hint that she had lost control of her wits. Nor does the form of the verse. The moment of an indescribable success deserved all the ornaments and decorations of exalted poetry. The alliteration damāh, daṃ, damanhāle; the mellifluous soft vowel sounds in 'prazalyom, naneyam, däph'; the picturesque metaphor aṅdryum prakāsh nĕbar tshōṭum (I winnowed the inner light out, scattering it in cascades)—, all this art cannot be the work of an insane, nude wanderer, off her head. The vakh describes a moment of emotional exuberance overflowing in a spurt of superb lyricism.

(ii) Some people read the first line of the vakh as under:

'Dama-dam kormas damanhale'.

'Dama-daṃ' is taken to mean application of all force and energy to the bellows. But they miss the point, viz., what is to be done to the bellows ? Actually the bellows are to be *restrained.* Therefore, 'dam kormas' is to be separated from 'dama'. Hence, it should read *damah* and not as *dama.*

Śiva being present in everything that exists, the luminosity of the individual self is an *a priori* conclusion.

A close study of the vakh is rewarding. She says: 'damâh daṃ kŏrmas damanhâle'—for a moment I checked and muffled his bellows. The bellows of Prāṇa are His (of the self) instruments. So the body with all its vital organs, such as the lungs and the bronchial tubes are not the self. The former are mortal while the latter is eternal. The self with the body is 'saguṇ' or has attributes. She wanted to realize it in the attributeless (nirguṇa) form. She had been putting herself through meditation tirelessly, so as to have a glimpse of Him who worked the bellows. She restrained the bellows and He could not help revealing Himself. The Self raised the veil ! Once hers, for ever hers. *It was not a passing vision.*

The most profound aspiration of man, from time immemorial, has been to discover the nature of Self. Just as by compressing the bellows gently, the feeble light of a lamp is made to shine brightly, in the same way she had by her acquired powers of meditation controlled and compressed Prāṇa, and the Self blazed upon her inward eye. But, according to mystics, realization of the individual Self is not the *summum bonum* of earthly life, especially for aspirants of Lalla's category. Final dissolution or reabsorption of the individual Self into the Self of the Macrocosm is their goal, in so much as this ensures spiritual salvation and freedom from the cycle of birth and death.

Having realized the Self, Lalla does not make light of the body. The aspiring yogi has ever to be alert against the inroads of the physical sense-organs and their shattering influence on meditation. She is not tired of expatiating on the theme of subjugating the insidious foe—the five 'indriyas'; nor does she forget the importance of controlling the vital airs. She says:

34. Shishras ẏuth kus raṭe,
Kus bŏke raṭi vāv;
Yus päṅtsh yiṅdray tsĕlith tsaṭe
Suy raṭe gaṭi rav.

शिशिरस बुथ कुस रटे
कुस ब्वके रटे वाव
युस पांछ इन्द्रिय च्यलिथ चटे
सुय रटे गटे रव ॥३४॥

Who can hold the drippings in freezing mid-winter?
Oh! who can hold the wind in one's clenched hand?
He and only he, who crushes the five sense-organs and tears them into shreds;
He alone can hold the sun (of Self) in the midst of pitch darkness.

In the freezing cold of mid-winter (in Kashmir) it would be a magical feat, an exercise of supernatural powers to stop the eaves from dripping: or to grasp the insubstantial air into one's grip, is surely an exercise in futility. But once man ceases to be a slave to his sense-organs, to the manifold of earthly experience, once he becomes dead to the external world, to speak nothing of holding back the drippings or grasping the air, he can climb the heights of higher mystical powers and behold the sun of Self in the enveloping darkness of ignorance. Restraining the sense-organs, withdrawing into himself, man can awaken in himself the consciousness of experiencing and standing face to face with his Self, shining as brilliant as the Sun.[1]

Miraculous powers come to the yogi, and the most miraculous of all is the power of Self-realization. But the prerequisite is the stupendous task of looking after one's five 'indriyas' and seeing that they do not disturb your meditation. Lalla had 'seen' the Self, resplendent as the sun, but she had also learnt, by personal experience, that the gateway to this spiritual heaven was the complete control on the sense-organs. By implication, we may say that she did not undervalue the undoing power of the sense-organs which act as instruments of Māyā, the governing force of obscuration of the Truth. The verse may be taken as a guide-line by the aspirants. "Die unto this world: thou shalt live unto thy Self."

In the first line of this quatrain, 'shishar,' may be interpreted as

1. *Bhagavad Gitā* VI. 18.

the 'shashikalā' or the topmost cakra — the Sahasrāra; and the line may, in that case, have reference to drippings of nectar from the Abode of the Moon. 'Vāv' may mean the void of the attributeless state of Siva, or Prāṇa as the cosmic Life-force.

So the two lines together may mean that to drink the nectar of the moon in the Sahasrāra Cakra, and to grasp the Parama Śiva are the destined achievements of a yogi who has controlled the sense-organs, and whose ignorance (Avidyā) has been removed by the Sun of knowledge of the Self. This vakh lays emphasis on the desirability and importance of restraining the sense-organs.

The study of the vakh that follows, however, shows that the mystical explanation given above does not fit in with the arrangement of this text. The stage for 'yoga', the final union, was still to come and the goal still tantalized her. She had grasped the Lamp of Self. Release from the never-ending gyrations of birth and death was yet to be achieved. And she worked hard for it. She says:

35. Pŏt zūni vathith mŏt bolanovum,
Dag Lalanävam Dayisañzi prahe;
Lali Lali karān lal vuzunovum,
Mīlith tas shrotsyom dahe.

पोत ज़ूनि वंथिथ मोत बोलनोवुम
दग ललनावुम दयि संज़ि प्रहे
ललि ललि करान लाल वुज़ुनोवुम
मीलिथ तस श्रोच्योम दहे ॥३५॥

Waking when the moon was about to set, I made my
mad-heart sing,
How I bore the pangs of my Lord's love!
Crying 'Lali'! 'Lali'! (I am a seeker! I am a seeker!)
I awoke the Ruby of my Self,
Meditating on Him, my body was sanctified.

The music of the verse touches the chords of the heart. The love-lorn heart of Lalla knew no rest. She says that long before daybreak, in the small hours of the night when the moon was about to set and the world of men and beasts was asleep, she woke up and madly sang for Him, for whom she pined and languished. She bore the heart-ache but could not help crying repeatedly that she was a seeker; till at last the Self awoke, the Lamp within her, and she was beatified and her body relaxed in plenitude of peace.

The vakh affirms that the first glimpse of Self had not been a passing phenomenon. She had dwelt on it then, and she could bring up to the foreground of consciousness, at will, that supreme experience. It was her immense capacity to bear the pangs of intense love for her Lord that helped waking the Self. Though a yoginī, Lalla does not rule out the efficacy of 'Bhakti' — intense, concentrated devotion — as a means to the awakening of the Self.

The verse has a rich, musical language and romantic content. Lyrical poetry in any language may not outdo this vakh in Kashmiri. 'Pŏt Zūni' — that is the background; and the nightingale seeking the mate sings with "full-throated ease" — "I am the seeker! I am the seeker!" And anon wakes up the Eternal Beloved, the Self; "Here am I to feast your mind upon!" The feeling of love, deepseated and burning, is readily answered and the lover is purified and transported into a state of ecstasy.

This vakh shows that she was still at a stage short of yoga. She had set as her goal the final salvation and she was yet on this side of the shore. She says:

36. Sahazas sham ta dam no gatshe,
Yatshi no prāvakh muktīdwār:
Salilas lavan zan mīlith gatshe,
Toti chuy durlabh sahaza vĕtsār.

सहुज़स शम तु दम नो गछ़े
यछ़ि नो प्रावख मुक्ती द्वार
सलिलस लवण ज़न मीलिथ गछे
तोति छुय दुर्लब सहु.ज़ु व्य.चार ॥

(Grierson, V. 29)

Alt. सहज़स शम तु दम नो गछ़ॆ
यछि प्रावख मुक्ती द्वार
... ... (Rājānak Bhāskara) MS.
... ... ॥३६॥

The Real is not attained by (mere) selfcontrol and continence,
The gateway to deliverance is not opened by mere wishfulness;[1]
Even after getting dissolved in Him, like salt in water,
It is difficult to determine the Reality.

She had recognized the Self by virtue of complete control over the sense organs and by withdrawing her mind from the external world. But her set goal was deliverance (mukti) from the bondage of life and death. Total dissolution in Him was what she had determined to achieve. Her ambition was not recognition of the *identity* but complete and never-to-be-severed *unification*. She says that 'śam' and 'dam' are not adequate means for that purpose. *The only solution is dissolution* and there is the rub. What spiritual struggle it involves is left to the aspirant's personal and individual experience when he goes through it. Like all masters, she just throws the hint: 'salilas lavan zan mīlith gatshe', as it were salt getting dissolved in water. She rounds it up with: 'Toti chuy durlabh Sahaza vĕtsār';[1] despite all that it is difficult to contemplate the Truth. By this note of warning an aspirant-novice may be clean bowled over and rendered helpless, unless he possesses the mettle that came natural to Lalla-ded. The alternative to this vakh, as given by Shri Rājānak Bhāskar,[2] reads:

Sahazas sham ta dam no gatshe
Yatshi prāvakh muktīdwār;
Salilas lavan zan mīlith gatshe,
Toti chuy durlabh Sahaza vĕtsār.

1. 'Does God really exist ?' Rama Chandra asked. 'Of course He exists,' Ramakrishna told him. 'You don't see the stars in the daytime, but that does not mean that the stars don't exist. There's butter in the milk, but how could anyone guess that by looking at it ? To get the butter you must churn the milk in a cool place. To get the vision of God you must practise mental discipline—you can't see Him just *by wishing*.' "
Ramakrishna And His Disciples. C. Isherwood. p. 169.

2. Ms. v 29. (Personal collection of Pandit Dina Nath, Rajabagh, Srinagar Rtd. official, Research Library, Srinagar).

Here stress is laid on the first word of the second line. The aspirant's 'yatsh' or Icchā i.e. intense desire is what ultimately matters for the attainment of 'mukti' or release from the cycle of birth and death. Withdrawing the mind from the external world and control of the sense organs etc. may be helpful for yoga but the Truth cannot be realized merely by these means. In fact, Sahaza or the One born with you does not need checks and restraints of the body if the "Will" to grasp him is firm and unfaltering. Concentration on the Self is difficult, even if apparently one gets dissolved in Him like salt in water and the redemption lies in a burning desire of the sādhaka.

The Lord confirms this point in the *Bhagavadgītā* when he says that out of thousands of people hardly one wills to attain Me.

मनुष्याणां सहस्रेषु कश्चिद्यतति सिद्धये ।

Gītā VII. 3.

And Shri Ramakrishna emphasizes the importance of a sincere, fervent desire of the aspirant for realization of God. When M. asked him what state of mind makes a man able to see God, Shri Ramakrishna said: "Cry to Him with a yearning heart, and you will see him." At another place he says: "When a man sheds tears and when his hair stands on end if he utters the name of Hari or Rāma even once, then you may know for certain that he no longer needs to perform rituals[1]..."

When we talk of Icchā, we have to differentiate it from a simple wishfulness. Lalla-ded recognises the force of a burning desire which presumes concentration of the whole mind. Śama and dama automatically lose their edge. Sahaza-větsar is not possible unless the will is firm.

1. *Ramakrishna And His Disciples.* C. Isherwood pp. 258, 267.
Also, cf. v.56 of this text. Lalla stresses 'Icchā' or burning desire of the aspirant.

10

COMPLETE SURRENDER

She too had finally to resign to His will and supplicate for (Anugraha) His grace. She says:

37. Mal vöṅdi zolum
Jigar morum:
Teli Lal näv drām
Yeli dali trävimas tati.

मल व्वन्दि ज़ोलुम
जिगर मोरुम
त्यॅलि लल नाव द्राम
यॅलि दॅल्य त्रॉविमस तॅती ॥३७॥

I burnt up the impurities of my mind,
I made away with my heart.
Then was I hailed by the name of Lalla (a seeker),
When I resigned myself completely to Him.

"The lives of saints are a history of successive renunciations of complication, one form of contact with the outer life being dropped after another, to save the purity of inner tone."[1] Lalla avers

William James, *Varieties of Religious Experience*. p. 349.

that she had purified her mind of all defilement. The impurities[1] of particularization of the Self, of dichotomy between the experiencer and the experienced etc., had, by a long intensive effort, been washed off her mind. The worldly desires had been totally done for. It is said that "mind limits consciousness so as to enable man to have finite experience. There is no mind without consciousness as its background, though supreme consciousness is Mindless (Amanaḥ). Where there is no mind (Amanaḥ), there is no limitation."[2] But the state of mindlessness is the state of final deliverance, the state of Śiva. She had, no doubt, transcended the impurities of Kārma and Māyā malas, but this was not enough. Oneness with the supreme consciousness may not be attained unless the Āṇava-mala is removed. She seems to have come to a halt in her yogic practice. She had to resign to His will. The distinction between (idam) 'this' and (aham) 'I' may not be removed by the powers of the individual mind: for, as a matter of logical necessity, non-duality cannot be attained so long as individuality obtains. This 'Mala' of differentiation cannot be cleansed off by individual effort. One has got to prostrate oneself at the feet of the Lord. The limitation is imposed by Śiva, and by some *function of His* (Anugraha)[3] alone the limitation of division into Three (Pāśa, Paśu, Pati) can disappear. Eternal bliss cannot be experienced unless the merger takes place, until the separated 'I' has the consciousness of reabsorption and dissolution into the Ultimate Being.

In view of this, Lalla submits without reservations to the Lord's will. '*Yeli dali trävimas tati*' is, in Kashmiri, an expression of extreme self-surrender. It is said that the Parama-Guru

1. श्राणवमायीयकार्ममलावृतत्वात् त्रिमयः ॥
"Owing to his being covered by '*mala* of *āṇava*, *māyā* and *kārma* (Śivabhaṭṭāraka) is of threefold build."

Pratybhijñāhṛdyam Sūtra 7.
Commentary Kṣemarāja. Tr. by Leidecker.

(i) The Āṇavamala or (mūlamala) transforms the soul into a limited aṇu of individual entity.
(ii) Māyāmala gives the soul its bodily form.
(iii) Kārmamala is the mala which enchains the soul by good and evil action.

2. Woodroffe. *Body-less consciousness.* p. 31.
3. *The Bhagavad Gītā* XVIII. 62.

is the Lord Himself. And His grace must attend on you.[1] "Anugraha is called the fifth phase in the cosmo-psychological process through which the soul finally overcomes the four other phases of sāṁsāra and reaps salvation."[2]

. "That Self cannot be gained by the Vedas, nor by understanding, nor by much learning. He whom the Self chooses, by him the Self can be gained. The Self chooses him (his body) as his own."

Kaṭh. Up. 1.2.25. Also, *Bh. Gītā.II.* 53.

2. Leidecker—Introduction p. 16 (*Pra. Hṛ.*). The other four being सृष्टि, स्थिति, संहार, पिधान ।

11

REALIZATION

Her Lord did not leave her long in the lurch. She was rewarded for her pains. She says:

38. Shĕ van tsaṭith shĕshikal vuzam,
Prakrat huṅzam pavana säti;
Lolaki nāra välinj buzam,
Shaṅkar lobum tamiy säti.

श्य वन च॑टिथ शशिकल वुज़म
प्रक्रथ हुं.ज़ुम पव़नु सूती
लोल़ुकि नारु वा॑लिंज बुज़ुम
शंकर लोबुम तमिय सूती ॥३८॥

Crossing the six forests, came the Shĕshikala oozing,
The Prakṛti was sacrificed (burnt out) with the air (Prāna),
With the fire of Love I roasted my heart;
Thus Śiva was realized hy me.

The esoteric import of this vakh is difficult to explain. Reference is made to the practice of yoga as laid down in the Sāstras. Exhaustive description of the Kundalinī Yoga is given in the *Ṣaṭ-cakra-nirūpaṇa*. Also reference may be made to slokas 9, 10 and 21 of *Saundaryalahari* — commentary by Swami Vishnu Tirthji Maharaj and *Devātma shakti* by the same author.

THE DIFFERENT YOGIC PLEXUSES

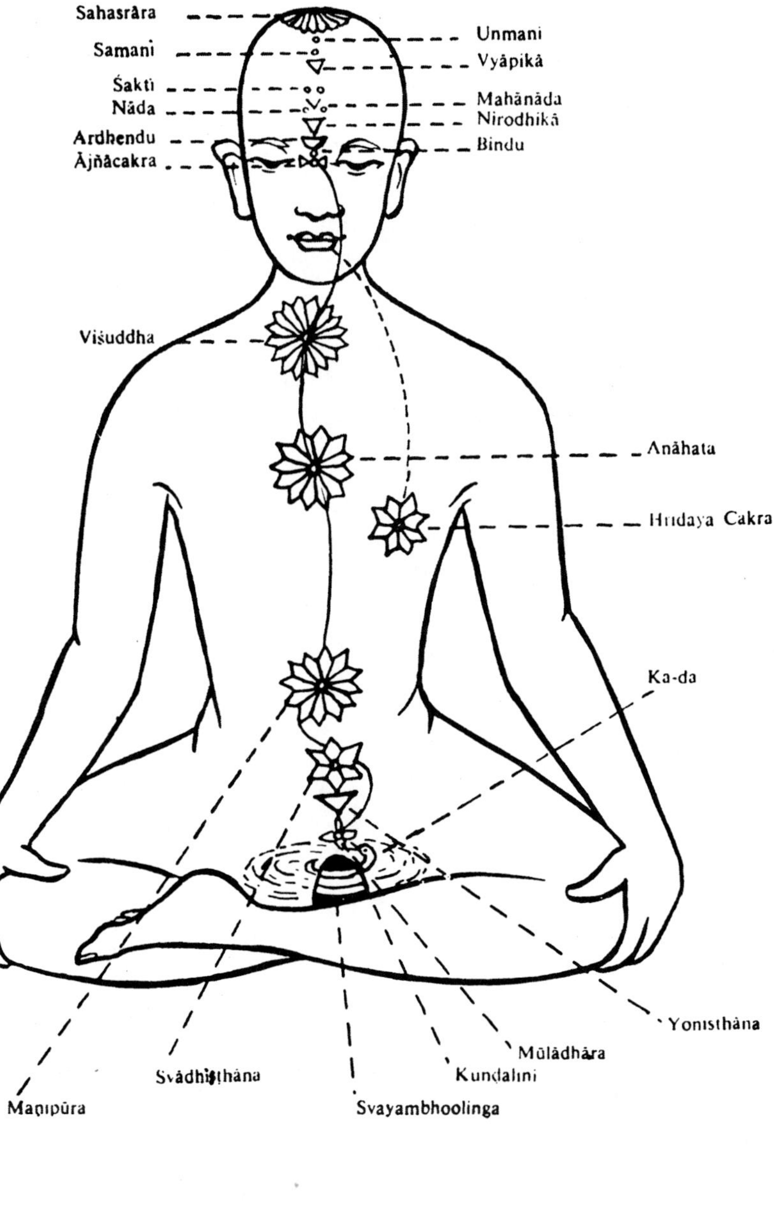

Lalla-ded may have been practising this mode of absorption and dissolution of the individual microcosmic self into the macrocosmic Self and this is evidenced by many other vakhs too. In an earlier vakh, she had wailed: zānha nāḍidal raṭith — how I wish I were able to grasp the nāḍis. In course of time, she seems not only to have discovered the nāḍīs, but also to have awakened the Devī Kuṇḍalinī, lying coiled round the Svayambhū-liṅga poised at the Mūlādhāra (the basal cakra), the 'home' of Śakti. With intensive practice, the Yoginī succeeded in awakening and raising the Cosmic Power in the individual through the six cakras. Then she came upon the digit of the Moon (Candrakalā or Śaśikalā) in the topmost cakra wherefrom oozes the manna, the honeyed nectar on licking which the Kuṇḍalinī bestows bliss to the individualized self. This state is said to be the harbinger of the state of yoga or final absorption. It is a prelude to samādhi wherein the yogi partakes of the bliss of Supreme Śiva. Lalla had attained this state. On bringing the Kuṇḍalinī down, she dwells on the experience.

She recalls that she had been able to ascend upward to the Sahasrāra after crossing the six difficult and risky stages which she compares with forests in which the aspirant may easily get lost, or be devoured by the wild beasts of the allurements and pitfalls of 'siddhis' or occult powers which are strewn on the path. If she had come out of the six forests safe and sound, it was because she had complete control on the vital airs and with their aid she had burnt out all the lower pulls and pressures of Prakṛti,[1] the elements of involution. As a matter of fact, she had

1. (a) The second line of the quatrain may also be interpreted so as to mean that she had aroused and kindled Prakṛti Śakti (Kuṇḍalinī) with the help of breathcontrol. 'Huṅzam' would mean *blazed up* as fire blazes up with a sudden whiff of air. In the evolutionary process, the five natural elements—earth (said to be the element at Mūlādhāra), water (at Svādhiṣṭhāna), fire (at Maṇipūra), air (at Anāhata), ether (at Viśuddha) and mind (at Ājñā)—are destroyed one after another so that the obstructions to the ascent of the Kuṇḍalinī Śakti are cleared away. The Yogadarśana of Patañjali refers to the siddhis of Bhūtajaya, Prakṛtijaya and Indriyajaya. "A yogi with the knowledge of separateness of Puruṣa (Ātman) and Sattva i.e. intelligence acquires all powers and all knowledge." "To detach the Purusha from all planes of Prakṛti is the main object of a yogi".

Saundaryalaharī 9, 10. Swami Vishnu Tirth.

performed a Mahāyajña, a 'Naciketa sacrifice'[1] which breaks the chains of life and death and opens the gateway of Heaven.

Her heart was parched and roasted, as it were, with the fire of love. Intense love of her Lord, unified energies of body and mind dedicated to Him, and complete control of the body on the mundane plane, and of the Prāṇas and nāḍīs on the subtle plane, had borne fruit. *She had experienced Śiva.* Attainment of Yoga, the phenomenon of Oneness, the absolute Unification of the individualized Self with the Absolute Being was to follow. She says:

39. Abhyāsi svavikāsi layi vothū,
Gaganas sagun myūl samitsraṭāh;
Shunya gŏl Anāmay mŏtū,
Yuhŏy vŏpadīsh chuy bhaṭṭā.

अभ्यासी स्वव्यकास्य लयु व्यथू
गगनस सगुण म्यूल समि.चरटा
शून्य गोल अनामय मोतू
युहोय वुपदीश छुय बटा ॥३६॥

By constant practice, (the individualized limited Self) was dissolved into the Unlimited (Self)!
The Qualified Being merged with *Ākāśa*, (The Ethereal Unqualified Being), into one homogeneous whole!
The Void melted away. Nothing was left over except the *Anāmaya*, — the Stainless, the Pure, the Weal, Parama Śiva;
That is the lesson to you, O learned man!

If this is not a condition of perfected yoga, what else can it be? The experience is ineffable and the pen is too frail an instrument to comment on it. It is not a stage of Sad-Vidyā or Śuddha-Vidyā — "the regions of true and pure knowledge."[2]

1. *Kaṭha-Up.* I. I. 16.
2. *Kashmir Shaivism* J. C. Chatterjee p. 77.

Sad-Vidyā may be a stage recognized in Śaktipāta, the Descent of Śakti into the sensible world. But in the 'Ascent' of the individualized Self as a reverse process, Lalla's supreme Experience defies description.

(Abhyāsi)[1] — with continuous practice (how long carried on, no one can tell), (Svavikās)[2] — the Being spread out in all directions, in all possible dimensions, immense and unfathomable. (layi vĕthu) — rose to reabsorb and dissolve the limited Self; and (Sagun) — the qualified immanent universe with all its attributes **(the Śakti aspect) (myūl)—merged (gaganas) with the Ethereal Void into a homogeneous Whole (samitsraṭṭa);** the two coinciding into one undifferentiated stretch of Light. But anon the Blank (Śūnya), the Ethereal void of Experience, (gŏl) melted away and what (mŏtu or mŏtsyov)[3] remained was (Anāmaya = An + āmaya) the Pure, the cleansed of (mala) the impurities gathered through (Prakṛti) immanence; the (svatantra, svayam prakāśa, svayam vimarśa Citti) Self-luminous, the All-pervading, the All-Consciousness, the Eternal, the Blissful (Sat-Cit-Ānanda) — Transcendental Śiva.

It is an awful experience. The 'Ascent' was completed; the summit of unification[4] was conquered. The very conception of the Nirbīja Samādhi Lalla had attained staggers the mind.

It is a state of samādhi[5] in which the seen and the unseen, the

1. *Bhagavad Gītā* VI. 23-25.

2. "That immortal Brahman is before, that Brahman is behind, that Brahman is right and left. It has gone forth below and above; Brahman alone is all this, it is the best."

Muṇḍaka. Up. II 2. 11

3. "When that incorporated (Brahman), who dwells in the body, is torn away and freed from the body, what remains then ? This is *That*."

Kaṭha Up. II.5.4.

4. मध्यविकासाच्चिदानन्दलाभः स एव च परमयोगिनः समावेश समापत्त्यादिपर्यायः समाधिः ॥

Kṣemarāja, *Pratybhijñāhṛdaya* Comm. Sūtra 18.

"From opening of the centre results attainment of spirit and bliss, and this is nothing else but the Samādhi of the highest yogin, for which we have as alternative terms besides others Samāveśa and Samāpatti".

Leidecker p. 85.

5. "When the five instruments of knowledge stand still together with the mind, and when the intellect does not move, that is called the highest state".

Kaṭha Up. II.6.10-11

heard and the unheard, the dynamic and the static, in short all distinctions sublimate into one vast encompassing Being. And merged in Him, it is a state of Bliss. No earthly joy can compare with it.

Lallayogeśvarī had attained Laya-yoga, a state of dissolution into the Absolute.[1] The duality had disappeared finally. Only one Universal Experiencing Principle, the "That" of the Upaniṣads, remained. No longer did she sob and moan 'dil chum bramān gara gatshaha' — I wish I were to go Home! The long course of struggle with herself had come to an end. 'What shall I pay the boatman to ferry me across?' No longer would such questionings torment her. She had reached safe and sound the other shore of (bhavasamudra) the ocean of earthly existence where her Lord waited for her and she had embraced Him and become One with Him. And fain would she tell the scholar Pandit that practical experience of Oneness is superior to theoretical knowledge.[2] Of the yogi who attains Samādhi it is said: "Thus, 'he attains samāveśa in spite of his outward gaze'; in other words, although he is busying himself with the sense-objects, the unfolding of the highest Śakti becomes for him an immediate reality and he (himself) becomes an 'accomplisher' i. e., a Yogin of the highest type."[3] "The peace of Blessedness reaches him who has reached the culmination of yoga."[4]

It is not a stray incident in an otherwise drab life, as may be the case with lesser spiritual accomplishments of inferior persons. For the Yogeśvarī, the yoga was a recurring experience. "This, the firm holding back of the senses, is what is called Yoga. He must be free from thoughtlessness then, *for yoga comes and*

1. "The fetter of the heart is broken, all doubts are solved, all his works (and their effects) perish when He has been beheld who is high and low (cause and effect)".

Muṇḍaka Up. II.2.8.

2. *Bh. Gītā.* **VI. 46.**
3. Kṣemarāja-*Pratybhijñāhṛdayam.* Tr. Leidecker p. 87.
4. युञ्जन्नेवं सदात्मानं योगी नियतमानसः ।
शान्ति निर्वाणपरमां मत्संस्थामधिगच्छति ॥

"Keeping himself ever steadfast in this manner, the yogi of subdued mind attains the Peace abiding in Me and culminating in Nirvāṇa."

Bh. Gītā VI. 15. Tr. by Swami Chidbhavananda.
Also *Ibid.* 28.

goes."[1] The vakhs of Lalla tell us that there was no letting go of the bliss. She must have basked repeatedly in the state of Samâdhi. She says:

> 40. Vākh, Mānas, Kwal, Akwal na ate.
> Tshwapi, Mudri ati na pravīsh;
> Rozān Shiv-Shakt na ate,
> Mvatiyay kuṅh ta suy vŏpadīsh.
>
> वाख मानस क्वल अक्वल ना अते
> छ़वपि मो_द्रि अति ना प्रवीश
> रोज़ान शिव-शक्त ना अते
> म्वतियय कुंह तु सुय व्वपुदीश ॥४०॥

Word, Thought, Kula and Akula cease to be there!
Neither silence nor yogic postures gain you admission there;
Neither Shiva, nor Shakti abide there!
Whatever remains is That; this *is* the Lesson!

(Vākh) Speech of which the Upaniṣad says: "Your Majesty, speech itself (is knowledge). For through speech, your Majesty, a friend is known (to be a friend), and likewise the Rig-Veda, Yajur-veda...... By speech alone, your Majesty, Brahman is known, speech indeed, O king, is the Highest Brahman. Speech does not desert him who worships that (Brahman) with such knowledge, all creatures approach him and having become a god, he goes to the gods,"[2] (says Yājñavalkya). (Mānas) Manas or mind about which is said: "Let the wise man without fail restrain his mind, that chariot yoked with vicious horses,"[3] and also

> "A yogin who has reached union with that incomparable happiness which consists in enjoyment of song and the other sense-objects,

1. *Kaṭha Up.* II.6.11.
2. *Bṛhad. Up.* IV. 1.2.
3. *Śvet. Up.* II.9

Possesses identity in essence with that (great bliss) because his *manas* is gaining,
Wherever there is joy of *manas*, there he may safely retain *manas*,
There the true nature of the highest bliss is shining forth;"[1] and further manas as '*Citta*' is nothing else than '*citi*' (Supreme Consciousness) in the form of the limited subject (and) descended from the stage of cetana, that is bent on comprehending objects ......"[2] ......, and (Kwal) Kula which has been explained in Tantras as the seat of Śakti in the microcosm of the human body, at the Mūlādhāra (the original abode) —"In the ordinary **condition,** Kuṇḍalinī sleeps quietly at the Mūlādhāra",[3] and Akula(Akwal)or Sahasrāra, the abode of Parama Śiva: *one and all of these disappear from view and have no relevance in the final experience of Yoga.* 'Tshwapi' (speechlessness) ... "In the Samādhi of Mantra-yoga the state of Mahābhāva is attained marked by immobility and speechlessness",[4] —(Mudri) Postures of Haṭhayoga, are of no consequence, even useless, *in the experience of Yoga which Lalleśvarī had attained.* Even the consciousness of Śiva and Śakti as distinct aspects of Reality is lost there. In the state of Samādhi, the names Śiva and Śakti as distinct conceptions on the intellectual plane disappear. We may ask: what is it that she found? The answer would be: 'Ineffable Bliss'. "In the Samādhi of Laya-yoga ... the yogi has no outer consciousness and is also immersed in the Ocean of Bliss."[5]

1. Quoted from *Vijñānabhairava* in *Praty.-Hṛ.* Tr. by Leidecker. p. 84.
2. *Ibid* pp. 35.36.
3. *Saundaryalaharī*—Pandit R. Anantakrishna Shastri

Note: We may compare this vakh with:

न यत्र वाचो न मनो न सत्त्वं तमो रजो नो महदादयोऽमी
न प्राण बुद्धीन्द्रिय देवता वा न सन्निवेशः खलु लोककल्पः ।
न स्वप्न जागर्नं हि तत्सुषुप्तं न खंजलंभूऽनिलोऽग्निरर्कः
संसुप्तवच्छून्यवदप्रतर्क्यं तन्मूलभूतं पदमामनन्ति ॥ —*Śrīmadbhāgavata*

4. *Ibid.*
5. *Ibid.*

Cf. pp. 281-86 (The Six Centres and the Serpent Power).—Woodroffe. ("The Samaya method of worshipping Śakti, called the Samayācāra is dealt with in five treatises by Sanaka, Sanandana, Sanatkumāra. Vasiṣṭha and Śuka"). These are Āgama Śāstras.

Lalla reveals to us glimpses, on the most subtle plane, of the highest Truth. In the sublime Samādhi, she experiences something, in which the common conceptions of mysticism are eliminated and set aside. The Śabda-Brahman, the activity of the mind, as on the lower plane, and even the view of Kula (the abode of Śakti, the power of manifestation coiled up at the Mūlādhāra) disappear when 'That Something' shines forth. The ordinary practices of the aspirants of penance and silence and of the mudrās (the yogic postures) are reduced to nullity. To speak nothing of other things, the philosophic thought of Śiva and Śakti[1] (as two aspects of the Absolute One) vanishes from consciousness. We may pose a question : What is 'That' ? And pat comes the reply: (Mwatiyay Kuṅh) *Whatever remains, is "That"*! This is quite in line with the Upaniṣadic teaching, with a difference. ***This is Revelation through personal experience.*** This is the lesson transmitted to the seekers of Truth. Surely, for us with our feet planted on the *terra firma*, this is abstraction raised to the power of infinity. But as surely, we tangibly realise that this is yoga, the final realization of oneness with the Lord. Eckhart says : "Thou must love God, as not god, not spirit, not person, not image, but as He is, a sheer, pure absolute One, sundered from all two-ness, and in whom we must eternally sink from nothingness to nothingness."[2] *Lalla lived the Thing.* Whatever remains? It is a query—pray one would like to know ? It upsets the ordinary powers of thought though she does not mean to upset, but to guide and advise. She rounds up the vakh with—(ta suy vŏpadīsh) "that is the lesson." This is exactly the same way as Naciketā is taught by

1. "Parama Śiva is beyond the limits of time, space and form; and as such is Eternal and Infinite....His nature has primarily a twofold aspect—an immanent aspect (Śakti) in which He pervades the Universe, and the transcendental aspect (Śiva) in which He is beyond all. Universal manifestation.... Indeed, the universe with all its variety of objects and means of experience, is nothing but a manifestation of the immanent aspect of Parama Śiva Himself. It has no other basis or ingredient in it".

—*Kashmir Shaivism*, pp. 44-45.

Again: cf. Commentary on Sūtra 1. by Kṣemarāja, *Pratybhijñāhṛdayam*. p. 21 Tr. Leidecker.

Also: Somānanda. *Śivadṛṣṭi* III. 2.3.

न शिवः शक्तिरहितो...शक्तिशक्तिमतोर्भेदः शैवे जातु न वर्ण्यते ॥

2. *The Perennial Philosophy*—Aldous Huxley. p. 44.

(Yama) Death; "When that incorporated (Brahman), who dwells in the body, is torn away and freed from the body, what remains then ? This is *That*."[1] Death lives with men, but talks from the vantage point of knowledge. Lalla too had her feet on the earth, but appears to talk from the pinnacle of mystical attainment. The panorama she delineates has no haze about it. It is not a statement of half-truths, or description of blurred pictures. "Whatever remains" is the Reality : there is no scope for cold logic or mathematical calculations. One has to raise the Self to that level. Analysis and elimination on an incalculable mystical scale !

Verse follows verse pointing at the bewildering and the ineffable Bliss. The Āgama Tantras say: "But this Kundalinī does not stay in the Sahasrāra for a long time. It always tends to return, and does return to its original position. The process should again and again be repeated by the aspirant several times until the Union of Sadāśiva and Cit is complete. The aspirant is then a Jīvan-mukta, or pure Sattva. He is not conscious of this material limitation of the soul. He is all joy, and is the Eternal itself."[2] The internal evidence of Lalla's vakhs corroborates this view. Yet another state of Samādhi is described as follows :

41. Tanthr gali tai manthr mwatse,
Manthr gŏl tai mwŏtuy tsĕth,
Tsĕth gŏl tai keṅhti na kune,
Shūnyas Shūnyāh mīlith gav.

तन्त्र गलि तय मन्त्र म्त्र्.चे
मन्त्र गो_ल तय मो_तुय .च्यथ
च्यथ गो_ल तय केंहति नु कुने
शून्यस शून्याह मीलिथ गौ ॥४१॥

When the 'tantra' melts away, Mantra remains,
Mantra too disappears, leaving behind citta,

1. *Katha. Up*. II. 5.4.
2. *Saundaryalahari*—Pandit R. A. Shastri.

When citta dissolves, 'Nothing' remains,
The void is reabsorbed into the Void !

From the Āgama Tantra Śāstras and from her guru, the Yoginī may have learnt the methodology of yogic practices. The Nirvikalpa Samādhi was attained after the stages of Tantric rituals, chanting the mantras and the stage of pure consciousness had been crossed by her one after another. Samādhi appears to have been attained not in one bound, but by changing over from one state to the next higher. The Tantra stage gave place to the Mantra yoga "in which the (sādhaka's) mind is controlled by means of its own object...that is, the manifold objects of the world of the name and form (Nāma-rūpa)...".[1] The transition though by steps, seems to have been too rapid to leave gaps. When the Japa completed its function what remained was higher consciousness; and the moment this individualized consciousness melted away, there remained 'Nothing'.[2] It was, she says, the experience of 'Nothing' getting dissolved into 'Nothing'. We may construe it to mean that the consciousness of individualized self got merged into the consciousness of the Absolute.

In the sublime state, the consciousness of body and mind was lost altogether. The Void of the Ātman got reabsorbed into the *Void*[3] of Parama Śiva.

1. *Serpent Power*, Woodroffe. pp. 224, 225

2. "Therefore according to their (Buddhist) 'Kṣaṇikavijñānavāda' every object, physical and psychic, and even life is transient and ever changing. And their ultimate goal is Nirvāṇa to Śūnya—complete Voidness, which is probably the same as the Absolute of Vedānta which regards the Absolute as Pūrṇa and not Śūnya."

यत्तद् ब्रह्म परं सूक्ष्मं शून्यं शून्यकल्पितम् ।
भगवान् वासुदेवेति यं गृणन्ति हि सात्वताः ॥

Bhāgvata 9-9-49.

"He — that Brahman, who is most subtle, and though not voidness is imaginable as voidness (Śūnya), is regarded by the sāttvatas (Bhaktas) as the Lord Vāsudeva."

Devātma Shakti—x1. p 106.

3. Grierson translates शून्य as transcendental Void. He quotes: "In Shaiva philosophy, the imaginary body in which one feels oneself in dreams, a vague,

indistinct and undefined something which is practically 'Nothing".
—*Kashmir Shaivism*. pp. 77,82.

He further says: " 'Śūnya, may be looked upon as the first stage in limited consciousness, and in reverse order (of the soul becoming united with the Supreme), it is therefore the last stage of limited consciousness before the soul becomes conscious of the Universal Experience as one with the Supreme, in one of the five phases or conditions prior to this association with Māyā. In the microcosm of the body, yogis locate this 'Śūnya' in the Sahasrāra. शून्यस शून्याह् मीलिथ गौ—With the acquirement of true knowledge, the unreality of the material existence is recognized, and the apparent reality disappears in the Transcendental Void."

In the above quotation, an error may be detected,. The Kashmir Shaiva philosophy *does not admit of the unreality of the material world.* On the other hand, it stresses the *reality* of the manifested universe, in so much as the Absolute Reality pervades everything that exists.

शून्य is also to be differentiated from the Buddhistic conception of the Void. cf. footnote to V. 13.

In Lalla's verse शून्य is a positive concept for the Ultimate, indescribable Being. The microcosmic 'Self' gets, in Samādhi, merged with the Unlimited Being.

The following references may help getting at the mystical concept of (शून्य) 'Śūnya'.

Trikoṇam tasyāntaḥ sphurati ca satatam vidyudākārarūpam
tadantaḥ *śūnyam* tatsakala-suragaṇaiḥ sevitam cātiguptam"
Ṣaṭ-cakra-nirūpaṇa. 41.

"Within the (Sahasrāra) is the full Moon. Inside it (Candra-Maṇḍala) constantly shining like lightning, is the Triangle and inside this again, shines the *Great Void* which is served in secret by all the suras".

The footnote to the above reads:

"Śūnya=Bindu — that is the Parabindu or Īśvara.........."

The Serpent Power Description of the Six Centres, p. 479.

Again, *ibid.* verse 42:

"Well concealed, and attainable only by great effort, is that subtle Bindu (Śūnya) which is the chief root of Liberation and which manifests the pure Nirvāṇakalā with Amā-kalā. Here is the Deva who is known to all as Parama-Śiva...."

Commentary: "The sense is that the void (Śūnya) is very secret and subtle being...like the ten millionth part of the end of a hair. It is attainable only by great effort consisting of long and incessant performance of Dhyāna and like practices... It is the Source of all the mass of great Bliss, which is Liberation...." *Ibid.* pp 481-82 Also, *Ibid.* p. 49.

The last line of Vakh 41 may also be understood with reference to *Bṛhad. Up*. II. 4. 12.13. and "......For knowing is inseparable from the knower, because it cannot perish. But there is then no second, nothing else different from him that he could know." *Bṛhad. Up*. IV. 3. 30,32.

[contd.

It is an experience which only an accomplished Yogi may expound ! Romantic poetry transports us to fairy-lands, but mystical poetry exalts and fills with hope. It raises us from the material plane and affords kaleidoscopic glimpses on the subtler planes of consciousness. Poetic alchemy surpasses material alchemy. The Yogeśvari's vakhs possess a very high potency for transformation of intellectual brass into mystical gold.

It must certainly have been a day for Lalla when she attained the Samādhi. It had been a tough long journey, the path all along strewn with thorns. She had a hard time of it picking out the thorns one by one, and smoothening the way. May be in her early years, the Tantra-Vidyā and the attendant formalities made her religious. The rituals, a binding on the orthodox devotees of Śiva, were later on replaced by inward repetition of sacred spells assumed to possess occult powers, and chanting of the hymns to the Lord. In course of time, the mantras and incantations yielded place to a mystic consciousness of the burning flame of Self. And now, at last, by a supreme effort of yogic practice, she was able to annihilate the lower fields of consciousness and in the Supra-mental state merge into the Absolute Being, which is attributeless, nameless and formless.

She uses the word (शून्य) Void, because the transcendental Being is ineffable. It may have been an experience approaching that of 'nothingness'. Nothingness is certainly difficult to describe; so is the experience of Self. Therefore, Lalla uses the word Śūnya, as the synonym for Self, immanent and transcendental, which in the state of yoga are said to be experienced as one.

Lalla's yogic experiences, have a flavour of originality and 'first-handness'. Her mystical poetry gushes out of the primordial springs of self. She sings in the first person, and the subjectiveness leaves behind indelible impressions of essential lyricism on the mind of the reader. It is not just a cry in the

Also *Śveta. Up.* IV. 14. 15.

Hence, Śūnya may be an equivalent of the Śiva-tattva, (both immanent and transcendental); and the last verse may simply be interpreted as the union of Jīvātma and Parmātma.

It may also be the state of Śuddha-Vidyā — the Experience of diversity in unity and identity (Bhedābheda), in the academic language. In any case, शून्य is a positive concept in the mystical language.

wilderness, reminiscent of poetic pangs of separation from the Beloved. She does not sing like Mīrā, her love-lorn songs, with the vibrating pitch of emotion, yearning for the Lord's 'darśan'. The mystical poetry of Lalla is of a different brand. And the planes of consciousness from which they sing may also, consequently, be different. For the common man, living on the earthly plane, it may not be easy to ascend to the plane of these exalted souls and comprehend their language. In fact, it is a job to interpret Lalla's verse. Nevertheless, her ascent has been along a slope and not a jetting up straight into the outer space of Truth. That has been an encouragement and a help in understanding her vakhs. *She reaches the heights by degrees and steps*; and when she finally comes up to the top, there is no coyness and hesitation on her part about its exposition. She says:

42. Tsĕta turug vagihĕth rŏṭum
Tsĕlith milavith dashināḍi vāv,
Tavai Shĕshikal vĕglith vatsham;
Shūnyas Shūnyāh mīlith gav.

च्यतु तुर्ग वगिह्यथ रो_टुम
च्यलिथ मिलुविथ दशिनाडि वाव
तवय शशिकल व्यगुलिथ व.छुम
शून्यस शून्याह मीलिथ गौ ॥४२॥

I drew the reins of the steed of citta,
I compressed the breath circulating through the ten nāḍis:
Lo ! the Śaśi-kalā melted and dripped,
And the void mingled with the Void !

The mystical experience is, by the compulsion of its nature, voiced in metaphors. The totality of fleeting psychical processes of mind (citta) is compared with a fleet-footed horse. This figure may have been borrowed from the Upaniṣads,[1] unwittingly though, because it is quite apt. The horse was reined in, lest it should work havoc with the yogic practice. Next essential, as already enunciated, was breath-control. There is no end to stressing this point in Lalla's verse. This becomes amply clear by

1. *Kaṭha-Upanishad.* I.3.4. Also *Śvetāśvatara-Upaniṣad.* II.9.

the bland statement (Tavai Shěshikal věgalith vatsham) "*By dint of this*, the digit of the Moon in the Sahasrāra melted and started trickling down.". The first word of this verse (Tavay) '*Therefore*' is significant. Yama, Niyama and Prāṇāyama are *sine qua non* for Samādhi. When the 'nectar' started dripping and the Śakti in the microcosm began licking the nectar, the condition of *bliss* came upon her. The Samādhi was perfected and yoga attained—(Shuněs Shunyāh mīlith gav) ! What all this adds up to is beyond our understanding. The aspirant needs must take it on faith, because the yogis realize it as a matter of fact. Lalla's vakh is so positive an affirmation that it leaves no room for sceptical disputation.

She appears, however, to forestall our half-hearted, doubtful, wavering faith. It is not a case of mere prescience, or understanding of the pulls and pressures of the common man's cast of mind. She seems to have pondered over the point that the world would be "too much with us", and by way of giving us a shaking and extending encouragement, she says :

43. Lūb mārun, Sahaz vetsārun,
Drŏg zānun kalpan[1] trāv;
Nishi chuy tai dūr mo gārun;
Shūnyas Shūnyāh mīlith gav.

लूब मारुन सहज़ व्यच़ारुन
द्रो_ग ज़ानुन कल्पन त्राव
निशि छुय तय दूर मो गारुन
शून्यस शून्याह मीलिथ गौ ॥४३॥

Give up imagining that the skill of killing (the demon of) desire, and meditating on the Self are too costly to buy;
He stands close by you ! Do not look for Him far away.
The void was dissolved in the Void !

Attaining Samādhi and merging with the Lord, in a state of super-consciousness, in a blissful state, appears to have become so

1. The word Kalpan may be exchanged with Kalapana. In that case it would mean "give up wailing and crying."

easy and so habitual to the Yogeśvarī that in her view anybody could accomplish it. The Lord is within you, she declares. Abandoning greed[1] and avarice and meditating on Him, anybody is assured of the success of yoga. It is anybody's destiny to realize the Self. What a vista of hope is spread out before the aspirant !

Browning is credited with an amplitude of optimism when he makes Pipa sing :

"God's in His Heaven,
All's right with the world !"

But Lalla's optimism far exceeds Browning's as it is bound to be, because Lalla was a Yoginī and had realised God in her own self. *The Heaven of happiness is within you*, she assures us. She seems to exhort us to experience the bliss of merging the individual self with the Absolute Being. The exhortation is couched in simple, direct language. No poetic ornaments, no figures of speech are needed to adorn *the appeal of a seer*. The fears of the common man are more imaginary than real, she wants to emphasize.

Renouncing hearth and home, wandering in the forests, looking for the Lord in mountain hermitages and making pilgrimages in search for Him are unnecessary ardours taken upon themselves by the ascetics, and religious mendicants and the ignorant. "The kingdom of God is within you !"[2] The aspirant has to curb his instincts of greed and desire, and take to meditation. The indescribable state of ecstatic Samādhi is sure to be gained. It is not a casual suggestion but a firm assertion on the strength of personal experience.

1. The Hereafter never rises before the eyes of the careless child, deluded by the delusion of wealth, "this is the world", he thinks, "there is no other;" —thus he falls again and again under my sway.

Kaṭha-Up. I.20.6

Also "When all the desires that dwell in his heart cease, then the mortal becomes immortal and obtains Brahman."

Ibid. II. 6. 14. 15.

2. Cf. *Bṛhad. Up*. II. 4. 5. Also *Ibid*-III. 5.3.

In another vakh, she says

44. Lal bŏh tsāyas **svamana bāgabaras,**
Vuchum Shivas Shakht mīlith ta vāh !
Tati lai karmas amritsaras,
Zindai maras ta mĕ kari kyāh.

लल बोह चायस स्वमन बागबरस
वुछुम शिवस शक्त मीलिथ त वाह
तति लय करमस अमृतसरस
जिंदय मरस त म्य करि क्याह ॥४४॥

I. Lalla, *willingly* entered through the garden-gate,
There, O Joy ! I found Śiva united with Śakti ;
There and then I got absorbed drinking at the Lake of Nectar.
Immune to harm am I, dead as I am to the world, though still alive.

'Svamana'[1] **literally** yields to the translation : 'with my own mind'. This may, therefore, be translated as 'willingly'. It may also mean 'with all my consciousness', on the earthly plane, which may be tantamount to saying that she entered the Samādhi, even while she was conscious of her physical surroundings, internal and external. It would, in that case, exemplify a very high state of mystical accomplishment. *The adept in yoga may choose to enter the Samādhi, the supramental state, at will even while ostensibly he is attending to the phenomenal world.*

In that state, what did she see ? Śiva, the Transcendental Being, united with His power of manifestation, Śakti. *Duality* as well as any residual doubts about it, *was totally wiped out.* The

1. Grierson has combined स्वमन with बाग to form a compound स्वमन-बाग and translated it as a garden of Jasmine flowers. सुमन is read for स्वमन and further सुमन is mistaken for योसमन, Kashmiri for Lilac and not Jasmine. Jasmine is English for Indian 'Chambeli." Therefore, Grierson's rendering "I, Lalla, passed through the door of the Jasmine-garden of my soul"— is untenable.

last of the Tattvas *in ascension* disappeared as a separate conception, and was dissolved in the Highest Being. The nectar of Bliss was at her disposal, not in drops now but in the form of a lake. She attained (Paramānanda) the state of the highest bliss.

The state of strife had at last ended. Mystical fruition had ripened to the core. She had become a Jīvanmukta,[1] freed from the bondage of births and deaths, even while she was with us in this mortal coil.

In yet another verse, Lalla describes her mystical experience.

45. Bān gŏl tai prakāsh āv zūne,
Tsaṅdr gŏl tai mŏtuy tsĕth;
Tsĕth gŏl tai kĕṅhti na kune; ;
Gay Bhŏŏr Bhwāh Swāh vĕsarzith kĕth.

बान गो_ल तय प्रकाश आव ज़ूने
चंद्र गो_ल तय मो_तुय च्यथ
च्यथ गो_ल तय कें्हति ना कुने
गै "भूर्भुवः स्व." व्यसर्जि़थ क्यथ ॥४५॥

When the Sun melted away, the Moon shone forth,
When the Moon disappeared Consciousness remained;
Consciousness too dissolved, there remained Nothing,
The three sacred Interjections (Vyāhṛtis) too departed at last.

The supreme experience is hard to explain in the language of everyday life. Step by step the samādhi deepens. The first stage of concentration on the lower abdominal cakras with the hot, dazzling orb of the Sun[2] yields place to the soft and soothing

1. "If a man is able to understand (Brahman), then even before the decay of his body, he is liberated."
Kaṭha-Up. II. 6. 4. Max Müller.

2. "(Mūla-cakrāntara-vivara-lasat-koṭi-sūrya-prakāśaṃ). She shines in the Mūlādhāra-cakra like ten million suns shining at one and the same time".
The Six Centres and Serpent Power verse 13. Woodroffe.
Also verse 19. "Meditate there (Maṇipūra-cakra) on the region of Fire, triangular in form and shining like the rising sun..." *Ibid*.

light of the Moon.[1] Lalla succeeded in 'building the bridge', as she called it earlier, from the Nābhisthāna to the Brahmāṇḍa. Dwelling upon the latter, the light of the Moon too withdraws, and there remains only the consciousness[2] of a blissful experience. But in the final state of samādhi there is total dissolution of the experiencing principle, the experiencer and the object of experience. 'Nothing' remains !

On our plane of thought and intellectual understanding, it may sound strange and fantastic; this conception of 'Nothingness' which is equivalent to the experience of the Highest Being. But the yoginī experienced *Something* the moment she became one with the Sat-Cit-Ānanda. The Trinity of Bhūr-Bhuvaḥ-Suvaḥ were bidden farewell too.[3] The three worlds—material, ethereal and the other world—wound up their show and disappeared.

1. "Above all these, in the vacant space (Parama-vyoma) where is Śaṅkhinī Nāḍī, and below Visarga is the Lotus of a thousand petals. This Lotus, lustrous and whiter than the full Moon, has its head turned downward."

Ibid. verse 40.

Also: "Anāhata Chakra is said to be the abode of the Sun and Ājñā Chakra is the abode of the Moon. Sun is the source of Universal Prāṇa and the Moon that of the Universal Mind."

Saundaryalahari commentary V.T.
Description of the chakras. pp. 149-165.

2. Commentary on v.40. of *Ṣaṭ-cakra-nirūpaṇa*:

"The Ācārya enjoins that Sādhakas, who wish to practise Samādhi yoga, 'should before such time with every consideration and effort dissolve all things in their order from the gross to the subtle in Cidātma.'"

Woodroffe.

3. "Bhūḥ, Bhuvaḥ, Suvaḥ, these are three sacred interjections (vyāhṛtis). Mahachamasya taught a fourth, viz. Mahas, which is Brahman, which is the Self..........

Bhūḥ is this world, Bhuvaḥ is the sky, Suvaḥ is the other world........."

Taittirīya-Up. 1. 5. I. 2, 3.

The meaning of the vyāhṛtis as given by Swami Dayānanda: "(Bhūr-iti-vai-prāṇaḥ: Yah prāṇayati chara-(a)-charam jagat sa bhūḥ, swayambhūrīśvaraḥ)-Supreme Lord (Parameśvara) who is the source and support of all life in cosmos, Who is more lovable than life itself, the uncreated Self-existent, and Bhūḥ, the Life-Principle in all.

Bhuvarityapānaḥ. Yaḥ Sarvaṃ duḥkhamapānayati sa (a)pānaḥ. He who is free from all sorrows, by whose contact or nearness beings become sorrow-free (pure and strong, therefore (His) this Supreme Lord's Name is Bhuvaḥ. Svaritivyānaḥ. Yo vividham jagad vyānayati vyāpnoti sa vyānaḥ). He who pervading (all) different and diverse existences, supports and sustains all, His Name, therefore, is Svaḥ."

Taittirīya Āraṇyaka: 7.5. (Taken from *Satyārth Prakāsh*).

Also: for detailed explanations: Cf. *The Grandeur of Gāyatrī*, Chiranjitlal (Vanaprastha) Tr. by C. Parameswaran.

The three principles of experience (the Īśvara-tattva, the Sādākhya or Sadāśiva Tattva and the Śakti Tattva),[1] in their ascending order, one after another ceased to function; and even the three aspects of Parama Śiva,.....as Bhūḥ ("the embodiment of Lifeforce"), Bhuvaḥ ("the Destroyer of all sorrows and Giver of immortal Freedom and Happiness"), and Suvaḥ ("the embodiment of Beatitude and Bliss")...... were bidden farewell in the state of Nirbīja Samādhi.

Is this not Advaita Śaivaism verified? Not a shadow of duality pursues Lalla in her state of yoga or Unification with Parama Śiva. It leaves no room for contrary argument because she sings out her heart. When we talk of Self-realization or God-realization, in our uncultivated way, we make use of our limited sense organs and limited perceptions to prove the Unlimited and we are baffled. But from the exalted, subtle planes the yogis dive into the ocean of Truth, far deeper than ever the plummet of limited faculties sounded.

1. "The moon and the sun represent, respectively, the uppermost and the lowest seats of action, or cakras. When by intense mental absorption, or yoga, these disappear, or cease to be present to the consciousness, the devotee is conscious of nothing except his (subtle) faculty of thought. When this is finally absorbed in the Supreme, all sense of difference between the individual spirit and the Universal Being (based on the three Principles of Experience) is sunk in the all-consuming consciousness of All-Being, All Light......

Bhūr-bhuvaḥ-svaḥ—also stand for the three denominations of time (the Past, Present and Future); they also represent the three cognitive states (Physical, Spiritual and Metaphysical) and may also denote the three conditions of being (matter, spirit and the void)".

—*Lallāvākyāni.* Grierson and Barnett

12

RECAPITULATION

Lalla-ded had cut the Gordian Knot by the sheer force of her spiritual stamina. Henceforth, she sings merely to recapitulate the *Blissful State* and to encourage the aspirant, by lighting the torch of Truth in poetic profusion which cannot escape the notice of sincere, zealous aspirants. She says:

46. Tshāṅḍān lūtshas päni-pānas,
    Tshĕpith Jñānas votum na kūṅtsh (kāṅh);
    Laị karmas ta vätsas althānas,
    Bari bari bāna ta cĕvān na kūṅh (kāṅh).

छांडांन लूसुस पानिय-पानस
छ़्यपिथ ज्ञानस वोतुम नु कूंछ़
लय करमस तु वा़चुस अलथानस
बंय बंयं बानु तु च्यवान न कूंछ़ ।४६॥

Tired was I and exhausted, seeking my Self.
Who could have access to the hidden knowledge (of self) within me?
(Once the Self was unveiled), I absorbed myself in it and reached the Abode of Nectar:
Jars lie filled to the brim, but few there be who drink from them !

Mystical nectar is offered to the seeker in poetic porcelain. Chalices of the highest joy lie about you. The only condition for drinking from them is 'Know Thy Self'. Hidden from view by the forces of obscuration and Māyā, the Self may prove elusive to the uninitiated and the unguided. It may tire out the aspirant and not infrequently leave him in the doldrums, spent and smashed. But the one who perseveres, like Lalla, emerges successful.

It is a cheering vakh to the experimentalist in mysticism, and, at the same time, it is a cry of regret that everybody does not attempt to get at the knowledge of the Self, which, though veiled at first, stands naked before the inward eye of the serious seeker. The stream of nectar flows by your doorstep.

In retrospect, a more sanguine note could not, perhaps, be sung by a perfected yogi. Verse upon verse throws light on Lalla's confidence that it is within reach of any aspirant to partake of the nectar of Divine Knowledge. If man suffers from scepsis, the fault lies with him. She says :

47. Tsa na bŏh na dhey na dhyān,
Gav pānai Sarvakriya mashith;
Aniyav dyūṅtḥukh kentsh na anvai,[1]
Gayi sath[2] layi Par pashith.

1. Anvai from Sanskrit अन्वय meaning relationship, order, support.

2. *Sath* may also mean the five external sense perceptions, mind and buddhi. According to Sūfism, it may mean the seven worlds—Lāhut, Jabrut, Malkut etc. All these melted away on apprehending the Lord.

"Indian cosmologists have described the sevenfold strata of Prāṇa (the first Principle which has evolved the whole living and the lifeless creation) separately as pertaining to the human body, the Earth, and Brahmāṇḍa (a cosmic unit) or the universe we see, there being innumerable universes of this kind......In the case of mankind, the seven strata are known as chakras such as Mūlādhāra etc. ......In the case of the Earth, they are called Dwīpas such as Jambu dwīpa, Kusha dwīpa etc....The ancients had divided the continental land of Jambū dwīpa into seven parts each being called a Varsha such as Hari Varsha, Ilāvrita Varsha, Bhārat Varsha etc....In the third case of Brahmanda, the seven Lokas are named as Bhurloka, Bhuwarloka, Swarloka, Mahaloka, Janaloka, Tapoloka and Satyaloka......(The above description has been given according to Vyāsa's commentary on Yoga Darśana).'

"Evolution of Prāṇa at its highest degree makes it merge in the universal Prāna and then in Brahman."

For more details, see *Devatma Shakti*, pp. 70-75.

If 'sath' in the last line of the Lalla-vakh means *seven*, the interpretation would be that the seven as detailed above were dissolved in the state of samādhi, on experiencing the Lord (Par). This is the highest state of evolution of the individualized prāṇa.

.चु ना बो_ह ना देय ना ध्यान
गौ पानय सर्वक्रिय मशिथ
अन्यव ड्यंठुख कैंछ़ न अन्वय
गय सथ लयि पर पशिथ ॥४७॥

There is neither you, nor I; neither the object of meditation, nor the process of meditation;
The Father of all action forgot Himself there.
The blind did not see any relationship and support there,
The devout merged with Him, the moment they saw the Lord!

Wearing the blinkers of limitations, gripped by the iron-hand of kleśas, involved in the whirlpool of earthly engagements, the worldly blind see no relationship with and no support in Him. Enveloped by the mist of ignorance, they cannot see a step ahead of themselves. The faithful, the wise and the devout see Him and reap the fruit of eternal joy by getting absorbed in Him.

All two-ness disappears in the state of realization of the Truth. The *ideal Unity* may be visualized by the fact that the cosmic power of all creation (the Śakti aspect of Śiva) forgets Herself when She is found united with him (the Transcendental Śiva) in the mystic's Supreme state of samādhi. It is one Paramaśiva, within and without, energetic and quiescent, manifest and unmanifest. Once a pious soul realizes Him, he sees nothing but Him all round.[1]

The pictures of the Being, painted in retrospect, are graphic and vivid. Simile and metaphor are the appropriate vehicles for transmitting her personal experiences in the realm of mysticism to us. She uses these means abundantly as much for precision of description as for poetic ornament. May be in mysticism, as in all provinces of abstract, higher knowledge, these are the only media for clarity of communication. Images are built and images are rebuilt by the superb poetic art of suggestion. Mystical

1. Rājānaka Bhāskara (quoted by Grierson):
"But godmen become absorbed in Him, when once they gain sight of the Supreme."

knowledge of this magnitude may not, perhaps, be clearly conveyed otherwise. She says:

48. **Tari salila[1] khota tai tare,**
Hĕmi trĕ gay byŏn-abyŏn vĕmarsha;[2]
Tsetani[3] rav bhāti sab same,
Shivamai tsrātsar[4] zag pashya.

तुरि सलिल खोतु तय तुरे
ह्यमि त्र्य गय ब्यो्न-अब्यो्न व्यमर्शा
चेतनि रव बाति सब समे
शिवमय चराचर जग पश्या ॥४८॥

Intense cold may freeze water (into ice): may be into snow.
Reflecting, you find water differentiated into three forms:
But when the sun of Cetana (supreme consciousness) dawns upon you, these again dissolve into One Cosmic Substance:
The universe of animate and inanimate beings is seen as Śiva.

In the higher consciousness, as the fruit of Self-realization and Samādhi, all differences are obliterated. If the seeker after Truth understands the Reality, the apparent differences, consequent upon

1. 'Salil'=Water; 'Hĕmi'=Snow; byŏn-abyŏn=Unity in Diversity.
2. 'vĕmarsha'=vimarsha="To the macrocosmic reabsorption, there corresponds the psychological experience of the yogin when in his *meditation* the empirical universe is vanishing. The word *vimarśa* means really 'touching', then investigating, scrutinizing, reflecting.........According to Kṣemarāja, *Sh. SV.* 116, 14, it is the experience of the Yogin by which he acquires knowledge of the true nature of his own self. Also, 'meditation''.
Pratyabhijñāhṛdaya p. 134. (Note by Leidecker)
3. 'tsetani'=Cetana
स्वेच्छया स्वभित्तौ विश्वमुन्मीलयति ॥
"By the power of its own will (citi) unfolds the universe upon its own screen." *Ibid.* Sūtra 2.
Again: "has Cetana, which is qualified by the contraction of Citi, been formed of the contracted universe." *Ibid.* Sūtra 4.
4. 'zag'=Jagat=The world. 'Pashya' =(पश्यन्ति)=will see (Śiva). 'tsrātsar=(चर-अचर)=The living and non-living.

the manifestation of Being through His Śakti Tattva, disappear in the recognition of the All-embracing Śiva in everything. The Diversity sinks into Unity and the thought of difference changes into one of sameness.

Kashmir Śaiva Philosophy enunciates: Transcendental Parama Śiva is the Absolute Being, without a second. His immanent aspect (Śakti) 'descends' or manifests Him and through 36 principles shows Him in the multitudinous forms that make the cosmos, the Parama Śiva continuing to be Transcendental as **well as Immanent,**[1] present even in the lowliest substance as the Ultimate Reality and essence of things. Thus it is a case of bhedābheda or Unity in Diversity. *Everything is Real* because Parama-Śiva the Ultimate Reality pervades everything, and is in and outside everything. In short, He is the only Being, the multiplicity being the result of the veil of ignorance and the limitations of time and space etc.

The multiplicity was reduced to the fundamental unity by Lalla, through yoga. Therefore, for the good of the aspirants, she makes use of an analogy. Water is converted into ice and snow, when temperature falls. But when the sun shines and the temperature rises, ice and snow change back into water. So is the case with the sun of knowledge of the Self and the recognition of Being. When the aspirant attains the spiritual realization, all thought of duality vanishes. Śiva, and Śiva alone, shines in His Divine effulgence everywhere, for a realized soul.

Stress is laid on raising the level of consciousness. She appears to carry us along through the stages of yoga, in yet another verse; but the substance is clearly recapitulatory. There is a tone of self-satisfaction: she appears helping the aspirants. She says:

49. Dĕn tshĕzi ta razan āse,
Bhūtal gaganas kun vikāse,
Tsaṅdar Rāhu-grās māvase;
Shiva pūzun gav cita-ātmase.

द्यन छ़्यजि़ तु रज़न ग्रासे
बूतल गगुनस कुन व्यकासे
च़ंद्र राहु-ग्रास मावुसे
शिवु-पू.जुन गौ चि़त्तात्मसे ॥४९॥

1. ॐ पूर्णमदः पूर्णमिदं पूर्णात् पूर्णमुदच्यते ।
पूर्णस्य पूर्णमादाय पूर्णमेवावशिष्यते ॥

The Day will decline and the Night will cast its pall,
The Earth will stretch in one vast expanse to the sky!
Rāhu[1] (the demon of Eclipse) will swallow the Moon on
Amāvāsyā, (the last day of the dark-fortnight);
The worship of Śiva means becoming conscious of self.

This vakh is a veritable parable. It is in the nature of (Sṛṣṭi) manifestation that the Day of Absolute Consciousness (Citi) declines. Then, as a consequent attribute of Prakṛti, the darkness of ignorance prevails. The (Jīva) limited soul is enveloped by one vast expanse of the darkness of duality of the experiencer and the object of experience, because the individual consciousness, receded from Absolute consciousness, is encased by sheaths of limitations. The darkness spreads over all that man now knows of the earth and sky, and he is buried in thoughts on the earthly plane. Coming away from the world of True knowledge and curtained off by the veil of (Avidyā) ignorance, like the moon on the last day of the dark lunar fortnight—'Amāvāsyā'—as it were swallowed clean and whole by the Demon of Eclipse, man on the material plane discriminates between the individualized

1. "Once the mind realizes the true nature of the Self as one with the Supreme Self, all things fade into nothingness......Nay, the demon of eclipse is eclipsed himself. *Absorbed in the Sahasrāra to the fully enlightened soul the day of earthly illusion disappears and all is night.* The apparent solid earth loses its bounds and becomes merged in the sky; in the illumination of the Self, so far from Rāhu swallowing (the nectar of) the (new) moon, it is the moon in the Sahasrāra that swallows the dark demon of ignorance......"

Lalla Vākyāni. Grierson.

Note:—It is not clear how all becomes "night" when "the day" of earthly illusion disappears ? Night is (tamas) darkness. As one of the attributes—Sattva, Rajas and Tamas of prakṛti, it is the lowest, and is said to be present in the final settling down or crystallisation of Divine manifestation into its most hidden state.

Again, what is meant by "Rāhu swallowing (the nectar of) the (new) moon" ? Amāvāsyā is the last day of the dark fortnight, not the first day of the new moon. It is the night of Total darkness, as Pūrṇmāsi is the night of full moon and total illumination. Secondly the "nectar" has always a reference to Sahasrāra, in the digit of the Moon, and Rāhu is the eclipsing Demon. Drinking nectar is a synonym for achieving the Bliss. How, therefore, the devouring Demon of Darkness drinks 'nectar' is not understandable.

soul and the Absolute Being, between himself and others. Quite naturally he falls a prey to the fallacy of considering the Experiencer (Pramātar), the object of Experience (Prameya) and the process of Experience (Pramāṇa) as three separate entities. On the gross plane this is inevitable. When the Truth is hidden by Māyā Śakti and other forces of obscuration because of the 'downward' process of manifestation, man automatically loses knowledge of Self.

By virtue of their innate spiritual potential and God's grace, yogis dedicate their lives to discovering and recognizing the Truth. They know that the Self in man, as in everything else, is the spark of the same Fire. Lalla had realized the Self, and like all generous yogis she does not hesitate giving away her knowledge to those who care to take it. She declares; "Shiva pūzun gav Cit-ātmase"—you worship Siva, if you become conscious of your Self. That is to say that one who makes an effort to realize his own Self, and becomes conscious of the nature of the Self, is the best devotee of the Lord.

She had gone through the harrowing Dark Night of despair. She had had moments of frustration and she had fallen at the feet of Śiva for His benign help. Finally, through the path of penance and yogic practice, the veil of darkness had lifted, the fountain of Nectar in the Digit of the Moon had oozed and dripped, and glad she was to recapitulate the scenes *en route*, and gladder still to announce on the house-tops for the benefit of all and sundry : *the essence of worship is to 'know Thy Self'*. Yogis like Lalla become amphibians in the spiritual sense, living simultaneously on the gross and the subtle planes. They become conscious of the Self, as we are conscious of the limbs and organs of the body.

Her mystical vakhs have a peculiar flavour of personal experience. In her own time, to begin with, she too had lost sight of the Self and run after inanities. She says :

50. Pānas lägith rovukh mĕ tsa,
Mĕ tsĕ tshāṅḍān lūstum dŏh;
Pānas maṅz yĕli dyūṅtḥukh mĕ tsa,
Mĕ tsĕ ta pānas dyutum tshŏh.

पानस लागिथ रोवुख म्यं .चु
म्यं .च्यं छान्डान लूसुम दोह्
पानस मंज़ यलि ड्यूंठुख म्यं चु
म्यं .च्य तु पानस ध्युतुम छ़ोह् ॥५०॥

Attaching myself to my body, I lost *You* clean and sure;
My day was spent searching for You !
Beholding *You* within me,
I brought my self and Śiva together in a thrill of joy !

One is reminded of Lalla's wail; 'Swaman swathi manz lūstum dŏh'—"The day is done in the middle of the dyke". She seems to remember the times when she had not recognized the Self as the Reality inhabiting the body. Her mental condition had been almost in shambles. But her faith and grit had stood by her. Continuing her search and struggle, she had found the Self within her. This was after her Guru had asked her to withdraw into herself (Nĕbra dŏpnam andray atsun). Discovering the Self with continuous yogic practice, she had realized the Supreme Śiva (Abhyāsi swavikās layi vŏthu). The one-ness of the two had been experienced in the state of Samādhi. That moment of Blissful embrace with the Lord is recapitulated in the above vakh.

The shift in mood is evident; it is a mood of glorification of the Lord; it is the excitement of discovery and recognition of the one-ness of the immanent and the transcendental Śiva. It is not merely an assertion that 'God made man in His own image', but the enunciation of the identity of man's self, and the Supreme Being. Man's Self, the driving force of the body and mind, is the Divine Self. There is no need to look for Him abroad. Lalla does not sing out of conviction and faith alone; ***she sings the song of personal experience.*** Her mystical attainment is transparent.

Yoga had brought a sea-change in her temper. Her verses gleam with satisfaction. They also evince the precious quality of humility. She says :

51. Makris zan mal tsŏlum manas,
Ada mĕ labam zanas zān,
Suh yĕli dyūnthum nishi pānas
Soruy suy ta bŏh no kĕnh.

मंकुरिस ज़न मल चो़लुम मनस
श्रद् म्यं लबुम ज़नस ज़ान
सु यलि ड्यूंठुम निशि पानस
सोरुय सुय तु बोह नो कॅह ॥५१॥

When my mind was cleansed of impurities, like a mirror of
its dust and dirt,
I recognized the Self in me:
When I saw Him dwelling in me,
I realized that He was the Everything and I was nothing.

She remembers how she came upon the Self. With perseverance and endurance, exemplary control on her sense organs, penance and righteous conduct, self-abnegation and a thousand checks and restraints, she had purified her mind. Long practice on the mystical plane had helped her shed off the impurities ('malas')[1] from which the individuals (jīvas) suffer. Her mind, therefore, became clear like a mirror, cleaned of its accumulated dust. That was how she had recognized the Self in her. Of course, it was not the end of her supra-mental experience. She had attained still greater heights. She had found her Self none other than Śiva 'individualized'. Furthermore, Śiva was the Master of the body. The little self or ego (individualized sense of I-ness, which dominates the Antaḥkaraṇas) was of no account. In fact Śiva pervaded within and without, and the separated ego-consciousness was but lack of knowledge of the Truth.h.

We should not read human *helplessness* or *fatalism* in this vakh. Nor is it a prop for those who shift their responsibility to the will of the Lord *because that attitude involves duality.* The argument briefly is that no extraneous power determines human destiny. Since the body is the abode of the Lord, the conduct of the body needs must conform to His divine nature. Therefore, the mirror of the mind must be cleansed of all its foulness, by restraint upon the senses and by pious conduct. Only then can we understand the true nature of the Self. Also, we come to understand that the phenomenal world of name and form is not Māyā or a mere illusion. *The phenomenal world is a reality* : it

1. cf. footnote, verse-37.

is an inseparable part of the Ultimate Reality. The manifested Being is part and parcel of the Absolute Being. The mystic's goal, therefore, sums up to Self-realization. And Vedānta, too, stresses that.[1]

Lalla had arrived at the goal of her earthly life. She had become a Jīvan-mukta. Fain would she help others to become free from the yoke of births and deaths. She says :

52. Tsĕdānandas jñānaprakāshas,
Yimav tsyūn tim zivantay-mukt;
Vĕshmas samsāranis pāshas,
Abŏdhy gaṇḍâh shĕth-shĕth dith.

च्यदानन्दस ज्ञानुप्रकाशस
यिमव च्यून तिम ज़ीवन्ती मुक्त
व्यषमस संसारुनिस पाशस
अबो_ध गंडाह् शथ शथ दित्य ॥५२॥

Those who realized the Consciousness-Bliss, The effulgent sun of All-knowledge,
Became liberated even while alive;
The unintelligent tied knots, by hundreds upon hundreds,
To the vastly spread meshes of the net of the world.

Knowledge of the Self had liberated her. She sings as an emancipated soul. She had attained the highest purpose of life —becoming united with the Lord who is All-Consciousness, All Bliss and All-knowledge. In the technical language of mysticism, we may say that *she had become a 'Jīvanmukta'* and glad she would be to haul up others to that State. But, to her dismay,

1. "Vedānta does not believe God to be far away; one has only to close his eyes and see Him within."

Swami Rama Tirtha, *The Woods of God-Realization*, vol. VI, p.60.

Also "It is only when we know that there is only one Self and that all the shapes and forms we see under the various names are really our Self, then there is rest......but when we Realize the Self, we dive below the surface into the realms of Absolute Truth".

Ibid. p. 43.

she found the mass of humanity wallowing in the mire of ignorance, caught up in the meshes of the worldly involvements, fastening knot after knot and getting more and more entangled. Attachment to the body, as the be-all and end-all of life, fettered them down. Lalla seems to be pained by the thought.

From the mystical heights she had gained, she looks through golden mists of Olympus down on the grey plains of human misery, and gives a call that there is a way out and up. Real joy can be gained even while we live on the earth and go about our daily round of work, provided we have freed ourselves spiritually from the meshes of involvement, and provided we know the true nature of Self—Consciousness-Bliss-Knowledge.

Lalla is not selfish, as no yogi of her stature can imaginably be. She draws the attention of the aspirants to the footprints she has left behind. She is not a lone conqueror, exulting in her solitary achievement. Since the world becomes the family of such as she was, gladly does she retrace the steps she had taken by way of help to others. She says :

53. Omkār yĕli layi ŏnum,
Vuhi kŏrum panun pān;
Shu-vot trävith sath-märg rŏṭum,
Tĕli Lal bŏh vätsas Prakāshasthān.

ऊँकार यॅलि लयि ओ_नुम
वुही कोरुम पनुन पान
शुवो_त त्राॅविथ सथमार्ग रो_टुम
त्यॅलि लल बो_ह वाॅचुस प्रकाशस्थान ॥५३॥

Focussing on the Praṇava and making it yield to me,
It was a process of burning myself to white-heat;
Forsaking the six cross-roads, I took to the path of Truth,*
Thus, I, the seeker, reached the Abode of Light !

*The third line may be interpreted esoterically thus: 'Shuh vot'—may mean the path of the *six Cakras*. She had awakened the Divine Sakti in the microcosm, raised her through the six plexi and finally fixed her up in the *seventh*—the Sahasrāra—which is referred to as the Abode of Light. But this interpretation does not fit in with the syntax of the vakh and the Kashmiri idiom she uses. 'Sath mārg' clearly means the path of Truth. 'Mārg' is a defini-

In retrospect, it is a 'résumé' of the line of spiritual action she had adopted. Her Guru had instructed her to concentrate on Oṃ at the Nābhipadma. She had done so with a will. It had been a consuming exercise. She had neither slackened nor left it half-way. Avoiding the six misleading roads—of the appeasement to the five Indriyas and the little Ego—, she had adopted the path leading to the Truth. The net result was that she had gained access to the Abode of Light. She basked in the Light of Knowledge and experience.

tive word for path, route or road. She does not even say '*the seventh*' which in Kashmiri should read 'satium!' By implication, therefore, 'shu-vot' is a crossing where six roads meet. This meaning is quite in accord with the Kashmiri idiom. 'Shu-vot' would imply the intense allurements besetting the wayfarer, charming him by sense-attractions and feeding his hungry, little self.

13

RAGGING THE IGNORANT

From the spiritual height she had gained, it is but natural that Lalla's religious perspective should change, not only enormously but wholly. With her knowledge that the diversity of phenomena is due only to the manifestation of the Lord whose essence is unity, it is not a matter of surprise or shock that she indulges in ragging the ignorant who begin their religion with formal ritualistic worship and *end it so*. The narrow outlook on religion and the prejudices hanging thereon, stirred her to song, the purport of which is to chasten the religious and heighten and broaden their outlook. If she shakes the chords of orthodox faith of the faithful, it is only a gesture of goodwill, not an act of disparagement. She does not depreciate the religious faith of the ignorant : she opens a more expansive vista of spiritual and religious understanding before them. She sends a fresher breeze of true knowledge into their closed rooms. Her verse, under the heading 'Ragging', may, therefore, be taken as neither a conundrum, nor a shock-therapy.

She sings from the Tower of Realization. If she appears to belittle our age-old beliefs and practices on the lower plane, we must take her in the right spirit. She says :

54. Dwādashānt-maṅḍal yas dīvasthaji,
Nāsikā pavana dāri Anāhaṭa rav;

Swayam kalpan anti tsaji.
Pānai su Dīva; ta artsun kas ?

द्वादशान्तुमण्डल यस दीवस्थजि
नासिका पवनु-दार्यं अनाहतु-रव
स्वयं कल्पन अन्तिह चंजि
पानय सु दीव तु अर्चुन कस ॥५४॥

Recognizing the Dwādashānt-maṇḍal as the shrine of the Lord;
Hearing the Anāhata-sound (dhvani) rising from the heart along the current of the air ending in the nose,
Automatically one gets rid of the fickleness of mind.
Verily he realizes his own Self as the Deity; whom should he offer worship then ?

'Dwādashānt-maṇḍal' has been translated as the Brahmarandhra,[1] which is indicated as the upper opening of the Suṣumnā Nāḍī, through which rises Śakti from the Mūlādhāra, at the lower opening of Suṣumnā called "the door of Brahma" (Brahmadvāra). Brahmarandhra is said to be the gateway to the uppermost cakra where dwells the Lord. But this rendering of Dwādashānt-maṇḍal does not fit in with the meaning of the verse. Dīvasthaja is a small domestic wooden or metallic shrine in which the orthodox Brahmins place the idols and icons after they are worshipped. The description of the Anāhata cakra is given as :

"Above that, in the heart is the charming Lotus, of the shining colour of the Bandhūka flower with the *twelve letters* (or twelve petals) beginning with ka (क), of the colour of vermillion, placed therein. It is known by its name of Anāhata, and is like the celestial wishing-tree (Kalpataru), bestowing even more than

1. Grierson & Barnett—*Lalla Vākyāni.*

Brahamarandhra: "a spot or cavity in the anterior fontanelle of the brain, under the frontal sinus".

Dwadashānt: Grierson refers to *Śiva-sūtra-vimarśinī* and says that it is "the name of a certain ventricle in the brain".

(iii. 16 translation p. 48)

(the supplicant's) desire. *The Region of Vāyu*, beautiful and with six corners, which is like unto the smoke in colour, is here."[1]

'Nāsikā' is nose; 'Pavan dāri' is the current of vital airs; 'Anāhata-rav' may be translated as the 'unobstructed' sound of Oṃ (the Primordial sound). 'Rav' may also be a form of 'Ravi' (the sun). Therefore, Anāhata refers to the Anāhata-cakra,[2] in the region of the heart where arises the (Rav) sound, humming along the current of the subtle air, Prāṇa.

Also : "Rasanand-Yoga, attained by Kumbhaka, in which the Sādhaka in a silent place closes both ears and does Pūraka and Kumbhaka until he hears Nāda, in sounds varying in strength from that of the cricket's chirp to that of the large kettledrum. By daily practice the Anāhata sound is heard, and the Light (Jyotih) with the Manas therein is seen, which is ultimately dissolved in the supreme Viṣṇu."[3]

This quotation is pertinent in explaining the second verse of this quatrain.

Also: ".........These sounds (Nāda) issue from Anāhata cakra in the cardiac region, for it is here that the Śabda-Brahma manifested by Vāyu and in association with Buddhi, and of the nature of manifested Nāda endowed with a special motion (Viśeṣa-Spanda) exists as Madhyamā speech. Though sound (Śabda) is not distinct and heard by the gross senses until it issues in the form of Vaikharī speech, the Yogi is said to hear this subtle Nāda when, through the various Bandhas and Mudrās, Prāṇa and Apāna have united in Suṣumnā. This combined Prāṇa and

1. Tasyordhve hṛdi paṅkajam sulalitaṁ bandhūkakāntyujjvalam
kādyairdvādaśavarṇakairupahitaṁ sindūrarāgānvitaiḥ,
Nāmnānāhatasamjñakam suratarum vāñchātiriktapradaṁ
vāyormaṇḍalamatra dhūmasadṛśaṁ ṣaṭkoṇaśobhānvitam.
Saṭ-cakra-nirūpaṇa. V. 22. Tr. by Woodroffe— p. 417.

2. "The Anāhata, or Heart Lotus, seat of the air element—(Vāyu maṇḍalaṃ)"."Within it is Bāṇa-Liṅga, lustrous like ten thousand suns, also Sound which is Śabda-Brahmamaya (whose substance is Brahman) and is produced by no cause (Ahetuka). Such is the lotus Anāhata wherein Puruṣa (that is, the Jīvātma) dwells".
Viśvanātha quotes. cited by Woodroffe. *op. cit.* p.4 18.
Also, for efficacy of meditating on Anāhata, see verses 23-27 and the summary. *Ibid* pp. 428-29.

3. Woodroffe. *op. cit.* p. 251. (quoting *Gheraṇḍa-Saṃhitā* Fifth Upadeśa.)

Nāda proceed upwards and unite with Bindu."[1] *Dvādaśānt-maṇdal* as given in the verse, *therefore*, clearly *refers to the Twelve-leaved-cakra* in the region of the heart, and *not* Brahma-randhra as suggested by Grierson.

The Yogeśvarī draws the attention of the devotees to a mystical appreciation of the Self. The Self (Puruṣa) resides in the Anāhata cakra. Ṭherefore, instead of posting the gods in the wooden or metallic shrines, installed in the domestic 'worship-room' or Ṭhakur-dwār', the aspirant-yogi must look for the Self in the twelve-petalled temple of the heart and permanently install him there. Concentrating on the Self in the Anāhata, along the currents of vital airs passing through Iḍā and Piṅgalā ending in the two nostrils, he would hear the Primordial sound (OṂ) constantly rising from the Vāyu-Maṇḍal, which is the place of "Bāṇaliṅga, lustrous like ten thousand suns." One who worships the Self here, automatically gets rid of the mental disturbance obtaining on the material plane. He does not suffer from imagining things and raising artificial barriers between himself and the Lord. Self-realization which is the end of all worship becomes easy by that process. Besides, even on the earthly plane, the Śaktis, seated in the Lotus of the Heart, grant boons, like the Kalpataru — the Blessed Tree of Heaven — to the supplicants who can be benefited more substantially, if they recognize Śiva as Self permanently dwelling in the shrine (Dīva-sthaji) of the heart.

Lalla says that when the Self is recognized and realized in one's own heart,[2] the devotee knows the Lord in him. The utility of formal worship is cut rather fine, in that case. When the indwelling Lord is realized, there is no need to seek him outside. She had been instructed, as an initiate, *to enter into herself.* She had followed the Guru's Word and found her Self, notwithstanding difficulties and dangers in her path. Now, she has no hesitation reminding the priests of the Lord where to find Him,

1. *Ibid* p. 252. (quoting from *Haṭhayogapradīpikā*).

2. "Although Kulakuṇḍalinī whose substance is Mantras, shines brilliantly as lightning in the Mūlādhāra of every Jiva, yet it is only *in the lotuses of the hearts of the yogis* that *She reveals Herself* and dances in Her own joy..." Woodroffe. *op. cit.* p. 260 (quoting from *Śāradā-Tilaka*).

quick and sure. If some, worshipping Him in their institutional ways, feel hurt incidentally, we cannot blame her. *There is no bitterness in her vakhs.* We may call it ragging and teasing with a view to inspiring the devotees with higher goals and subtler glimpses of Truth.

She feels that man has fallen into a rut and drags the wheels of life screeching all the way to the end of his days. The religion of perfunctory routine might well have appeared to her a process of stagnation. The cosmos was pulsating with the presence of The Absolute Being. Little wonder, therefore, that she should try to uplift people out of the bog, on to the firmer, more solid path of Self-realization.. She was impelled to sing so as to direct the aspirants to surer means of salvation. From the inert stone to the most evolved form of life, everything was imbued with Śiva. As such formal rituals of worship had quite lost their meaning and purpose for her. She says:

55. Dīv vaṭā, dīvar vaṭā,
Pĕṭẖa bŏna chuy īkavāṭẖ:
Pūz kas karakh hūṭ bhaṭā,
Kar manas ta pavanas sangāṭh.

दीव़ बटा दीवर बटा
प्यठॖ - ब्वनॖ छुय ईकॖवाठ
पूज़ कस करख हूटॖ बटा
कर मनस तॖ पवनस संगाठ ॥५५॥

Idol is but a stone, so is the temple,
Above and below it is joined in one mass;
O ignorant Brahmin! Whom would you offer worship to?
Bring about the communion of the mind and the vital airs (Prāṇa).

In the practice of yoga, as has been already said. Prāṇāyāma is said to be efficacious in bringing under control the restless, roving mind, as a preliminary step for dhāraṇā and dhyāna.

This verse may be understood in the light of her own axiomatic aphorism: (verse 48):

Tsetanya rav bhāti sab same
Shivamai tsarātsar zag pashyā.

Her consciousness of Truth shone like the sun, and in its encompassing light everything was levelled and realized as the manifestation of Śiva. Her mystical knowledge turned out, in a sort of way, pantheistic. All objects of sense-perception, animate and inanimate, were permeated with Being. If man looked for Him, away from himself, it was sheer nescience. In short, we have no reason to be shocked if idol-worship should have become meaningless for her, and should have appeared a travesty of true religion, viz., recognition of the Self and its oneness with the Lord.

She does not negate the faith that Śiva was present in the stone. But what she appears to disparage is the ignorance of man because of which he considers Śiva in the stone and the Siva in himself as different, separate, discrete entities, so that the dualism which ensues leads one to worship the idol as the bestower of boons. As a realized soul, she had resolved the doubt of duality. Her castle of Advaita (non-duality) had become impregnable. From its high turrets, looking down upon humanity, she could hardly brook and suffer the people who would not rise to those heights wherefrom was visible the One Cosmic Spirit which saturated everything that was manifest in the universe. Lalla may have felt the urge of uplifting people to her own post.

The last line of the quatrain makes it clear that *she was not an iconoclast*. She lowers her hand from her tower to haul up others to the position where shone the light of knowledge. She gives a positive advice and direction to the aspirant. She lays down the first principle of spiritual self-realization. One has to develop the process of breathing and subjugating the fickle mind, so that mind and breathing co-ordinate and function in harmony as a preliminary step to yoga.

It may not be out of place to mention here that the Yogeśvari had her day of idol worship. In her early days, her visits to the holy cave of Lord Siva at Harshishwar are a pointer to the fact that her subsequent spiritual attainments had a sound base. From the folk-tales, it is sufficiently borne out that she was an orthodox devotee of Śiva. But she had transcended her early phase of worship. Now that her problem had been solved, the stone-image and its utility as a help to mental concentration became superfluous. Prayers and formal worship have, no doubt, a great value for bringing about peace of mind.[1] But a mystic, particularly of Lalla's order, is not content merely with peace of mind. Yoga is quite a different thing. It is the gateway to the innermost sanctuary of the Lord. Therefore, Lalla considered it proper to advise the worldly to come out of the shell of the limited field of faith and dogmatic religion. As a generous soul, she sings to help others experience the Infinite.

The spirit of this verse becomes clear from the following. She says:

56. Kush, posh, tel, dīp, zal na gatshe,
Sadbhāva gwara kath yus mani heye,
Shambhuhas swari nĕth panani yatshe,
Suy dapize sahaza akriyi, na zĕye.

कुश पोश़ तेल ड़ूफ ज़ल ना गछ़े
सद्बावु ग्वरु-कथ युस मनि ह्यये
शोम्बुहस स्वरि न्यथ पनुनी यछ़े
सुय दपिज़े सहज़ु-अक्रयी ना ज़्यये ॥५६॥

Kusha-grass, flowers, sesame-seeds, a candle and water are not essential (for worship);
Adopting the Guru's word with all one's heart,
One who daily meditates on Siva voluntarily with genuine faith,
Verily becomes actionless and is not born again.

The paraphernalia deemed essential for the performance of Brahmanical, ritualistic worship are of little importance to a

1. "When a man sheds tears and when his hair stands on end if he utters the name of Hari or Rāma even once, then you may know for certain that he no longer needs to perform any rituals. Then only does he have the right to renounce them—or rather, they themselves will drop away from him. Then it will be enough merely to chant the name of Rāma or Hari, or just the word Oṃ......Ritualistic worship becomes merged in the sacred Gāyatrī mantra, and the Gāyatrī likewise becomes merged in Oṃ."
Sri Ramakrishna. C. Isherwood. p. 258.

mystic who has gained direct knowledge of Truth (Brahma-jñāna). Lalla's spiritual attainment was a sufficient authority for considering the traditional Hindu rituals unnecessary and barren; and one may say, all traditional, hackneyed religious formalities had become meaningless to her. The crux of the matter was to gain liberation from the ever moving wheel of birth and death. To this end, the Guru was the guide. He alone could break off the bonds of birth and death, who cherished the word of the Guru, acted upon his guidance and meditated on the Lord round the clock, with single-minded devotion and faith. *If* the Guru's word touched the heart-strings of the aspirant, and his mind vibrated to Him, the usual wares of worship were redundant.

She had risen far above the plane of formal worship and could well afford depreciate rituals. To get rid of 'Kārma-mala',[1] the fruit of the action which results in births and deaths, the ritualistic methods of worship were of little avail, in her view.

This verse is an important pointer to the much debated problem of actionlessness. Lalla does not advocate *inaction*, much less does she speak for running away from responsibilities, social and domestic. While doing one's duties, 'actionlessness' can be achieved. The prescription is very simple and easy to act upon. The aspirant's mind must be wholly and solely concentrated on the Lord. Meditation on Him with every breath which one breathes is the key to salvation. Of course, no spiritual step may be taken without the guidance of a spiritual teacher. And man's *will* is of utmost importance. She says:

57. Gagan tsåy bhūtal tsåy,
Tsåy chukh dĕn, pavan ta rāth,
Arg, tsañdun, posh. poñi tsåy
Tsåy chukh soruy ta lägizi kyāh?

1. "Action—(selfish) works, desires etc.,—is the great enemy of absorption in the Supreme and causes perpetual rebirth. By recognizing the identity of the Self with the Supreme, as taught by the Guru, a man becomes free from the bond of action".

—Grierson.

गगन .चुय बूतल .चुय
.चुय छुख द्यन पवन तु राथ
अर्ग चन्दुन पोश पोञ चुय
.चुय छुख सोरुय तु लांगिज्यि क्याह ॥५७॥

You are the sky so are you the earth;
You are the day, the atmosphere and thé night;
You are the grains, the sandal (wood), flowers, and water;
When you are everything, what may be offered to you in worship?

Everything in the universe is the result of Divine manifestation: and Parama Śiva inheres all that exists. "This Caitanya or Parama Śiva is the Reality which underlies, as *its innermost and true self,* not only every experiencing being but also everything else in the universe, both separately, i.e. individually, as well as a totality, i.e. as the entire universe as a whole.

As the underlying reality in everything and being in the universe, Parama Śiva is one and the same in them all — undivided and unlimited by any one of them, however much they may be separated either in time or in space. In other words, Parama Śiva is beyond the limits of time, space or form and, as such, is Eternal and infinite.

Again, as the underlying reality in everything, He is all pervading; and *at the same time* He is also all-transcending. That is to say, His nature has primarily a twofold aspect — an immanent aspect in which He pervades the universe, and a transcendental aspect in which He is beyond all Universal Manifestations."[1]

When the *Advaita* Śaiva Philosophy, of which Lalla was not only a staunch follower and a protagonist but also a literal

1. *Kashmir Shaivaism* pp. 44, 45.

"And again, the entire universe so constituted, from Śiva to the earth, flashes in identity with the blissful Parama Śiva."

Cf. *Pratybhijñā. Hṛ.* p. 29.—Leidecker.

इह हि सर्वत्र अप्रतिहतशक्तिः परमेश्वर एव तथावभूषस्तथानवति; न तु अन्यः कश्चित परमार्थतः अस्ति इति असकृदुक्तम् ॥

Pratyabhijñavimarshini. I. I. 7
Abhinavagupta.
(*Kashmir Shaivaism* p. 44)

verifier through yoga, propounds a theory like this, one certainly feels it difficult to choose what to offer in worship to the Lord. Religious sacrifices and offerings are enjoined upon the devotees in most formal religions of the world. But the yoginī appears to pooh-pooh the practices. In a state of Self-realization one would surely repeat the query: what shall I offer to Him? (Lāgizĕs kyāh?). No material aids are needed in His worship, in an accomplished spiritual state when the haze of duality disappears for good.

14

THE VISIONS AND THE RIDDLES

It is admitted on all hands, that mystics enjoy experiences denied to the unrealized souls. They command (siddhis) occult powers which may dumbfound the layman. They have visions which have not unoften been misinterpreted as instances of psychoneurosis. But the siddhas and the realized souls would not be declared neurotic, if their perceptions were appreciated from higher planes of consciousness. The seers, sages, oracles and prophets, admitted as such for their divine inspiration and revelation, do not fall outside the category of mystics though the latter enjoy a privileged position of their own in the galaxy of *Supermen*. The mystics are said to be in direct communion with the Cosmic Reality, but oracular advice and prophesies are not fundamental to their objective.

Lalla too had her share of incursions from the Supraconscious realms, and sub-liminal fields. The invasive explosion of thought seems to have unravelled to her pictures of the efflux of the Supreme Being into Cosmic existence and backwards into non-existence, the folding and un-folding processes — the Mahā-Kalpa and the Mahā-Pralaya. That the *play-spirit* at Creation and Annihilation is inherent in the Supreme Being *has to be taken on faith*. Lalla testifies to the truth of the same through her visions. She says:

58. Trĕyi nĕṅgi sarāh sari saras,
Aki nĕṅgi saras arshas jāy;
Harmukha kauṅsara akh sum saras,
Sati nĕṅgi saras Shunyāhkār.

त्रयि न्यंगि सराह् संयं सरस
अकि न्यांगि सरस अर्षस जाय
हरुम्वखु कौंसरु अख सुम सरस
सति न्यंगि सरस शून्याकार ॥५८॥

Three times did I see a Lake but a waste of waters,
Once saw I the Lake extended even to the sky!
Over the Lake sprawled a spanless Bridge from the Harmukha peak to the Kauṅsar springs,
And seven times the Lake appeared as the Void !

The vision is hard to make out. Dr. Paul Brunton, explaining the meaning of Mentalism, says: "If the similarity of sensations has to be accounted for, this arises because the higher consciousness which stimulates all individual minds into the activity of sense perception is one and the same thing — a common universal Mind. . . . There is indeed a hidden unity enclosing all human minds as larger circle encloses many smaller concentric ones. . . . Put into practical language, the World-Mind is the Soul of Nature."[1] Again he says: "It is through mutually acting Karmic processes that this universe becomes possible. The World-Mind brings forth its general world images not by any arbitrary fiat but by their natural continuity as the consequences of all those that have previously existed. . . . When the collective Karmas of all individual and planetary centres exhaust themselves, a cycle of world history closes. The manifested universe then retreats and the World-Mind rests from its labours. But dawn follows night and the cosmic dawn witnesses the re-imagining of all things once again. . . . This antithesis of work and rest, of Becoming and Being, of a rhythm curiously like that of the in-breathing and out-breathing of living creatures, immediately confronts us when we try to understand the World-

1. *The Wisdom of the Overself.* Ch.: The Meaning of Mentalism. p. 22.

Mind's relation to the universe. . . . The history of universal existence is, therefore, the history of an endless chain of alternations between potential being and actual becoming. . . in the end everything must return to its divine source, if not before by its own evolution then certainly at the end of a cosmic cycle by the universal dissolving movement which then attains its climax. If we turn backward in thought to such a time when the universe was not in visible tangible existence, to one of those cosmic periods when the World-Mind had taken in its breath as it were, we find a mysterious state of nothingness that is yet not a nothingness. Mind alone is, a great Void alone reigns, it is as if there were no existence at all. There is not a thing, not a thought and not a creature. . . ."[1]

The Lake of which Lalla speaks may be the Lake of Cosmic exisience in the potential form, what Dr. Brunton calls the World-Mind. Having achieved perfection in yoga, she had had visions of the past formations and dissolutions of the Cosmos over the Kalpas. She recollects having been a witness, as Omniscient Śiva and the everlasting 'World-Mind', to the creation and dissolution of the universe. Out of the Void of Being, the Becoming sprang into the universe of form and back again the latter was folded up into the Void. This had been experienced seven times.

In this connection, we may quote the Śiva Sūtra: "Then — as a result of penetrating into the perfect self (ahantā) which in essence, is the bliss of light and, in its character, the great mantra-power — there follows obtaining of lordship over one's inborn circle of the deities of consciousness which works con-

1. (a) *Ibid.* Ch., The Birth of the Universe. pp. 29-31

(b) "When Śakti expands or opens herself out (unmiṣati) the Universe comes to be, and when She gathers or closes herself up (nimiṣati), the universe disappears as a manifestation, i.e. as 'predicable' in terms of discursive thought and speech (vācya). . . She alternates herself eternally between a phase of manifestation or explication (Sṛṣṭi) and a phase of potentiality (a Pralaya or dissolution). . . ."

Kashmir Shaivaism pp. 48-49.

He refers to *Pratyabhijñāhṛdaya* of Kṣemarāja p. 2.; also *Spanda Kārikā* (Kallaṭa). *Also Pra. Hṛ.* Sūtra II.

tinually the emanation and reabsorption of the universe,"[1] — as the fruit of samādhi.

Esoterically it may mean anything. In her samādhi, or mystical absorption, she had three times a vision of the Lake of Nectar full to the brim in the digit of the Moon. Once only the top of the Lake had come to the fore for a concentrated view. On the subtle plane, she had ascended from the Anāhata cakra (the Harmukh or the dwelling of Śiva) to the Sahasrāra (the Kauṅsar spring of Nectar) over a spanless bridge, in a leap as it were. Practice of yoga had become a second nature with her, and the Samādhi was accordingly attained with ease. Seven times she had had the realization of merging with the Absolute Void,[2] so that the Lake of Nectar and her Self had become one ineffable Void of Consciousness. It was the state of Parama Śiva — the State of Eternality - Consciousness - Bliss.[3]

But when all is said and done, and the intellectual capacity to interpret the vakh is stretched to its farthest limit, the vision remains an unsolved riddle. The archetype, ideational Lake is referred to in yet another verse. She says:

59. Yath Saras sariphŏl na vĕtse,
Tath sari sakalay poṅi cĕn;
Mrag, sragāl, gaṅḍi, zalhasti,
Zĕn nā zĕn ta tŏtuy pĕn.

यथ सरस सरिफो_ल नु व्यच़े
तथ सरि सकुलुय पोञ चन
मृग सृगाल गंण्डय ज़लहस्यती
ज्यन ना ज्यन तु तो_तुय प्यन ॥५९॥

The Lake in which a mustard seed cannot be contained,
Is the one from which all (the sakala) drink water;
The deer, the jackals, the rhinoceroses and the sea-elephants,
Are no sooner born than they fall into *It*.

1. *Pratyabhijñāhṛdyam* Sūtra 20. tr. by Leidecker. p. 89.
2. Cf. "Shunĕs Shunyāh milith gav". —verses 41, 42, 43.
3. Grierson feels that the verse "emphasizes the eternal pre-existence of the soul."

This vakh lends itself to different interpretations. The Lake is the manifested universe. It is already full to capacity, though compared to the Total Being (both manifest and transcendental) it is but tiny, and cannot contain an additional mustard seed. Notwithstanding its tiny extent, all the sakalas[1] — the creatures of this universe — derive their sustenance from it. They live and die in it. Their life is so short and limited, when compared to the unlimited Time, that they appear to die as soon as they are born. They are caught up in a cycle of quick succession of births and deaths. According to this exposition, Lalla's vision transcends the manifested universe. She basks in the Total Being in which the conception of Time and space vanish completely.

Another interpretation is that the Lake of pure spirit brooks no defilement and desecration, even to the extent of a grain of mustard-seed. From this Lake all the creatures drink and sustain themselves. This Spirit is the Life Force, the Śakti aspect of Being, which is ever active in creation and dissolution. For creatures devoid of knowledge and realization of the ultimate Truth, births and deaths are inevitable. The deer and the jackals etc. are instances of the unsaved souls who cannot escape the Wheel. Man too would fall in this category of creatures unless he wakes up to realize the Self and be freed from this bondage through knowledge and yoga.[2]

There are quite a few hard sayings among the vakhs of the Yogeśvarī, and an attempt has been made to put them in this section to allow the reader rack his brain to get at the mystical meaning these may hide. The language of these vakhs is too plastic and baffling to refuse being moulded into any shape of interpretation. She says:

1. 'Saklīy' in Kashmiri means, before taking the breakfast early in the morning. This meaning does not fit into the verse. Sakala, creatures of the world who are tainted with all the three impurities (malas)—the Āṇavamala, Kārma-mala, and Māyīyamala. *The sakala souls are embodied.* The Sakalas include men. They are to be differentiated from Vijñānākala (who suffer from Āṇava-mala alone) and the Pralayākala (who are tainted with both Āṇava and Kārma malas). The three types of soul in bondage are recognized in Trika (Kashmir-Śaivaism).

2. The riddles are open to interpretations, and it would be sheer presumptuousness to say anything as a final word on them.

60. Kyāh Kara päṅtsan dahan ta kāhan,
Vakhshun yath lĕji yim karith gay;
Säriy samahan yĕthi razi lamahan,
Ada kyāzi rāvihe kāhan gāv.

क्याह् कर् पांच़न दह़ुन तु काह़न
व्वक्षुन यथ ल्यजि यिम करिथ गय
सारिय समुह़न यथ्य रज़ि लमुह़न
अदु क्याज़ि राविहे काह़न गाव ॥६०॥

What shall I do with the five, ten or even eleven?
They have upset and disturbed the contents of this pot.
Could they come together and tow this same line !
Then the cow would not have been lost to the eleven.

The five are interpreted as the five factors constituting the materiality of the sensible universe, viz. the Tattvas of the Earth (Pṛthvī), the water (Āpa), the Fire (Agni), the Air (Vāyu) and the principle of Vacuity (Ākāśa).

The ten are: Five powers of the motor-nervous system (Karma indriyas) and five powers of sense preception.
The Eleventh is the antaḥkaraṇa Mind (Manas) along with Ego (Ahaṅkāra) and Reason (Buddhi).

She had been troubled and put in disarray by the five Tattvas and the ten Indriyas[1] and her mind, because they dragged her self—the spiritual Cow—this way and that. They operated for

1. The five powers of the motor-nervous system are:
 i. Upastha—The capacity of enjoying passively,
 ii. Pāyu —the capacity of rejecting or discarding,
 iii. Pāda —the power of locomotion,
 iv. Hasta —the power of handling,
 v. Vāk —the power of expressing or voicing.

The five powers of sense-perception are:
 i. Sense of smell (Gandha-indriya).
 ii. Sense of taste (Rasana-indriya)
 iii. Sense of sight (Darśana-indriya)
 iv. Sense of touch (Sparśa-indriya)
 v. Sense of hearing (Śravaṇa-indriya)

[contd.

their individual satisfaction in ways which upset her scheme of thought. If all of them were set to pull the same line, their cooperative combined strength might help one to arrive at the ultimate Reality. But so long as one is a slave to the whims of one's earthly elements and power of sensory preceptions, the individual self is apt to get confused and lost; much the same way as the cow, owned by several masters and driven in different directions, is likely to be lost.

The implication of the riddle is that on the path of yoga, a unified effort of all the energies at one's command is the pre-requisite for success. The absorption of the individual Self in the Universal Self demands total exclusion of interests other than the spiritual. A half-hearted will and scattered irons in the fire cause confusion. The chances are that one may get lost for ever. It is as dangerous as sitting on two stools to permit our mind and its natural inclinations (vṛttis) to have a free, loose rope to wander and at the same time to aspire for Self-realization and salvation. Another such hard saying is:

61. Ase pŏnde zwase zāme
Nĕthay snān kari tīrthan;
Vahari vaharas nŏnuy āse,
Nishi chuy ta parzāntan.

असे प्वन्दे ़ज्वसे ज़ामे
न्यथ्य स्नान करि तीर्थन
वहुर्यं वा़हुरस नो_नुय आसे
निशि छुय तु प्रज़ानतन ॥६१॥

These five collectively are called the five Jñāna-indriyas or Buddhi-indriyas.

Grierson translates व्वक्षुन into scraping out. But 'vokshun' is used in Kashmiri for disturbing the contents of a fire-pot so as to stir the hotter contents below, to make the pot feel warmer. The comparatively cooler ashes at the top are sent down and the lower contents with live charcoals raised up with a special wooden or metal paddlet made for this purpose. If nothing is handy, a Kashmiri uses his hand for stirring the coals.

For scraping out we have a specific word क्वलुछ करुन. His note reads: "The 'pot' which they have scraped out is the soul. Just as people take a pot of food, and ladle out its contents, scraping out the last dregs; so these have taken the dregs of worldly enjoyment out of the soul for their own purposes and have gone away and left it helpless. They themselves have gained temporary joys, while the soul has lost its opportunity of union with the Supreme."

He laughs, sneezes, coughs and yawns:
He bathes daily at the holy places:
He remains naked all the year round.
He is so close to you ! Recognise Him if you will.

The reference is to Śiva or Self in man. Bereft of Him, human body is but mortal flesh. It is He who laughs and sneezes and coughs and yawns. The activities of the body derive their dynamic energy, in all our moods, from Him. When the ascetic bathes at holy rivers and springs, it is the Self who gets the joy of the bath, the body being only His temporal abode. The Śiva in us does not wear clothes. Being other than the body, He does not need apparel and raiment whatever the weather or season may be. Pleasure and pain, heat and cold are not His attributes. The attributeless, indescribable He is within us. The need is to recognize Him.

The quatrain has a kink in the second line and the third. Who bathes at the sacred places daily? Are the sacred places the ordinary places of pilgrimage of our world? Aren't they the seven lotuses located by the yogis on the subtle plane within us? What is the implication of 'bathing at the sacred places' ? Does it involve the experience or ecstasy and bliss which are the privilege of yogis ?

We might ask a host of questions. 'Vahari vaharas nŏnuy āse'. Does this mean that he has no need of clothes and remains naked all the year round ? Doesn't it reflect on the ascetics who don saffron clothes to indicate their religious order, or on others who put on rags and motley gowns or even sack-and-hair-cloth to demonstrate their renunciation of the worldly goods ? One wonders what the cryptic language signifies. 'Nŏnuy āsun' *may even mean that He is not hidden at any time of the year from those who seek Him.* We have to develop the specific mystical insight to recognize Him, especially when we are told that He is so intimate with us; in fact our tears of joy or sorrow are owing to Him.[1] *The stress*, in any case, *is on the recognition of the Lord within us.* Lalla repeatedly exhorts the

1. (a) "Call them not blind who have no eyes, O Nanak ! Such in fact are blind who see not the Light of God within them",—*Godman* by Kirpal Singh (Ruhani Satsang), Sawan Ashram, Delhi, p. 47. (contd.

aspirant to realize the Self in him. The next 'vakh' throws more light on this.

62. Prathay tīrthan gatshān saniyās,
Gārān Swadarshan myul;
Tsĕta parith mo nishpath ās,
Deṅshakh dūre dramun nyūl.

प्रथय तीर्थन गछान सन्यास
गारान स्वदर्शन म्युल
च्यत्ता परिथ मो न्यशपथ श्रास
डेंशख दूरि द्रमुन न्यूल ॥६२॥

A Sanyāsi goes on pilgrimages to all the holy places :
He is in search of his Lord.
O mind ! lose not the path even after receiving education;
The grass looks greener from a distance !

The Kashmiri Śaivite does not believe in abandoning his domestic duties.[1] He need not wander about in search of his Lord.

(b) One of the recorded anecdotes about the Sufi 'Bāyazid of Bistam' reads: "When Bāyazid was asked how old he was, he replied: 'Four years'. They said:. 'How can that be' ? He answered: 'I have been veiled from God by the world for seventy years, but I have seen Him during the last four years. The period during which one is veiled does not belong to one's life'."

The Perennial Philosophy-Aldous Huxley, p. 24.

(c) Note: It was the Sūfi who was veiled, not God. God is always visible to those who have the power to see Him.

"The knower and the known are one. Simple people imagine that they should see God, as if He stood there and they here. This is not so. God and I, we are one in knowledge."

Eckhart. *Ibid.* p. 25.

(d) "Śiva as Śakti manifests Himself as a correlated order of knowers, knowables, and means of knowledge. This threefold self-division of Śiva appears on the back-ground provided by Śiva Himself. It presupposes a limitation imposed by Śiva upon Himself. The self-limited Śiva is designated the paśu or animal, Jīva, Saṁsārin etc.....To realize the unfettered condition, to recognize oneself as that which has become, or even is, everything, to have unlimited power to be, to know, enjoy, and manifest self-bliss, to be infinite and eternal...rather to recognise oneself as Śiva is the goal of the Jīva."

Kashmir Shaivaism- *The Cultural Heritage of India* IV. p. 92.

1. *Bh. Gitā* V.2.

(a) The blessed Lord said:

"Renunciation and performance of action both lead to freedom; of the two, performance of action is superior to the renunciation of action".

[contd.

Since distance lends charm to things, the places of pilgrimage may attract Sanyāsis. But one who has received true religious and spiritual education will not go astray. "The kingdom of heaven is within you." Since Śiva is within us as much as He is without us, we can well meet Him at home.[1] 'Syadarśan' can mean 'God' as well as seeing one's Self. Sanyāsis wander about to find their own Self as if He were residing outside themselves. According to Lalla, it is an anomaly of religious understanding. She seems to pity them for their lack of knowledge, more so because they usually boast of their religious scholarship.

Sometimes the riddles and parables are couched in compressed, obscure imagery so that one is at a loss to interpret them satisfactorily, for example :

63. Jñāna-mārg chai hāka-vār[2]
Dizĕs shama-dama krĕyi poñi,
Laṃ--cakra pŏsh.prāni krĕyi där,
Khĕna-khĕna mwatsi väray chĕn.

ज्ञानुमार्ग छ्य हाकु-वा़र
दि़ज्यस शमु-दमु क्रयि पोञ
लमु-चक्रु पो़श प्रानि-क्रयि दा़र
स्यनु स्यनु म्वचि़य वा़रुय छ्यंन्य ॥६३॥

The path of knowledge is a kitchen-garden,
You should water it with action based on self-restraint and continence,
The Lam-cakra is the beast and past actions the gateway,
And the vegetables may be eaten up, (as the fruit of your past actions), by and by denuding the kitchen-garden.

(b) "The inexperienced player at a game of dice wants somehow to secure a victory and he is intent on it. But an adept in it takes to the display of his talents first and attends to the gain next. Sādhakas who want to escape from the turmoils of the world are second to those who serve the world but are not bound by it." —Sri Ramakrishna.

1. This vakh repudiates the hearsay that Lalla wandered about from place to place in a naked condition of the body.

2. Hāk is a leafy vegetable particularly grown in Kashmir, and 'Vär' is a kitchen-garden in which 'hāk' is usually grown. Hence, *hāka-vär*.

The rendering by Grierson reads :

"The way of knowledge is a garden of herbs,
Thou must enclose it with the hedge of quietism and self-restraint and pious deeds (poñi kriya).
Thus will thy former deeds be offered like beasts at the Mothers' sacrifice.
And by steady eating of its crop the garden will become empty and bare."

'Laṃ-cakra-pŏsh' is translated as 'a beast devoted for sacrifice in the joint worship of all these mothers (Mātṛkā-maṇḍala)—used metaphorically to signify anything devoted, or destined to destruction.'

"In the garden of knowledge, the herbs are the deeds of the present life. It must be carefully guarded from outside temptations by the performance of the daily obligatory religious rites and the practice of quietism and self-restraint."

The interpretation of Sir Grierson does not stand close examination. Firstly, he has translated 'Kriya-poñ' into pious actions by combining the two words and inverting the normal Kashmiri compound 'Poñi-Kriya', for pious actions. The combination and inversion are unwarranted. Secondly, he uses the word 'enclose'. 'Dizĕs' in Kashmiri cannot, by any stretch of idiom, mean the process of enclosing.

Therefore, I have read 'Kriya' with 'Shaṃ-daṃ', as actions based on self-restraint and continence, and 'poñ' as water. 'Poñ dizĕs'—*You must water it.* A vegetable garden needs watering, i. e. nourishment. The third line is again translated in a faulty manner.

(där)—a window, has been totally ignored in translating this line. It appears that Sir Grierson has been misled by the prevalent practice of offering a sheep or a goat as a sacrifice to the Divine Mother, Śakti. But he confuses the issue. If the herbs are the deeds of the present life, what are the 'Prāṇi Kriya' or past actions, and how do past actions help you get rid of the present actions ? Again we know, in Kashmir, growing Hâk in a kitchen-garden is a cherished thing; none would like the garden to become denuded of the vegetable. No one would like to get rid of a 'Hāka-vär', particularly when in the first line it is compared with the path of knowledge.

In the light of the above, I have attempted to interpret the parable differently. The path of knowledge, of course mystical knowledge, is a very loveable thing. It is a way of arriving at the Truth. We must nourish it by all means possible, particularly by the 'Sādhanas' or yogic means of self-restraint, continence and penance. The Divine Mother, the Śakti aspect of Śiva, coiled at the Mūlādhāra or Laṃ-cakra, the seat of Dharā-Bīja (Laṃ) on the back of the elephant Airāvata, lying asleep in a state of nescience, acts in the immanent world.[1] Also by the Law of Karma, past actions must bear fruit. It is feared that the *beast of retribution* functioning as the Laṃ-cakra, through the aperture of the past actions, may eat up the vegetables and, by and by, render the garden empty, so that the path of knowledge on which we may be moving is destroyed completely. Immersed in the world of sensuousness, we may find that the cherished leaves of True Knowledge are destroyed one by one.

The parable seems to stress three things : firstly, that on the path of knowledge, we must walk warily, by resorting to abstention from indulgence of the body, by voluntary temperance and self-control. Secondly, the fruit of our past actions must be borne. We have to be careful lest the fruit of past actions should undermine our present determination to walk on the path of knowledge and self-realization. The temptations of the worldly pleasures should not supervene our smooth movement on the path of understanding of the Truth. And thirdly, the Śakti at the Mūlādhāra must be stirred from its lambent state to the dazzling ecstasy of knowledge in the Sahasrāra.

When Lalla had attained yoga, she appears to have wondered at the mystery of Śiva's immanence. The mystic may solve the problem of apparent duality; still the puzzle of puzzles "Why all this diversity ?" remains unsolved.[2] She poses the riddle :

1. Cf. Description of Mūlādhāra, the Lotus of four petals. Description of the six centres. Woodroffe, op. cit. p. 400.

2. Swāmī Rāma Tīrtha answers this question in the Chapter on 'Māyā or The When and the Why of the world'.

—*In The Woods Of God-Realization*. Vol. VI. p. 97.

64. Aṅdariy āyas tsaṅdaray gārān,
Gārān āyas hihĕn hih;
Tsay hai Nārān, tsay hai Nārān,
Tsay hai Nārān, yim kam vih ?

अन्दुरी आयस .चंद्रय गारान
गारान आयस हिह्यन हिह
.चुय है नाराण .चुय है नाराण
.चुय है नाराण यिम कम विह ॥६४॥

Looking for the Moon within me,
I came out in search of the like of Him;
I found Nārāyaṇa (Śiva) in this and Nārāyaṇa in that,
I found Nārāyaṇa permeating everything :
Why does He assume the multitudinous forms ?[1]

1. "In the Trika (Kashmir Śaivaism) philosophy, Reality is conceived both as Transcendent and Immanent. As transcendent, it is described as Śiva; as immanent, as Śakti. Śiva and Śakti are not two separate realities., but two phases or conceptual aspects of the same Reality.

Śakti is always in the state of perfect identity with Śiva, but for the purpose of clear understanding the two are distinguished in thought only. The integrality of Śiva and Śakti is designated as Paramaśiva. Śakti is described as the heart, the sāra or essence of Śiva."

Cf. *Īśvara-pratyabhijñā* I.S.14.

"Cit, pure Consciousness, illumination, cannot be without self-consciousness, without self-illumination. Cit is also Caitanya. Caitanya is the Śakti aspect of Reality, regarded as feminine. Thus Consciousness is self-consciousness. Śakti is Śiva's power of turning upon Himself. This is called Cit-Śakti, or the power of Cit to reveal Itself and to know Itself. The Trika makes a five-fold distinction of the fundamental modes of Śakti: Cit, Ānanda, Icchā, Jñāna and Kriyā. Cit is the power of self-awareness; Ānanda, the power of absolute bliss; Icchā is Śiva's power of absolute will to manifest the universe out of Himself, Jñāna is the power of knowing the inherent relations of all manifested or manifestable things among themselves and with his own Self; and Kriyā is the power to assume any form. These five are only aspects of the selfsame Śakti and not five different entities.

Sakti is also known as 'Svātantrya' independence or freedom because Her existence does not depend on anything extraneous to Herself. She is also 'Vimarśa'—various things at the same time; it is Śiva's awareness of Himself as the integral and all-comprehensive ego.

She had found the Light of Truth in the digit of the Moon, in the Sahasrāra Cakra. Back on the earthly plane, she made search for the likeness of Him. By her yogic knowledge, she discerned Him in every atom of which the universe is constituted. She realized Him in all the creatures, animate and inanimate, sentient and non-sentient. She tangibly felt the presence of God in the immanent form, as she had become conscious of the Transcendental Being, in the state of samādhi. Nevertheless, one riddle remained unsolved. Why this Becom-

When there is reflection of Śiva in Śakti, there emerges in the heart of Reality the sense of 'I' which is described as aham-vimarśa.

This is the original bimba or reflection, of which everything in the universe is prati-bimba or ābhāsa, a secondary reflection or shadow. (This system is known as Ābhāsavāda).

The Universe in the Trika conception is a system of subjects and objects, grāhakas and grāhyas. All subjects or Knowers are reflections of the original subject, the integral I, which Śiva is by virtue of vimarśa.... The relation between Śiva and Śakti is one of identity, tādātmya, and of perfect equilibrium (*sāmarasya*). They are regarded as two in one, or rather *one as two*. The relation of substance and attribute holds between them.

Śiva, by virtue of its inherent power, becomes Śakti and the latter in turn is also regarded as substance, because all manifestable objects are taken to be inherent and latent in Her womb. They have no existence apart from Śakti."

The Cultural Heritage of India, IV, p. 82.

Further in this connection the following may be relevantly quoted:

तत्रान्तरं तत्त्वमेकम् 1 "The internal Reality of things of diverse nature is unity."

· *Iśvarapratybhijñā* II. 2.

and व्यपदेशमात्रं एतत् कारणं अकारणं च "The cause or no-cause are one and the same; so unity and Plurality can be the attributes of one and the same object." *Ibid.*

Also, नीलं पीतं अविकल्पं सविकल्पमित्यपि सर्वं मायापदे व्यवहारमात्रम् ।।

"So in essence the objects internally are one consciousness, but, practically speaking, as being differentiated by the 'blue' and 'yellow', unchangeable or changeable, indeterminate or determinate, imply multiplicity externally at the illusory level." Abhinavagupta. *Iśvarapratybhijnā Vimarśini* II. 35-36.

Also, स्वरूपविश्रान्तिहृदयं परमेशितुः

हृदयं (heart) really means Love, joy and bliss. Śakti-tattva is really the Universe as a potentiality. It is the *yoni* or *bijāvasthā*, as referred to in *Pratyabhijñahṛdaya* Sūtra II, p. 24.

ing ? Why should He assume the myriad forms and guises ?

Yogis may realize that Being and Becoming are only two sides of the same coin; all the same the question arises : Why this play at creation and dissolution ? We are told that Becoming is in the nature of Being, because the seeming product of becoming —"All This"—is already present in Being, in the latent state. The quest for knowledge, even for a yogi of perfection, seems to have no ending. Where lies the necessity of the dichotomy of Śiva into the Transcendental and the Immanent ? Why should Śiva assume limitation through Śakti, even by way of sport ? That is the question Lalla poses. The Vedānta, as well as speculative philosophies of the west, leave it unanswered.

15

THE MONOLOGUES

Lalla's poetry has a variety with a peculiar charm of its own. She stimulates the reader with a mystical conundrum and directly supplies the solution. A few typical verses are given below.

65. Shiva gur̥ tai keshav palanas
Brahma pāyrĕn vŏlasĕs
Yūgi yūga kali parzānĕs
Kus Dīva ashwavār pĕṭh cĕḍĕs (khŏtus) ?

शिव गुर तय कीशव पलुनस
ब्रह्मा पायर्यन व्वलांस्यस
यूगी यूगु-कलि परज़ान्यस
कुस दीव अश्ववार प्यठ चडयस ॥६५॥

Śiva is the horse and Keśav (Viṣṇu) the saddle,
Brahma adorns the stirrups,
The yogi, by the art of yoga, recognizes Him.
Who is the god that rides the horse ?

66. Anāhata kha-swarūp shuñyālai
Yas nāv na varan na guthr na rūp
Ahaṃ vimarsha Nāda-Binduy yas vŏn,
Suy Dīva ashwavār pĕṭh cĕḍĕs (khŏtus).

अनाहत ख-स्वरूप शून्यालय
यस नाव न वर्ण न गुथर न रूप
अहं विमर्श नाद-ब्यंदुय यस वो न
सुय दीव अश्ववार प्यठ चडयस ॥६६॥

It is the perpetual, unobstructed sound (Om), beyond time and space, permeating everything, the principle of absolute vacuity, whose abode is the Void (of the Sahasrāra),
Who has no name, no complexion, no pedigree and no form;
Who by Its own reflection on Itself emerges as 'I-ness', first as the Sound and the Dot, and is called as such,
He is the God will mount the horse.

This duet, in one voice, contains all the essentials of Kashmir Śaivaism. The Powers of Creation, Preservation and Destruction, — the processes of universal life, — personified as Brahmā, Viṣṇu and Śiva respectively, are but the stirrups, saddle and the horse. They are only vehicles and agents of the Supreme Being, and carry out His behests. The description is a superb allegory. The Deities worshipped by people derive their power from the same ultimate source. In fact, they are not separate gods, but personifications of the Supreme Being in His different capacities, vis-à-vis the creatures of the world.

Out of their ignorance, the men of the world take Śiva, Viṣṇu and Brahmā as separate, distinct individual gods and attach themselves in religious faith to one or more of these as potential Lords in their own right. But the yogi knows the Truth. The Absolute Being is the indescribable One. Brahmā, Viṣṇu and Śiva function in Him and by Him. He cannot be categorized by any name, form, complexion, or lineage. Vacuity is his substance. He permeates everything. Time and space cannot be related to Him. He is omnipresent, omniscient and omnipotent. He is self-contained and self-sufficient and independent of attributes. In His static-form he is transcendental. But by virtue of his own illumination (Prakāśa) on His ownself, the reflection of the heart of Reality emerges as 'I-ness' — the dynamic power of Śakti. This process of the Being transformed into Becoming is 'ahaṁ vimarśa'. Thus the Being and Becoming, Paramaśiva and

Śakti stay in eternal unity. Since the Transcendental and Immanent are one, the Primal sound of Oṁ—the first emblem of immanence — is unobstructed, continuous, eternal and beyond the relations of time and space: this sound is simultaneously accompanied by the Primal-light (the dot) of the Being. The sound, Śakti aspect, and the dot of light, the transcendent Śiva aspect, together symbolize the Supreme Being. This is Nāda-Bindu. The sound of the sacred syllable Oṁ is perpetually heard by the yogi, who by his hard-won art of yoga has a supra-consciousness of the Supreme Being realized by him in Sahasrāra Cakra or the abode of the Void. There as Void, as Lalla calls Him, dwells Parama-Śiva. Oṁkār as the symbol of Parama-Śiva becomes, therefore, the rider of all the symbolical Cosmic powers that be there, because it is by virtue of Him that all the life-processes function.[1]

Another monologue dwells on a physiological enigma expressed in metaphysical symbolism.

67. He gwrā Parameshwrā,
Bāvtam tsĕyi chuy antar vyŏd;
Dwashavai vŏpadān kanda-purā,
Häh kava turun ta hāh kava tŏt ?

हे ग्वरा परमीश्वरा
बावतम च़्य छुय अन्तर व्यो़द
द्वशिवय व्वपुदान कंदु-पुरा
ह़ह कवु तुरुण तु हाह कवु तो़त ॥६७॥

O my teacher ! Thou art as God to me !
Explain thou to me, for the inner meaning (or the difference) is known to thee;
Both the breathings take their rise from the region of the Bulb :
Why then is 'häh' (short breath) cold and 'hāh' (long breath) warm ?

1. The use of the word 'horse' for a comparison appears to have been borrowed from the Upaniṣads. Cf. *Kaṭha Up.* I.3.4. *Svetā. Up.* II. 9.

68. Nābhisthānas chai prakrath zalavani,
Hidistām yĕti prān vatagŏt,
Brahmāṇḍas pĕṭh shīt nad vahavani;
Häh tava turun ta hāh tava tŏt.

नाबिस्थानस छ्य प्रकथ ज़लुवुनी
हृदिस्ताम यॆति प्राण वतुगो_त
ब्रह्माण्डस प्यठ सूत नद वहवनी
हह तवु तुरुण तु हाह तवु तो_त ॥६८॥

Alt.

Nābhisthānas tsit zalavani
Brahmasthānas shishirun mwakh,
Brahmāṇḍas chai nad vahavani,
Tavai turun 'häh', 'hāh' gav tŏt.

[Alt. नाबिस्थानस चित ज़लुवुनी
ब्रह्मस्थानस शिशिरुन म्वख
ब्रह्माण्डस छ्य नद वहुवनी
तवय तुरुण हूह तु हाह गव तो_त ॥].

The region of the navel is glowing with fire, by its very nature,
The hot air rises up to the throat which is the passage for inspiration and expiration,
But, from Brahmāṇḍa there is a cold stream flowing downwards,
The short breath is cold, therefore. and the long one is hot.

On the subtle plane, the coolness of short breath and the warmth of a long breath are related to two facts accepted by the yogis. The navel region or 'Kanda-pura' is the region of the sun where the abdominal heat glows perpetually. It is here that the 'dot' of light explodes with a perpetual reverberation with every breath. The vital airs[1] rising from this region along Piṅgalā or Sūrya nāḍī are naturally warm in character as they are exhaled from nose in the process of 'Prāṇāyāma', or exercises in breath-

1. The two breaths are called 'Prāṇa' and 'Apāna'; the cold breath from the head and the warm from the navel region.

development. The long expiration is said to get warmed up by the heat of the Bulb at the navel.

Against this, the yogis also assert the presence of the microcosmic Moon in the Brahmarandhra or the upper extremity of the Suṣumnā nāḍī. The region of the Moon being cold, by its very nature, gives out a cold current down the Suṣumnā. This current cools the breath as it is carried by Iḍā nāḍī or Candra nāḍī, in short breathing.[1]

69. Kus dingi ta kus zāgi ?
Kus sar vatri teliy ?
Kus Haras pūzi lāgi ?
Kus Paramapad meliy ?

कुस डिगि तु कुस ज़गि
कुस़ सर वत्रि तेलिय
कुस हरस पूजि़ लागि
कुस परमुपद मेलिय ॥६६॥

Who remains asleep and Who keeps awake ?
Which is the spring which continuously oozes out ?
What is that which one may offer in worship to Lord Śiva ?
Which is the Supreme station which one may attain ?

70. Man dingi ta Akwal zagi,
Dädi Sar pancayandi vatri teliy,

1. Cf. *Saundaryalaharī*. Swami Vishnu Tirth. pp. 149, 150 for detailed description of Nāḍis.

Note: The Guru is addressed as Parameśvara for two reasons. Firstly, he must be a yogi of known perfection and, as such, one who is spiritually one with Parameśvara. Secondly, the Guru or guide is not only a preceptor and a means to the spiritual development of the aspirant but is also his bulwark against his spiritual ailments. In the last analysis, Parmeśvara Himself, through His grace, becomes the guide and mentor of those who have unshakable faith in Him.

Therefore, it is not necessary to mistake the two vakhs as an address to Siddhmol and his reply. On the other hand it is a 'monologue' in which the Yoginī, out of sheer wonder at the functioning of the human organism, poses questions and replies to them herself. The mechanical organism has a mystical background and significance.

Svavĕtsāra poñi Haras pūzi lāgi,
Paramapad tsītnā Shiva meliy.

मन डिगि तु अक्वल जागि
ड्ंड्य सर पंचु-यंदि वक्रि तेल्लिय
स्वब्यचारु पोञ हरस पूजि लागि
परमुपद चीतुनायि शिव मेलिय ॥७०॥

The mind remains asleep[1] and the Akula[2] keeps awake.[3]
The spring of the five sensory-organs continuously oozes out.
The water of self-analysis and introspection is fit to be used in the worship of Hara (Parama-Śiva);
The consciousness of the Supreme station is the meeting of Śiva.

The last line may also be translated as:

1. "Māyā makes the Experiencer feel himself one with the experienced which is no longer what it was in the Sādākhya and the Aiśvara states, but is already perceived, more or less, as an Anātman or not-Self, i.e. other than the Self of the Experience. This is necessary, because there can really be no change in the Experiencer himself—he being, by his very nature, Caitanya."

J. C. Chatterjee *op. cit.* p. 81.

"With absorption and, therefore, with identification thus produced by Māyā, the Experiencer loses the realization of 'himself' as the Self of the Experience; and as this happens he becomes *sleepy.*"

Ibid. p. 83.

सुप्तस्थानायमाणम् *Tantrasāra Āhn.* 8.

"As the Experiencer falls asleep, the perception of the 'All this' itself, in which he had himself been at first lost, grows dim......"

Ibid. p. 84.

"This Experiencer (called Puruṣa), *thus put into sleep by Māyā* who has hidden away from him his own Divine State and Glory...." (under the effect of the five limitations of Kāla, Niyati, Rāga, Vidyā and Kalā).

"And while Māyā, together with the five other Kañcukas, makes the existence of the limited Individual spirit as such—i.e. of the Puruṣa—possible ... he still remains as he ever was ... as Parama Śiva, or Parā Saṃvit, the Supremest Experiencer. That is to say, the All-Experiencer becomes the Puruṣa, to use the technical language of the (Trika) system, following the Ābhāsa process which leaves entirely unaffected the Primary as well as each successively originating source, even when products come into manifestation."

Ibid. p. 86 [contd.

With the consciousness of (Parama-pad Akhĕr) perpetual vibration of Oṃ in the vital airs, one may attain Śiva.

So long as it devotes to the worldly activity of thought and feeling in obedience to the five organs of sense, the mind remains asleep in relation to true knowledge. It remains tied down to 'Kula'.[1] Speaking figuratively, it is not awake to the

"And remaining *always* what he is in his aspect as *himself*, in another aspect he also *constantly falls asleep: that is to say; he is falling asleep or is assuming a limited aspect every successive moment of time....* But while the aspect, in which he ever remains himself (Akwal Zagi), is and must be one and the same, the 'sleeping' or the limited aspect he assumes every moment of time cannot be so. That is to say, while he is always one and the same in his aspect as himself, what he assumes as a 'sleeping' or limited aspect every moment of time is a fresh or a new one."

Ibid. p. 88

"But, although blind and moving and working in the dark, still Manas is an experience of groping, of seeking.... It is, therefore, the seat of desires. Indeed Manas is 'desire' incarnate."

Ibid. p. 119.

यदा प्रार्थयते किंचित् तदा भवति सा मन:

Mahābhārata

Also, "संकल्पविकल्पात्मकं मन:"

"Thus it is, that Manas is intensely active and restless as it moves constantly, on the one hand from sense to sense, and on the other from the senses to the Ahaṅkāra.... "

Ibid. p. 117 Also: *Bh. Gītā.* VI. 34.

Note:—This extensive quotation from *Kashmir Shaivism* by J. C. Chatterjee, should adequately throw light on Lalla's allusions to *sleep* and *wakefulness* and the overflowing stream of sense-perceptions and their mystical meaning.

2. For explanation of 'Kul' and 'Akul', Cf. Vakh-40 and for 'Cit' see footnote to vakh 30.

3. Also: "He, the highest Person, who is *awake* in us while we are *asleep* shaping one lovely sight after another, that indeed is the Bright, that is Brahman, that alone is called the Immortal. All worlds are contained in it, and no one goes beyond. That is That."

Kaṭha Up. II. 5.8. Also cf. *Bṛhad. Up.* II. I.16,17.

1. Mūlādhāra, the sacral plexus, is said to be a lotus of four digits where rests the Kuṇḍalinī (the Serpent Power). This is the basic cakra and is also named Kula or the 'home' of Kuṇḍalinī. This is the sphere of cosmic action. The Kuṇḍalinī remains in a state of sleep, coiled up with its tail in the mouth. Sahasrāra, "in the Medulla Oblongata, the uppermost cakra, is

[contd.

Self. But when the mind with its concomitant psychological functions is subdued, the consciousness transcends 'Kula' and reaches a state of ever wakefulness on the higher plane of 'Akula'—the negation of Kula.

The spring of five sense-organs is perpetually oozing out. There is no possibility of its drying up, of its own accord. Therefore, the aspirant has, with an effort of will, to pull up his mind, carry on Self-analysis and concentrate on his Real Self. That is true worship of Śiva. Canalizing the waters of the spring of the five senses is a process of sublimation, so as to enable the yogi to remain conscious of nothing but the supreme state, the oneness with Śiva. For the realization of the Supreme Śiva, stress is laid on control of the mind and the five senses, introspection and self-analysis and developing consciousness of the Truth through redirecting sense-organs inwards and purification of thoughts'. 'Swa-Vĕtsār' may mean asking oneself 'Who am I ?' It may also mean right and pious thoughts. The paraphernalia of worship, like water and flowers, are not needed by a yogi, if he realizes the Śiva in himself and in everything that comes within the purview of the sense perceptions.

Similar thoughts are expressed below.

71. Kus push tai kwasa pushäni ?
Kam kusam lägizĕs pūze ?
Kami sara gŏḍ dizĕs zaldäni,
Kava sana mantra Śaṅkara swātma vuze.

कुस पुष तय क्वस् पुषांनी
कम कुसुम लागिज्यस पूजे
कमि् सर गो्ड दि्ज्यस ज्लुदांनी
कव् सन् मन्त्र् शंकर स्वात्म् वुज़े ॥७१॥

the abode of Parama-Śiva, who by His nature is in a state of perennial wakefulness. This is the antithesis of Kula at the lower end of Suṣumnā nāḍī, and is styled as Akula or N-kula."

Śiva-saṁhitā-V.151.

Note:—The interesting feature of the duets is that each line in the second stanza gives an appropriate and complete answer to the question posed in the corresponding line of the preceding stanza and each line is weighted with a literal and a mystical image and impregnated with spiritual philosophy.

Who is the male and who the female florist ?
Which flowers may be offered to Him ?
Which spring is the water to be drawn from for anointing the idol of Śiva ?
Which mystic mantras may rouse the Śiva of one's Self?

72. Man push tai yatsh pushāni,
Bhāvaki kusam lägizĕs pūze,
Shisharas gŏḍ·dizĕs zaldāni,
Tshwapi mantra Shaṅkara swātma-vuze.

मन पुष तय यछ़ पुषानी
बावुक्य् कुसुम लागि ज्यस पूज़े
शिशिरस गो̱ड दिज्यस जलदानी
छ्वपि मन्त्रु शंकर स्वात्मु वुज़े ॥७२॥

The male florist is the mind and the female florist, the fervent desire (to realize Him),
The flowers of faith and devotion ought to be offered to Him,
The nectar in the digit of the Moon in the Sahasrāra Cakra should be poured on Him for anointment,
And the spell of silence will arouse the consciousness of Śiva in one's self.

The answers do not stand in need of further explanation. Our whole mind is to be converted into one inextinguishable fire of desire for self-realization.

Absolute faith, unalloyed devotion and silent concentration on the Primal Sound – these are the steps which lead to the consciousness of Self within us.

16

LALLA'S PHILOSOPHY AND TEACHING

Lalla-yogeśvarī did not found any school of thought, nor do her teachings specify any scholastic line to be attributed to her exclusively. She was an emancipated soul who had realized her oneness with the Supreme through yoga. She was not a mere theoretician. From her own 'vakhs', we glean sufficient evidence that she had achieved her goal; and what she sang from her plane, she sang with conviction and out of first-hand knowledge. There is no arbitrariness or artificiality hanging about her verse. That is why her didactic language comes home.

Her philosophy is the same as the philosophy of Kashmir Śaivism, known as Trika. Parama-śiva, through His '*descent*', presents Himself in the Puruṣa-Prakṛti aspect. And the individual's aspiration is to *ascend* back to the original state, through self-realization and yoga. It is a philosophy of non-dualism. The experiencer and the experienced are one. Prakṛti, the manifested universe, is real and not an illusion. The individual subject of experience, Puruṣa, and the object (Prakṛti) are aspects of the same final essence. The transcendental aspect of Being includes the immanent aspect as also the power of obscuration. The manifested universe exists in the Being in the ideal state, and the former appears in the limited aspect by virtue of Ābhasa or self-illumination. The manifestation is a case of involution. "But although the Tattvas and universes as experiences are thus different for different experiencers, they in each stage yet form a unity ... as ultimately the whole is a single unity in and as Parama Śiva."

Apart from this, the individual human being is a microcosmic structure corresponding, in detail and potentiality, to that of the macrocosm. This is the spring-board of yoga,—the practical realization of the Divine macrocosmic Self through the gateway of realization of the microcosmic Self. The upshot of Lalla's mystical poetry is the experiencing of the union of the limited and the unlimited Self which is beyond the bounds of space and time. Lalla does not lay down any creed; for in the path of yoga, the barriers of creeds are automatically demolished. Superficial and superimposed walls of multitudinous, institutional religious faiths crumble down. We are knit up into one religious pattern of His manifestation. The colour schemes and designs are various, but the texture of the warp and woof is one and the same.

A few vakhs are quoted to illustrate the tenor of her teaching and philosophy.

73. Azapā-Gāyatri Haṃsa-Haṃsa zapith,
Ahaṃ trävith suy ada raṭh,
Yĕmī trov ahaṃ suy rūd pānai,
Bŏh na āsun chuy vŏpadīsh.

अजपा गायत्री हंस-हंस जंपिथ
अहम् त्राविथ सुय अद रठ
यंम्य त्रोव अहं सुय रूद पानय
बोह न आसुन छुय व्वपदीश ॥७३॥

Chant the Ajapā Gāyatri (mantra) with every breath, as Haṃsaḥ,
Give up the Ego (I-ness) and be absorbed in Him;
Whosoever abandoned his Ego, verily became He.
The lesson to be learnt is to efface the sense of separateness.

This is the sum and substance of her teaching and philosophy. In the cosmic existence there is not a shadow of duality. To realize the oneness of the self in man and the cosmic Self, there is a regular method, and that is of *yoga*.

Haṃsa is the Jīvātmā manifesting as Prāṇa.[1] With every breath (Pūraka, Kumbhaka and Recaka) the aspirant has to chant the Ajapā Gāyatrī mantra[2], without a break. In Tantra-śāstras, this practice is said to have the efficacy of restraining the Antaḥkaraṇas—Manas, Buddhi and Ahaṅkāra (the Ego or I-ness), — which are active at the lower plane of consciousness and must be subdued before entry into the higher, subtle planes of consciousness can be gained.

"The mind under the influence of Haṃsa moves to and fro, over different subjects; by restraining Haṃsa, the mind is restrained".[3]

The aspirant's individual self encompassed by the individual body has to cross the boundaries of its imprisonment and bondage of ignorance as a separate entity and realize the knowledge of Oneness with the Lord.[4]

1. *Saṭcakranirūpaṇa.* Footnote by Woodroffe. verse 36. p. 454.
2. For description of Praṇava or mantra Oṃ, cf. verse 35 (commentary). *Ibid.* p. 450.

(i) Also, cf. *The Grandeur of Gāyatrī* by Prem Bhikshu Ji (The New World-Order Publications.)

(ii) Also; "The mystic formula or *mantra of silence* is the so called 'Ajapā' mantra, in which the devotee utters no sound, but simply performs various inhalations and exhalations. It is also called 'Hamsaḥ' in which word the anusvāra or bindu represents Puruṣa and the visarga Prakṛti. *Tāntrika-abhidhāna* defines Ajapā as haṃsa, or inspiration plus expiration, or Śvāsa-praśvāsa, saying that:

60 Śvāsas = one prāṇa, 60 prāṇas = one nāḍī,
60 nāḍīs = one ahorātra (day and night).

Thus, in one day and night, there are 21600 śvāsa-praśvāsa or 'haṃsa-japas' "—Grierson.

(iii) Also: cf. *Saundarya laharī:* Śaṅkarācārya: Commentary by S.V.T. śloka I. p. 32.

3. Śruti quoted by Woodroffe, Commentary on v. 36 of *Ṣaṭcakra-nirūpaṇa* p. 453.
4. "Beginning from Sad-Vidyā upto Śiva-tattva, the endeavour of the aspirant soul is to absorb and integrate the object progressively into itself. The complete identification results in the realization of Pūrṇāhantā, or complete subjecthood, which means nothing but the experience of identity between the self and the universe."

Cultural Heritage of India iv, p. 91.

[contd.

When the consciousness of 'I-ness', as a limited Ego disappears, what remains is the Self in man who is also the Cosmic Self. Therefore, Lalla emphatically pronounces her lesson which is to bid farewell to the Ego, as the little self. One has not to run away from the world to discover the unity underlying the apparent diversity. *The ego-centric life is to be abandoned*; and by that way one may discern the cosmic Self present in all manifested things. Recognition of One Universal Soul leads to freedom and bliss. A study of her vakhs shows that she is not tired of hammering this lesson home to the aspirants. She says :

74. Par tai pān yĕmi sŏm mon,
Yĕmi hyūh mon dĕn kyoha rāth,
Yĕmisay adwai man sänpun,
Tamiy dyūṅṭhuy Sura-Gurunāth.

पर तय पान यंम्य सोम मोन
यंम्य ह्युह मोन द्यन क्यहो राथ
यंम्यसय अद्वय मन सांपुन
तमिय ड्यूंठुय सुरगुरनाथ ॥७४॥

He who has deemed another and himself as equals,
He who has deemed the day (of joy) and the night (of sorrow) alike;
He whose mind has become free from duality,
He, and he alone, has seen the Lord of the chiefest of gods.[1]

The vakh may also be translated as: He who has deemed the self in man and Parama-Śiva as one and the same; he who has borne the day of joy and the night of sorrow with equipoise of mind: he alone can develop a consciousness of non-duality and

Note: "Duality is the considering of God and nature to be distinct. The true believer, who sees God, is one who recognizes that God is all in all, and that all creation and all experiences, are but modes of Him"

—Grierson.

1. Sura-Guru: The Preceptor of gods, i.e. Bṛhaspati. Sura-Guru-Nātha may, therefore, mean the Lord of Bṛhaspati or Śiva.

he alone has seen the Lord, the Guru of Gurus. 'Par' may be short form of Paramātmā, so that the individual has to recognize the Lord within himself. In the state of recognition, man would not lose mental equilibrium in weal or woe. He achieves stability in non-duality and thereby stands face to face with the Absolute Being.

75. Śiva Śiva karān haṃsa-gath swarith
Rūzith vĕwahäri dĕn kyŏha rāth
Lāgi-rŏst yus man karith
Tasi nĕth prasan Sūra-Gurūnāth.

शिव-शिव करान हंसु-गथ सो_रिथ
रूज़िथ व्यवहारि द्यन किह्रो राथ
लागि-रोस्त युस् मन् करिथ
तसि् न्यथ प्रसन्न सूरगुरुनाथ ॥७५॥

Chanting the name of Śiva repeatedly, concentrated on 'Sūhaṃ' as the inaudible vibration of every breath,
Even while conducting one's worldly duties day and night,
One, whose mind, without attachment to any worldly object becomes truly non-dualistic,
Finds that Parama Śiva is always pleased with him.

The devotional attitude to the Lord is expressed by chanting His name with every up-breathing and down-breathing, even when the devotee is otherwise engaged in his or her worldly duties. Hamsa,[1] the Jīvātmā as Prāṇa, repeated with every breath quite naturally gets converted into 'sūham'—I am He. Thus with every breath, the identity between 'I' and 'He', the self in man and the Absolute Self, is recognized. Concentrating on this yogic practice, carried out day and night, the individual is freed from the impurity of separateness and the Lord smiles on him ever afterwards.

1. Haṃsa-gath: the way of the Swan: the mystic formula 'Suham' or I am He, with each rise and fall of breath. cf. तत् त्वम् असि "That art Thou" of the Upaniṣads. This is the Ajapā mantra, the soundless, primordial Mantra.

The apostles of 'Bhakti' or devotion to the Lord have extolled the value of Bhajan and Kīrtan — reciting hymns and saying prayers. The bhakta may have to take some time off his daily round of work for this purpose. When the kīrtan is over, he may descend back to his separateness and smallness. Lalla-děd exhorts the bhaktas that it is not the prayer of an hour that will solve the problem of man. *Nor is it a case of begging for boons.* Her precept is to realize One-ness of all that exists. When that realization dawns upon you, the Self is satisfied.

We have to note particularly the guidance advanced in this vakh. Fix the mind on the Lord with every breath, she says. This is quite a simplified formula for yoga. She uses the words lāgi rŏst'—unalloyed, without attachment. Non-duality is a concept which brooks not even an infinitesimally small ingredient of duality. Attainment to that consciousness should be the objective of the aspirant. When that happens, all the knots are cut.

Next, our mind is rivetted to the two pregnant words; (Rūzith věvahäri) — Karma-yoga in a nutshell. Day or night, the aspirant may go about his routine of work. Of course, the crux of the matter is *non-attachment* which is the quintessence of the teaching of the Lord in the *Bhagavadgītā.* When the ego is annihilated, and self is experienced as the Self of the Macrocosm, the individual little self has no reason to get upset by the fruit of action. Kārma-mala or the impurity of action automatically disappears. The individual becomes merely an instrument of action. Therefore, he must function and act, as it were per necessity, so long as he remains locked up with life and death. Shirking one's duties is neither advocated, nor thought conducive to realization of the Self. There is, as such, no contradiction between our earthly duties and spiritual aspiration.

The recluse and the mendicant have no place in her philosophy for *she does not preach 'escapism'.* Renunciation of hearth and home is not necessary for Self-realization. The following vakh unambiguously states this:

76. Kaṅděv gěh těza kaṅděv vanvās,
Věphŏl, man na raṭith ta vās;
Děn-rāth gaṅzarith panun shwās,
Yuthuy chukh ta tyuthuy ās.

कंह्यौ गेह् त्य जु कह्यौ वनवास
व्यफो_ल मन नु रटिथ वास
द्यन-राथ गंजुरिथ पनुन श्वास
युथुय छुख तु त्युथुय प्रास ॥७६।

Some renounced their hearth and home, some took to living
in the forest hermitages,
All in vain! so long as the mind is not tethered at home;
Counting your breath day and night,
As you are, so shall you be.

It is fruitless to run away from domestic duties and seek peace of mind, or the Lord, in forest hermitages. To the purpose is the difficult task of controlling the fleeting mind and tying him down at home.[1]

If the mind roves, it is of no avail and of no spiritual significance to desert your domestic post. On the contrary, even while attending to one's mundane duties, if the aspirant brings under his citta-vṛttis, and reins in the steed of his mind and focuses his consciousness on his breath, as the regulated, unpronounced 'japa' or chanting of the Lord's name, the aspirant shall realize the Blissful nature of the Self, as He has been always. The Self of man, as the vital spirit, is Sat-Cit-Ānanda and the aspirant will realize it as such. Otherwise mental flux will shroud the Self in a dark mantle of ignorance and defilement, whether one stays at home or runs away to the forests.

A fickle-minded person is unfit for yoga-practice, wheresoever he may dwell: in the midst of a throng or in the mountain-solitudes.

Śaivaism of Kashmir, of which Lalla appears to have been a practical exponent in her own way, does not absolve the householder from the desirability of living in concord with the religious spirit which is the yogic realization of his Self. Her teaching holds good as much for a person immersed in material affairs as for a Sanyāsi. *The Soul of humanity, in parts and in the aggregate, is One.* Only if man were to recognise this! In that

1. Reading these verses, one cannot bring oneself to believe that she tore off her garments and wandered nude.
vās=avasthāna, Gṛha=home.

recognition and realization lies the *raison d'être* of all world religions.

Lalla's teaching avoids the controversial issue of renunciation of hearth and home, as an essential step towards realization of the Self. According to her, it is immaterial whether one continues to live at home or takes to a hermit's life by dissociation with the social ties and living in a forest. The place of residence has little importance, so long as one continues to be ensnared by desires leading to actions woven into the web of time. Such actions by their very nature bind the individual in a chain reaction of cause and effect. She says:

77. Kalan Kāla-zäli yŏdvai tsĕ gŏl.
Vĕndiv gĕh vā vĕndiv vanvās;
Zänith sarvagath Prabhu amŏl;[1]
Yuthuy zānakh tyuthuy ās.

कलन काल्-ज़ालिय यो़दवय च्यं गो़ल
व्यंदिव गीह् वा व्यंदिव वनवास
ज़ानिथ सर्वगथ प्रो़बू अमो़ल
युथुय ज़ानख त्युथुय आस ॥७७॥

1. 'Amol' means without impurities.

"The impurities are three in nature: Āṇavamala, Māyīyamala and Kārma mala. The impurity of the bound self, aṇutva or āṇavamala, is responsible for the non-intuition (akhyāti) of the true nature of the Self.

The three types of soul in bondage are recognized as:
(a) With Āṇavamala, it is called Vijñānākala;
(b) With Āṇava and Kārma malas, Pralayākala;
(c) and with all the three malas, it is called Sakala.

"Āṇava-mala can be removed not by soul's own effort, but by some function of Him who imposed the limitation. It is His grace (*anugraha*). As a result of grace, 'idaṁ' is absorbed into 'ahaṃ'."

For so long as the 'experiencer' and the 'ojbect of experience' are separate, there is no complete attainment of 'I-ness', the *Pūrṇāhantā* by the soul, and without that there is no bliss. Beginning from Sad-vidyā upto Śiva-tattva, the endeavour of the aspirant soul is to absorb and integrate the object progressively into itself. The complete identification results in the realization of *pūrṇāhantā* or complete subjecthood, which means nothing but the experience of identity between self and the Universe."

Cultural Heritage of India IV, pp. 88, 89, 91.

"The process of overcoming the sense of separateness between 'I' and 'It' is the process of *ātmasāt* or 'making the other One's own."

Pratyabhijñāhṛdaya. Leidecker p. 15.

If your desires have snapped the threads of the web of time,
You may live at home or take your abode in a forest;
Knowing that the Pure Self is all-pervading,
As you will know, so shall you be.

Time is one of the limitations. Actions, as the offspring of desires for things bound up in the limitation of time, are snares for the Ātman. The individual self remains tethered down to the Puruṣa-Prakṛti state by the force of desires directed at the earthly objects. Desire for material things involves man in the web of Time. Therefore, for release from action and its fruit, desires are to be concentrated on the spiritual, timeless, objective only. If the individual succeeds in *disintegrating the web of time* in regard to his desires, it is of no consequence whether he stays at home or goes to live in a forest. The only desire which is not tainted by the 'impurity or limitation' of time is the desire of Self-realization, for Self is beyond all limitations. Once the aspirant realizes the fact that the Supreme pervades all that is, he has no need to give up hearth and home. His spiritual status will depend on the degree of his true knowledge[1] of the Self.

Three things are laid down clearly. Desire for worldly things involves the individual into the limitation of time, which is a handicap for the yogi. Self-realization should be the only potential desire with the aspirant for spiritual knowledge of Pure Reality. For the fulfilment of this desire, there is no need to give up one's home. (Kashmir has lots of instances of mystics and saints who carried on household duties upto the last). And lastly, the Ātman of the individual comes closer to or recedes from the Parmātmā, according to the individual's own understanding and knowledge of the Supreme Being. For the perfect in knowledge, there is no duality. The Parama-Śiva, the Puruṣa and the Prakṛti are one, indivisible and inseparable. Lalla's teaching does not, therefore, involve abandoning action as such, but it does imply non-attachment to the fruit of action, which comes off in time. *Desires in relation to 'time', i.e. of temporal nature, are enemies of yoga.*

1. Cf. ज्ञानं बन्धः: Knowledge is bondage. *Śiva Sūtra*. I.2.

Freedom from desire, and knowledge of the nature of the Self give ultimate release, whether man leads a life of a householder, or confines himself in a hermitage. The mode of life is immaterial. With this knowledge, his own soul becomes harmonized to his conception of the nature of the Supreme, and he becomes spiritually one with Him.

The essence of her spiritual philosophy is laid down in the following vakh, which sets the tenor of her basic teaching:

78. Atshĕn āy ta gatshun gatshe
Pakun gatshe dĕn kiho rāth;
Yorai āy ta tūri gatshun gatshe;
Kĕṅh na-ta kĕṅh na-ta kĕnh na-ta kyāh?

अछ़घन आय तु गछु न गछ़
पकुन गछ़े छन किहो राथ
योरय आय तु तूयं गछ़ु न गछे
कॅह नतु कॅह नतु कॅह नतु क्याह ॥७८॥

We have been coming into existence continuously, and we cannot escape death;
It is inevitable to move on this path night and day.
We ought to go back to the place wherefrom we came.
There must be Something in this; otherwise what is (all-this)?

On the physical plane we observe a ceaseless cycle of birth and death. We come into existence and day and night we wend our way to the grave. Transmigration is inescapable, as the law of Karma is inexorable. If the soul is immortal, it must have a source from where it comes. The human endeavour must, therefore, be to get back to the source of life, so as to be freed from the pangs of birth and death. Mukti or freedom from the bondage of the cycle of life and death; Nirvāṇa or attaninment of ultimate rest and peace, mark the goal of individual, limited self. If the uninitiated have doubts and the ignorant ask what that ultimate origin of manifested creation is, the answer is quite plain. If the mysterious source is not 'Something', why and how do life and death come about? What is the secret of all this coming into existence and ceasing to be?

There is nothing woolly and involved in her logic. If there is 'Nothing' behind the screen of this stage of life, how is all this sport carried on?

Deliverance is achieved even in this life through realization of the Supreme. It is not enough to say: 'Nothing, nothing'. He must be 'Something',[1] for the very reason that we are alive, we argue and that we have a limited life. And to realize that 'Something', and to get united with the Unlimited, consciously, is the goal of human life. That achievement brings rest and peace. That is the 'Home' we must seek and get back to. Not that we are anything apart from Him, but to realize the Non-duality, that He is within us and without us; in fact, it is He alone who exists; to realize Him through penance and yoga is to return Home. Otherwise, we live in perpetual darkness. We pray to the Lord; 'Tamaso mā jyotir gamaya' — May you bring us out of darkness of ignorance into the light of Knowledge! And Lalla, in her mystical aphorism, calls it: "We must go back to wherefrom we came". She calls the Supreme: 'Keṅh nata Keṅh' — 'The Something or Other', and leaves the rest to us.

Her instruction to the aspirant is definite and her teaching, of course, has a universal application. She says:

79. Tsĕth amarpathi thävize,
Ti trävith lagi zūre;
Tati tsa no shīṅkzi saṅdärize
Dwadashur ti kwach no mūre.

1. चैतन्यमात्मा[1] —*Śiva Sūtra.* I.1.

"This Caitanya or Parama Śiva is the Reality which underlies, as its innermost and true Self, not only every experiencing being but also everything else in the universe, both separately i.e. individually as well as a totality, i.e., as the entire universe as a whole."

Kashmir Shaivaism J.C.Ch. p. 44.

Note: Sir Grierson's translation: "What is anything ? It is nothing, nothing" of the fourth line of the vakh is faulty and his quotation, 'Vanity of Vanities, saith the Preacher, all is vanity' (Koheleth, XII.8.) is obviously inappropriate.

च्यथ अमरपथि थाविज़
ति आविथ लगिय ज़ूरे
तति च़ नो शींक्यजि संदायंज़
ह्वदुशुर ति क्रछ़ नो मूरे ॥७९॥

Thou must fix thy mind on the path of immortality,
Straying from that, it will get involved in evil ways;
There (on the path of the Eternal) thou shouldst entertain neither doubts nor fears,
There should not be any deviation, even to the extent of a stir of a baby in its mother's lap.

The Divine path cannot brook a divided personality. The instruction to man is not to swerve and falter and go astray. Whole attention must be devoted to the realization of the Self. Yoga cannot be practised by people with a scattered mind. Mental concentration is the preliminary condition. Besides, God-realization is a structure which stands on the foundation of unshakable faith. A mind full of doubts and fears cannot ascend to the top. The preconditions to salvation are *faith*, *determination* and *absence of fear and doubt*. A sceptic has no truck with spirituality. Lalla's teaching is not meant for academics and intellectual hair-splitting,

Among other things, the food we eat is supposed to have a great bearing on the yogic art. Aristotelian[1] golden-mean, also enjoined on his disciples by the Buddha, is upheld by Lalla too. Neither the ascetic practice of fasting and self-mortification, nor over-indulgence of the stomach like a glutton are approved of by her. She says:

80. Khĕna khĕna karān kun no vātakh,
Na khĕna gatshakh ahaṅkārī:
Sŏmuy khĕ māli sŏmuy āsakh
Sami khĕna mutsaranai barñen täri.

ख्यन् ख्यनु करान कुन नो वातख
न ख्यनु गछ़ख अहंकारी
सो़मुय ख्य मालि सो मुय आसख
समि ख्यनु मु.च़्रुनय बरन्यन तारी ॥८०॥

1. "The Seven Wise Men (of Greece) had established the tradition by engraving on the temple of Apollo at Delphi, the motto *meden agan.*—nothing in excess". The Story of Philosophy: Will Durant, p. 77.

Overeating will not permit you reach the goal,
Wilful abstention from food makes you conceited.
Therefore, you must eat moderately so as to be a normal person,
And moderate eating would surely lead to unbolting of the gates!

'Eating' may even mean indulgence of the senses. 'Reaching the goal', pertains to yogic attainment. Not a few ascetics become a prey to their self-opinionatedness, because of their staunch practice of fasting and mortification of the body. Lalla considers the body a sacred abode of the Ātman; as such putting it to hardships as the 'Haṭhayogis' do, is not at all helpful to the accomplishment of self-realization. "Ahaṅkāra is what gathers and stores up the memory of *personal experiences,* and 'identifies' and 'assimilates' the experiences of the present, of which experiences the sum-total, thus held together by it, constitutes what makes the artificial or made up 'I' of an individual, as distinguished from the real and innermost 'I', which everyone is as Parama Śiva. The artificial 'I' is only produced by the identification with and assimilation to the real self of the now produced not-Self."[1] "From Ahaṅkār again is produced... Manas."[2] Submission to the *not-self* obviously needs must be a stumbling block on the path of yoga. Since Ahaṅkāra or egoism produces the mental activities and gives the latter a fillip, fasting and emaciating the body are not laudable and useful practices, as are not over-indulgence of sense-organs, and gormandizing. Middling way acts as a magical charm of 'Open-sesame' for the gates of Heaven. The body remains in good trim and the mind can easily be withdrawn from the outer world to the inner. Stark starvation of the mind is prone to result in complexes and abnormality.

Harping on the same note, she says :

81. Yava tär tsali tim ambar hĕta,
Khyŏd yava gali tim āhār ann;

1. अहंकारो येन बुद्धिप्रतिबिम्बिते वेद्यसम्पर्के कलुषे पुम्प्रकाशे अनात्मनि आत्माभिमान शुक्तौ रजताभिमानवत् ॥
Tantrasāra Āhn. 8. J.C. Chatterjee p. 103.

2. *Ibid.* p. 115.

Tsĕtā swa-par vĕtsāras pĕtā,
Tsentan yi dīh van-kāvan.
(vana kyāh vŏñi)

यवु तूर चलि तिम अम्बर ह्यता
क्षवद यवु गलि तिम आहार अन्न
च्यत्ता स्व-पर व्यचारस प्यता
चेनतन [छुनतन] यिँ विह वनकावन ॥८१॥
(वन क्याह व्वञ)

One ought to put on clothes to keep off cold,
One ought to eat that food which satisfies hunger.
O citta, rest thou in meditation on the individual Self and the Supreme,
Consider this body to be food for the forest ravens.
(Understand this body; what more shall I tell you)

Bound down by materialistic views, people believe that we live to eat and put on clothes more as a mark of 'material progress', as Rabindranath Tagore calls the western civilization, than as a necessity to protect our body from cold. Lalla does not advocate doing away with food or clothes.[1] She does not stand for nudity and starvation of the body. The body must be maintained in health and fitness. Even for a yogi, it is necessary to keep off discomforts of cold weather and heat. She advises that we must eat to live; and being physically comfortable, we should concentrate our mind with whole attention on realizing the Self. These are the fundamental problems which man must face squarely and solve them for his ultimate good. For the rest, the body is dust and ashes, or food for ravens. The body does not deserve the sole care of our mind all the time.

She is not tired of telling us that lust, anger and greed are the fell enemies of man on the spiritual path.... Having subdued the passions and reaped the fruit thereof, she sees no end to expatiating on this subject. She says:

1. This vakh shows that the Yogeśvarī considers putting on clothes a necessity to protect the body from cold. In the face of the severely cold winters of Kashmir, one cannot bring one-self to believe that she wandered nude. Cf. Vakh. 27.

82. Mārukh mārabhūt kām krūd lūb,
Nata kān barith māranai pān;
Manai khĕn dikh swavĕtsāra shaṃ,
Vishai tihuṅd kyāh-kyuth dŏr zān.

मारुख मारुबूथ काम-क्रूद-लूब
नतु काण बरिथ मारुनय पान
मनय ख्यन दिख स्वव्यचारु शम्
विषय तिहुंद क्याह्-क्युथ दो़र जान ॥८२॥

The agents of the Evil One, — Lust, Anger and Greed,— should be done for,
Otherwise they will dart their arrows and kill thyself.
Feed them with a careful mind and calm them down by righteous thoughts,
Learn thoroughly the nature, functioning and effects of these passions.

On the path of self-realization, the human passions of lust, anger and greed may entrap the individual and act on him as three Deadly Sins.[1] They may sap his spiritual energy. If they

1. "But he excels, O Arjuna who, restraining the senses by the mind unattached, directs his organs of action to the path of work".

—*Bhagavadgītā*, III, 7.

For killing the deadly enemies of men, Lalla refers us to the third line. Evil must be nipped in the bud by redirecting and sublimating the instincts. This is to be achieved by vigilance against their inroads, so that their fire is extinguished by and by. "The curbed senses are like the inactive snake almost beaten to death. The sublimated senses cause harm to none while elevating their owner to sublimity."

—Shri Ramakrishna.

Note: The following Brahma-Sūtra may be referred to in connection with the restraint on senses.

अथातो ब्रह्मजिज्ञासा । (*Brahma-Sūtra* I.1.1.)

"Now, therefore the inquiry (into the real nature) of Brahman."

Commentary by Swami Vireswarananda.

Explaining the significance of the word 'now' in the Sūtra, it is said that 'now' does not refer to an antecedent of the "study of the vedas,..., nor the knowledge and performance of rituals prescribed by the Karmakāṇḍa, for these in no way help one who aspires after knowledge, but to certain spiritual requisites. The spiritual requisites referred to are: (1) discrimination

are not killed in time, they may get an upper hand and kill man's spirit of quest for Truth. The instincts of sex, bellicosity and acquisitiveness are to be sublimated before setting sail on the spiritual voyage. Getting rid of them is not advised. A correct psychological diagnosis of their working and an appropriate redirection in healthy channels are the remedies suggested. The individual cannot starve the instincts, but with careful thought they can be controlled and brought under. One cannot be too careful in dealing with them.

It is interesting and important to note that Lalla does not believe in a wild-goose chase. The power of instincts is admitted. As an astute teacher, she tells us (Manai khĕn dikh, swavĕtsāra shaṃ) that we must feed the instincts with mental consideration and hold them in check by constant meditation on the Self. The instincts and natural propensities of lust, anger and greed, if not sublimated will disturb the aspirant's spiritual equipoise. With constant restraint they are likely to lose their intensity and in course of time may wither away. The same subject is touched in the following verse :

83. Yĕmi lūb manmath mad tsūr morun,
Vata-näsh märith ta logun dās;
Tamiy sahaza Īshwar gorun,
Tamiy soruy vyŏndun sās.

यंम्य लूब मनमथ मद चूर मोरुन
वतु-नाश मारिथ तु लोगुन दास
तमिय सहज ईश्वर गोरुन
तमिय सोरुय व्योन्दुन सास ॥८३॥

between things permanent and transient, (2) renunciation of the enjoyment of fruits of action,(3) the six treasures, viz:, not allowing the mind to externalize, and checking the external instruments of the sense organs (śama and dama), not thinking of the things of senses (Uparati), ideal forbearance (Titikṣa), constant practice to fix the mind in God (Samādhāna), and faith (śraddhā) ; and (4) the intense desire to be free (Mumukṣutvam)."

Brahma Sūtra pp, 21, 22.

Unless, the aspirant brings the body and mind and sense organs under control, not by obstinate, unreasonable self-mortification but by the proper understanding of their function and thoughtfulness, he cannot set out on the path of enquiry for the Brahman. The control of passions is an antecedent to the search for Truth.

He who has slain the thieves — greed, lust and pride—
And having slain these waylayers, has become humble,
Has been able to meditate on the Lord, naturally,
Considering the worldly goods but dust and ashes.

For a seeker after the Truth, it is essential to retract the mind from temptations. Greed, lust and egotism act like thieves stealing one's attention from experiences of Reality and appropriating it to themselves. Caught in the snare of passions, man gets atop the whirligig of time. And a never-ending cycle of action and its fruit follows as a logical corollary. For the aspirant to salvation, the passions for material objectives are accordingly robbers. They rob you of your spiritual wealth. In Persian Sūfism, they are metaphorically called 'Ghoul-i-rah' or 'vata näsh' as Lalla calls them—cheats who waylay and misguide you. Subduing them, you can meditate on the Lord, easily. She says :

84. Pavan pärith yus ani vagi,
Tas bŏvi na sparsh na bwachi ta tresh;
Ti yas karun anti tagi,
Samsāras suy zĕyi nech.

पवन पॗरिथ युस अनि वगि
तस ब्ववि नॖ स्पर्ष नॖ ब्वछि तॖ त्रेश
ति यस करुन अन्तिह् तगि
संसारस सुय ज़्यॆयी नेछ ॥८४॥

One who controls the breath after inhaling it,
Will not be tormented by sensations of touch or hunger or thirst;
In the last analysis, one who can do this
Makes his birth in the world profitable.

Regulation of breath is enjoined on the aspirant as an essential preliminary condition for self realization. Stress is laid on the utilization of this life as a means to the end of spiritual perfection. Breath-control is said to make the yogi immune to the onslaughts of external sense-stimuli.[1] The sense organs are laid to sleep, as it were, during the breathing practice and as a culminating end-result of it.[2]

Yoga, by its very nature, is individualistic; as it means self-realization. It is not a collective or mass action. Each individual is answerable for his or her actions and the fruit too are to be borne individually. In this connection, Lalla has a word of advice :

85. Yuh yi karm kari partsun (pĕtrun) pānas,
Arzun barzun bĕyis kyut.
Antih lāgi-rōst pusharun swâtmas,
Ada yūri gatsha ta tūry chum hyōt.

युह यि कर्म करि पर्चुन [प्यतुरुन] पानस
अर्जुन बर्जुन ब्यॅयिस क्युत
अन्तिह लागि-रोस्त पुशुरुन स्वात्मस
अदु यूर्य गछ़्तु तूर्य छुम ह्योत ॥८५॥

Whatever actions I do, their burden is to be borne by me alone,
The gains of my (worldly) actions are shared by others.
(Therefore actions ought to be performed) without attachment to their fruit, all actions being entrusted to the care of the Self which we are;
Then wherever I may go, it shall be to my benefit.

This verse focuses light on a very important issue in the common man's life. She does not teach actionlessness. But the motive of action is to be carefully studied. The ordinary worldling performs actions for the sake of what he may gain thereby. The gains are often shared by others. But the net effect of our motives and the actions issuing from these, cumulatively, produce a chain reaction of cause and effect, binding the individual to a

1. *The Bhagavadgītā,* II.14.15.
2. Dr. Paul Brunton, in his *Search Into Secret India* refers to many instances of yogis who were dead to the external world while in a state of breathless trance.

life of birth after birth, as the actions are performed purely as born of Prakṛti.

Since it is not possibe for an individual to live without action, Lalla repeats the lesson taught by Lord Kṛṣṇa in the *Bhagavad-gītā*.[1] Actions are to be performed without attachment to their fruit, for the fruit lies in the hands of the Lord. But in addition to regardlessness for the fruit, we are told that all action should be dedicated to the service of the Self,—not anything extraneous, but the Self that we are ourselves. This attitude involves a basic recognition of non-duality. Parama-Śiva is very much within us. We live in Him and through Him. All action on the earthly plane is to be performed consciously as His action, by Him, for fulfilling His design. Then limitations are automatically eroded. The bondage due to action in time is broken and the individual is free from the burden of the chain of cause and effect. Evil deeds motivated by evil designs, for the acquisition of worldly goods, have no room in this philosophy. It can be only due to the impurity of knowledge as the outcome of limitations of Prakṛti that one may ascribe one's evil thoughts and evil deeds to Him who is pure, unqualified and without a taint. Otherwise, One-ness with the Almighty leaves no scope for wickedness committed consciously and wilfully.

The individual embedded in spiritual equilibrium is not disturbed by storms of actions or their results. Wheresoever he goes, whichever path of action he takes, it brings peace and plenty to him. He lives in Bliss.

In another verse, the futility of sensuous enjoyment is explained. She says :

86. Hĕth karith rāj pherina,
Dith karith trapti na man;
Lūb vĕna zīv marina,
Zīvantay mari tai suy chuy jñān.

ह्यथकरिथ राजफेरिना
दिथ करिथ त्रप्ति ना मन
लूब बिना जीव मरिना
जीवन्तुय मरि तय सुय छुय ज्ञान ।।८६।।

1. *Bhagavadgītā* III. 3 and 5, II.39, X.20 and 39.

Human mind is not satisfied even when a man ascends a throne and rules over a kingdom;
There is no satisfaction even in renunciation of power and place;
Without greed man will not die;
True knowledge lies in *dying while alive*.

There are followers of Epicurus who hold that maximum sensuous enjoyment is the highest good. They are choice and dainty in food and drink. Lalla would permit them the pleasure of physical, and material life, only if they could turn their mental gaze inwards after having had their fill of enjoyment. But that is not to be. Give man the kingship of the earth, his lust for power and the earthly possessions knows no satisfaction. He sinks deeper and deeper into the bog of desires. It is not easy to extricate himself out of it, and set his mind on the essential process of discrimination between what is ephemeral and what is everlasting. It is not easy for man to come back to the path of true knowledge, — the knowledge of the Self. Man gets entangled, by the force of instincts, into the meshes of lust, avarice and egotism and the more he has a taste of these, the less easy he finds to stage a come back.

Human mind is not set at rest by abdication of power either, or even by taking to charitable, philanthropic deeds. It is a queer fish, this human *mind.* There is no saturation point in its indulgence. Living to the world, it dies to Eternity.

Lalla stresses one point, however. Without greed and avarice man will not die physically or spiritually. It is possible to lead a happy earthly life wlthout greed. Sublimated instincts and contentment pave the way to Self-realization. "My mind to me a kingdom is," sings the contented man and in the end reaps a greater harvest of happiness, and mental peace.

Therefore, her precept is to die while one lives. Death in life may mean not indifference to the comforts of life but surely restraint over the mind lest it should yield to temptations and be overpowered by the 'robbers' on the path.

Lalla's teaching has many facets. But the thread running through the apparently multi-coloured beads of the rosary of precepts is the same spiritual thought of renunciation and yoga. She says :

87. Kĕṅh chiy nĕṅdrihati vudi,
Keṅtsan vudĕn nĕsar pĕyiy,
Kĕṅh chiy snān karith aputi,
Kĕṅh gĕh bazith ti akryiy,

कॅंह् छिय न्यंद्रिह्‌ती वुदी
कॅंचन वुद्यन न्यसर प्यंयी
कॅंह् छिय स्नान कॅरिथ अपुती
कॅंह् गेह् बॅज़िथ ति अक्रयी ॥८७॥

Some there are who wake even while asleep,
And some, apparently awake, lie in slumber deep;
There are some smelling foul even after a bath,
Quite a few, apparently engaged in household duties, remain actionless.

Gold and brass cannot be told by their mere appearance. There are people who seem to be asleep i.e. busy with the affairs of the temporal world, yet the Ātman in them is wide awake. The formal activities of the day to day life are no hindrance to self-realization. By contrast, there are persons who exhibit traits of spiritual wakefulness, yet in truth are asleep in regard to their knowledge of the Self. The body may remain in a state of sleep or wakefulness.[1] What really matters is the consciousness of the eternally waking Self within us. Bathing at sacred rivers may not remove the pollution of spiritual ignorance.[2] On the other hand, there are householders who conduct their

1. For explanation of sleep and wakefulness, see foot-notes to vakhs 69 and 70.

2. (a) 'Keṅh geh bazith ti akryiy'. The meaning of this line is made clear by the following:

"With the mind purified by Karma Yoga, and the self disciplined and senses subdued, one who realizes one's self as the Self in all beings, though acting, is not affected."

The Bhagavadgītā. V. 7
Tr. by Swami Chidbhavananda. Also, *Ibid.* V. 8.9
[contd.

domestic duties in a normal way. Nevertheless, through the realization of the true nature of the Self, they have trained their mind to act in a detached way. The long and short of it is that, in spiritual matters, the Grace of Śiva is very much needed. It is difficult to judge an individual's spiritual stature by his external conduct.

Lalla cautions the naive and the gullible. We cannot be too careful against the fake mystics. She advises us not to be misled by the occult powers of some because by using their powers they harm themselves.

88. Paṭanac san dith thavān Maṭan
Lūba bwachi bolān jñānac kath,
Phaṭi phaṭi nerān tim kati vaṭan;
Trukai māli chukh pūra kaḍ kath.
Alt. (Trukai māli chukh päri kaḍ path).

पटनच सन दिथ थावान मटन
लूब ब्वछि बोलान ज्ञानच कथ
फटय् फटय् नेरान तिम कति वटन
त्रुकय मालि छुख पूर कड कथ ॥
Alt. [त्रुकय मालि छुख तु पर्यं कड पथ ॥] ॥८८॥

The stolen property of Pattan is deposited in Mattan,
There are people who talk about matters of spiritual knowledge out of sheer greed;
Such people get exposed, for they fritter away their powers and cannot store and conserve.
If you are wise, you can understand all that I mean.
Alt. If you are wise, retract your steps from this path.

(b) "An individual has the delusion, 'I am the doer', as long as the philosopher's stone has not converted the base metal of his mind into the noble one of the divine eye. When he is in ignorance, he entertains the feelings of agency such as 'I am the doer of this virtuous act', and 'I am the doer of this vicious act'. This attitude is the cause of the continuation of the wheel of birth and death. But when one realizes God, one is freed from the feelings of agency and bondage. One remains convinced in the truth: God is the real doer of everything." —Shri Ramakrishna.

It is common knowledge that many a mystic makes forecasts of events. They develop occult powers of clairvoyance and thought-reading. They cannot restrain themselves from making use of the powers they have gained. And frittering them away, because of greed for money or social importance or simply to gain respectability, they lose the stamina and resource for further ascent. They sell their mystical knowledge as vendors of tinsel do. The result is that the gorgeous mists at the foothills hide the Summit of knowledge from them. They fall off halfway in their mystical ascent. For the perfected yogi, the culmination is consciousness and realization of Unity, resulting in Blissful silence.

The yogeśvarī, therefore, warns the aspirant of the pitfalls on the yogic path. The crevasses in the glacial route are treacherous. Sometimes a sudden flow of knowledge may be difficult to control. Quietism of a sort is necessary to avert the risk of a fall.

There is another category of men who may be called pretenders to mysticism. They pose to be sententious soothsayers and diviners. They practise as thieves and stealers of information. The naive and the gullible fall an easy prey to these swindlers. No amount of care and caution is misspent when one comes across such an one. Exploitation of mystical powers has been the bane of spirituality. And Lalla indirectly expostulates with such Pseudo-mystics.

The reproof and remonstrance to those who expose their mystical power and thereby bring about their own downfall from yoga, is repeated in unequivocal, strong language. The display of occult powers is nothing short of fraud. It is the work of jugglers and magicians because achievement of these powers is not the aim of a true mystic. She says:

88-A Zal thamuno hutva turnāvano
Ūrda gamano par-varzĕt carit
kāṭha deni dwad shramanāvano
Anti sakalo kapaṭh carĕth[1].

1. *Lallāvākyāni* —Bhāskara. Acc. No. 797. R. L. Shl. 38.

In spite of the above vakh, many miracles are attributed to Lalla-dĕd. It is said that "Siddh Shakt, a Brahmin of known austerity and asceticism, wanted

Checking the flow of water, cooling fire,
Walking in the air, contrary to natural laws
Getting milk from a wooden cow,
All this, in final analysis, is fraud and legerdemain.

In the next vakh, a pointed reference is made to a mystic of some attainment. He may have realized the Self within him which experience proved too much for him. He could not contain the divine knowledge. Lalla is sore against such shallow minds.

89. Tĕmbar pĕyas kava no tsäjin,
Maś-ras (or Mansūras) kava ahanäjĕn gav;
Shāṅtĕn haṅz krĕya tola-mwala väjin,
Andrim gaha yĕli nĕbar pĕyos.

त्यंबुर प्यांयस कवु नो चांजिन
मसरस [मनसूरस][1] कवु अ्रहनांजिन गोस

to bring Lalla-dĕd within the fold of his disciples and followers. He bragged of his spiritual attainment by demonstrating how he had moulded his physical system so that he could subsist on very little food. He would eat just one grain of rice on the day of the new-moon and, with the passage of each day, double his ration of rice till the day of the full-moon and then decrease his food by half till the next new-moon day. It was a proud claim to austerity, fasting and self-mortification. He demonstrated his absolute control on his body.

But Lalla-dĕd wanted to teach him a lesson to be humble. She asked him to fetch two unbaked earthen plates. She placed one plate under her feet and the other over her head, on the day of the fullmoon. She asked Siddh Shakt to lock the door from outside and to unlock it again only on the day of the Amāvasyā—the day of new-moon. When he unfastened the door on the appointed day, to his consternation he found that Lalla-dĕd was not there in the room. The two plates lay in the middle of the room closed up one above the other. Hastily he shut the door, locked it, put the key in his pocket and left the place, disconcerted and ruffled..

Charged with curiosity and equally upset with distress, he reappeared on the day of the full-moon. His amazement was too great for exclamations when he saw Lalla-dĕd standing between the plates whole and sound. Siddh Shakt no longer boasted of his asceticism."

Birbal Kachroo: *History of Kashmir:* p. 100.

1. Hussain ibn Mansur El-Hallaj, the great Sufi martyr, dismembered alive and done to death, in 922 H for allegedly claiming that he was God. *The Waq of the Sufi.* Idries Shah, p. 51.

शांत्यन हुंज कयि तोलु-म्वलु वाजिन
अंदुयं गाह यालि न्यबर प्योस ॥८६॥

Why did he not bear a spark that affected him?
Why did the wine of knowledge become too heady for him ?
or [Why did the wine instead of getting down the gullet, get into the wrong (wind) pipe?]
He depreciated the weight and value of the action of the yogis with mental equipiose,
The moment his inner effulgence sparkled out.

Mahendranath Sircar makes a distinction between empiric intuition and transcendental intuition. He says that the empiric intuition "embraces even the intuitions of supersensuous consciousness.... They must differ from the apprehension through transcendental or philosophic intuition!"[1] He has made yogic intuition synonymous with psychic intuition. But in yoga, as envisaged in Lalla's poetry, all intuitions dissolve in Cit or Citśakti, light of Self-consciousness. "Brahman is Existence, Knowledge, Infinity."[2] "Brahman is Knowledge, Bliss".[3] Self-consciousness becomes synonymous with knowledge. The yogi's strength lies in containing the all-consuming fire of Self-knowledge. It is all-consuming in the sense that it burns 'avidyā'—ignorance, and lifts the veil of Māyā. For perfect yogis, the effulgence of Self-consciousness leads to the bliss of quietude. It brings in its wake the peace sought for. But the immature and shallow-minded and imperfect practitioners spill out the light and in the process stop short of the goal.

The aspirant is explicitly taught to guard against high emotion on receiving 'siddhis' or occult powers. The mystical journey, subtle and tortuous, is to be undertaken with care, endurance and tight lips. Visions and revelations are to be taken in one's stride without agitation or exuberance of spirits. The inner light of God-realization is to be contained within.

(It is said that Mansur could not contain himself with joy and declared: 'I am God!' The spark of knowledge proved too

1. *Hindu Mysticism*:pp. 18. 19.
2. *Taittirīya Up*. 2.1
3. *Bṛhad. Up*. 3. 9. 28.

much for him with the result that he had to pay the price with his own life.).

In the event of total merging of the individual self with the Cosmic Self, the Yogi's lips are sealed.[1]

In the lever of yoga, 'Practice' is the fulcrum. Lalla lays due stress on practice. She says:

90. Parun swalab pālun dwarlab,
Sahaz gārun sikhim ta krūṭh,
Abhyāsaki ganirai shāstra mŏṭhum.
Tsetan Ānand nĕshcai gom.

परुन स्वलब पालुन द्वलंब
सहज़ गारुन सिखिम तु क्रूठ
अभ्यासुकि गनिरय शास्त्र मोठुम
चीतनु आनन्द न्यश्चय गोम ॥९०॥

To con the scriptures is easy, but to act upon them is difficult,
The quest for the Reality is a difficult, subtle process.
I clean forgot the scriptures in the thick of (yogic) practice,
(Nevertheless), I attained the state of Conscious-Blissfulness.

To the majority of men, study of scriptures becomes the be-all and end-all of religion. Very few there are who act upon scriptural teachings; and very rare are the instances of god-men

1. "A wise man should keep down speech and mind: he should keep them within the Self which is knowledge; he should keep knowledge within the Self which is the great; and he should keep that (the great) within the Self which is the Quiet."

Kaṭha Up. 1.3.13. Tr. by Max Müller.

Note: People say that this vakh has a reference to another great mystic of Kashmir, Swami Rishi Pir. But this guess seems incorrect insomuch as Swami Rishi Pir is said to have been a contemporary of another saint of Kashmir, Sheikh Hamzah popularly known as Makhdum Saheb, who, according to Hassan, died in 1576. Both Makhdoom Saheb and Rishi Pir are said to have performed many miracles.

whose goal of life becomes the realization of the Self.[1] 'Who am I?' is an eternal question, but how many of us can muster strength to face the question squarely and find an answer to it? Surely it is a formidable question and to find an answer to it a delicate, subtle and difficult job. The names of saints who found an answer to it cannot be counted by the legion. The Buddha, Mahāvīra, Śaṅkarācārya, Sri Ramakrishna Parmahamsa, Ramana Maharshi, and Lalla-dĕd were born to know the Truth and benefit the world by their divine knowledge.

As a practical teacher, Lalla makes no bones about hammering home to the aspirant that mere theoretical scriptural knowledge[2] does not bring light to the yearning soul, but yogic practice carried on with patience, endurance and perseverance, does bring one to the threshold of God.

She says:

91. Avĕtsäri pothĕn chi-ho mâli parān,
Yitha tota parān 'Rāma' panjaras;
Gita parān ta hīthā labān;
Param Gita ta parān chĕs.

1. "Of thousands of men, some rare soul strives to realize Me; of those striving yogis, again, some rare one (devoting himself exclusively to Me) knows Me in reality".

Bhagavadgitā VII.3.

2. शास्त्रयोनित्वात् ॥ *Brahma-Sūtra*. 3. Tr. by Swami Vireshwarananda.

"The scripture being the means of right knowledge." This Brahma-Sūtra lays down that the study of scriptures is a '*means*' of right knowledge (with regard to Brahman), but their study is not an '*end*' by itself......But after reading the scriptural texts like:

"I am Brahman", —*Bṛh. Up.* 1.4.10. or "He who knows the Supreme Brahman becomes Brahman indeed",—*Muṇḍ. Up.* 3.2.9. or "There is no manifoldness in It",—*Kaṭ. Up.* 2.4.11., the question is: how many learned scholars of scriptures turn their mind from things external and direct it inwards ?

Lalla does not discount or undervalue the reading of scriptures. "The scriptures themselves say, 'One who is ignorant of the scriptures cannot know that Brahman'." But realization of Brahman as a practical experience needs something besides the knowledge of scriptures. It involves the application of scriptural knowledge, which is the special privilege of perfected yogis.

अव्यचा़र्यं पोथ्यन छिहो मालि परान
यिथ्‌ तोत्‌ परान राम पंजुरस
गीता परान त्‌ हीथा लबान
परम गीता त्‌ परान छ्यस ॥९१॥

Without discernment they read the holy books,
Just as the parrot repeats 'Rāma! Rāma !' from its cage;
To them reading of the Gītā is just a pretence:
I have read the Gītā and am reading it (every moment of my life).

The holy books are not to be read parrotlike without making out the deeper import of the lessons taught therein. These books are to be chewed and digested, as Sir Francis Bacon says. The reader ought to live upto the teaching of the scriptures, otherwise mere reading is a facade put up for an exhibition of religiosity. She had read the *Bhagavad Gītā* and made the Lord's teaching part and parcel of her thought and conduct in life. "A worldly man may be as much informed in religion as the spiritual man; or he may even excel in learning and intelligence. He may even be endowed with the discipline of a Yogi's life and the detachment of a Sanyāsin. In the midst of these merits his life may degenerate if he utilize them all not for the glory of the Lord but for self-glorification, name, fame and wealth,"[1] says Sri Ramakrishna.

The vakh sums up the need of close correlation between reading and living the lessons.

In yet another verse, the same theme is touched. She says:

92. Parun polum apŏruy rovum,
Kesar vana volum raṭith shāl,
Paras prŏnum ta pānas polum,
Ada gom molūm ta zīnim hāl.

1. *Shrimad Bhagavadgitā.* VI. 46.47. Swami Chidbhavananda

परुन पोलुम अपो_रुय रोवुम
केसर वनु वोलुम र'टिथ शाल
परस प्रो_नुम तु पानस पोलुम
अदु गोम मोलूम तु ज़ीनिम हाल ॥६२॥

I put into practice whatever I read, the unread was lost to my consciousness;
I dragged the lion down the forest by his silken mane as if he were a jackal!
I preached what I practised,
That way did knowledge dawn on me and I won the goal.

Since it is not possible to read all the scriptures, she made a judicious selection of these and ignored the rest. But she lived the lessons she learnt from the scriptures. It was not just a walk over. A Herculean courage and hard struggle it meant for her, as may metaphorically be compared with catching hold of a lion in the forest by his mane and dragging him down as if he were a mere jackal. The figures of speech beautifully illustrate Lalla's confession that yoga is a very difficult practical feat. She had read the *Gītā*, as many of us do. But to realize the Lord's presence in all that exists as His manifestation, and to dedicate all action to Him without regard for the result thereof, is the peculiar prerogative of the yogis like Lalla. On the mundane level, we are asked to bear in mind that we must resolve to act upon what the scriptures teach. The secret of mystical success lies in bridging the gap between precept and practice. Religion should not be consigned to the lifeless leaves of books. *Religion in practice* is the essential thing. Mere chanting of scriptures is acting the parrot. That is not the way of getting freedom from the cage! We are all encaged parrots and release ought to be our goal. Lalla is a practical philosopher.

17

ON AHIṀSĀ

Lalla has a 'vakh' against animal sacrifice. She says:

93. Laz kāsiy shīt nĕvāriy,
Trana zala karān āhār;
Yih kami vŏpadīsh kŏruy hūṭ baṭā,
Atsītan vaṭas satsītan dyun āhār.

लज्ज कासिय शीत न्यवारिय
त्रिण् जल् करान ग्राहार
यि कम्य् वञपुदीश को्रुय हूट् बटा
ग्रचीतन वटस सचीतन द्युन ग्राहार ॥६३॥

It will cover your shame and keep off cold from your body,
It feeds on grass and has water for drink.
Who has taught you, foolish Pandit,

Note: It is said that Lalla found a Brahmin leading a sheep to be sacrificed to propitiate a god, in order to secure redemption from sin. Directly this verse issued to admonish the foolish man. She could not stomach the fact that any true scriptures or a truly religious man could advise him to go in for the animal sacrifice. With her knowledge of the all-pervading Śiva, animal sacrifice was a symptom of total ignorance.

(Certain Tantric practices involving animal sacrifice are prevalent to this day in India.).

This verse may relevantly be connected with verse 13.

To offer as food the living creature to propitiate an insentient stone?

This 'vakh' does not need any elucidation.

According to the Trika, true knowledge consists in realizing Śiva in everything, animate or inanimate, sentient or insentient. The philosophy of immanent Śiva as Śakti leaves no scope for animal sacrifice.

18

ON DEATH

There are a few verses of Lalla which throw light on life and death. But 'life' and 'death' have a different meaning and connotation in the mystical parlance. Life signifies release from the cycle of birth and death. It is identical with yoga or the union of the limited and unlimited Self, which are essentially one but are considered separate, owing to the effect of Māyā or power of obscuration and 'āṇavamala'. In this context, 'death' does not refer to the body, as we understand it ordinarily. Death is *isolation* and bondage of the jīva, the individual soul. So long as the Jīva is wrapped up in the cloak of darkness and does not recognize, realize and experience the oneness of the individual and the Cosmic Self, he does not attain deathlessness.

The yogesvarī had had the personal experience of deathlessness; and, as a matter of course, she speaks on the subject with authority. She says:

94. Tsāmar chatra rath siṁhāsan
Āhlad[1] nāṭiya-ras tūla-paryaṅkh,

1. 'Āhlad', in Sanskrit, means 'joy'. 'Tūl' means 'cotton'. 'Paryaṅkh' means 'bed'. 'Tsāmar' in Kashmiri is the same as the decorative piece in the crown, usually made out of peacock-feathers or yak-hair. 'Siṁhāsan' is the whole tiger-skin with the head of the animal on, used as cover to the seat.Now simply the throne. 'Sheṅkh' is equivalent of śaṅkā: doubt, fear. 'Sthir' is steady; fixed; firm; changeless; permanent.

Kyāh mänith yĕti sthir āswani?
Kawa zana kāsiy maranañ shĕṅkh?

चामर छत्र रथ सिहासन
आह्लाद नाटिरस तूलु-परयङ्क
क्याह मानिथ यति स्थिर आसुवनीय
कवु ज़न कासिय मरुनञ शङ्क ॥६४॥

The decorative crown of peacock feathers, the royal canopy, chariot and throne,
Merry-making, a taste of dance, a bed stuffed with cotton:
How did you expect these to be permanent and lasting?
How do you expect Him to relieve you of the fear of death?

Leading a life of luxury, man misunderstands the nature of Self. Physical pleasures engross him to the total neglect of his self. Buried in joys of life, mists of illusion blur his understanding. He takes the evanescent joys of the present sense-perceptions for permanent fixtures. He forgets that flesh, by its very nature, is destined to destruction. He has not the sense of discrimination between the transitory and the everlasting and gives himself up to the present pleasures of the body and casts the care of the self to the winds. Yet, if such an individual, swept clean off his feet by the gusts of self-forgetfulness, expects to gain release from the yoke of birth and death during aeons to come, he is deluded.

The point to note is that Lalla does not denounce the luxuries of physical life as such; she does not emphasize or advocate mortification of the body; she does not decry sensuous satisfaction and the enjoyment of worldly glory; she is not antagonistic to aesthetic pleasures of different sorts; but that she does certainly reprimand the person who is so overtaken and absorbed by the worldly pleasures of the body that he mistakes them for permanent, and everlasting things. He runs after them day in, day out to the utter disregard for his immortal Self. He becomes shortsighted. Drunk with the wine of material pleasures, he shoves the thoughts of spirit clean out of his mind.

Verily, such a one cannot hope at all to escape the wheel of birth and death through the passage of 'kalpas' and 'Mahākalpas'.

Death in the mystical sense, stares him in the face. He is doomed and cannot taste the nectar of immortality.

In another verse, she says:

95. Kyâh bŏḍukh muha bhavasŏdra-dāre,
Swŏth lūrith pĕyiy tamapaṅk;
Yama-bhāṭh karanaị käli choradāre,
Kawa zana kāsiy maranañ shĕṅkh.

क्याह् बो_डुख मूह् बवुसंद्रु दारे
सो_थ लूहरिय प्य'यिय तमु पङ्क
यमुबाठ करुनय काल्य छोरुदारे
कवु जऩ कासिय मरुनुञ शङ्क ॥९५॥

Why have you got drowned, out of ignorance and attachment, in the current of the ocean of existence?
Why have you dismantled the embankment and got stuck up in the morass of darkness?
The apparitors of Death[1] will drag you bleeding in due time.
How do you expect Him to relieve you from the fear of death?

As in the temporal so also in the spiritual field, ignorance of law is not accepted as an excuse. The embankment is the raised path of knowledge above the level of flood of ignorance.

1. In the *Mratva* Tattva (Bhṛngeśa Saṁhitā), there are given blood-curdling scenes which the subtle body of man has to face at the hands of the Servitors of (Yama), the god of Death. They drag the sinful body on a road strewn with thorns and make him bleed like hell. The Purāṇa is read and explained by the priest for a week, after the death of any elderly member of the family. This practice is in vogue here among the Hindus.

'Muha' is Kashmiri equivalent of 'Moha' meaning ignorance, illusion; attachment. 'Bhavasŏdra' is the ocean of existence. दार from दारा is a current. Kāl is from 'Kāl' or time. Tam from तमस is darkness; ignorance; absence of knowledge. *Paṅka* in Sanskrit means mud.

(*Paṅkh* has been written by Grierson for *Paṅk*. The former is a misreading).

Demolishing the path of knowledge surely leads to getting drowned in ignorance. A person who wilfully gets involved in the vortex of wordly life at the cost of knowledge of his Self is like a man who demolishes a dyke to let in the flood waters to drown himself. He spends his earthly days, as it were, in mire. He will not be forgiven his negligence at the end of the physical life. Retribution awaits us because of karmic laws. We shall have to pay the price for our ignorance and negligence. Under the circumstances, we have no reason to hope for redemption and release.

This life is a sort of testing ground. Even as we are wallowing in the mud of ignorance, somewhere at the back of our mind is a streak of the light of Truth. But we put out the light and choose to stay in darkness. Indulging in actions under the limitations of Prakṛti, we lay the self to sleep. Instead of making the self arise and evolve, we choose to stay on in the sheath of the body. If the pangs of birth and death attend on us, we are ourselves to blame for it. It is absurd to hope for salvation (Kaivalya) in this state of ignorance. Death dies only when the self is roused and helped ascend to the consciousness of Self. *Immortality is another name for ascension backwards to the origin of our being.*

Lalla's approach to the problem of 'death' is not negative as may be the impression gathered on reading the last two vakhs. She has a positive advice to give in order to help the aspirant to attain immortality. She says:

96. Karam zah, Kāran trĕh kŏmbith,
Yava labakh paralūkas aṅkh;
Vŏth khas Surya-maṇḍal tsŏmbith,
Tavai tsaliy maranañ shĕṅkh.

कर्म जह् कारण त्रेह् को͞म्बिथ
यव् लबख परलूकस अङ्क
व्वथ खस सूर्यमण्डल चोंम्बिथ
तवय चलिय मरनञ शङ्क ॥९६॥

Works are two and causes three. Overcoming these with the Kumbhaka or control of breath,

You may discover the symbol of and cue to the other
world;
Piercing the disc of the Sun,
That is the way of getting rid of the fear of death.

Liberation from 'Death' is possible only through knowledge of the Self. The actual practice of Yoga is summed up in the four compressed lines of this verse. The vakh has the likeness of a Sūtra, an aphorism or a clue to knowledge. She says that there are two actions, but she does not dilate upon it. Filling in the blanks, we may add that the two kinds of actions are good and bad: the actions which help and those which hinder a cause; i.e., forward and backward movements in time and space. There are three causes as laid down by Śaivaism, viz. the three 'malas' or impurities.[1] These impurities are considered as the causes of the apparent existence. Due to the first the soul is deemed as finite. The second leads to the cognition of difference between one thing and another, and the third produces action, both pleasurable and painful.

Now Lalla's vakh is a lesson in the practice of yoga. Breath-control is recognized as a means of ridding the Prakṛti-enveloped Puruṣa from the two Actions and the three Impurities or causes of apparent existence. In the Kumbhaka-yoga practice, the individual self is said to be awakened from sleep by breaking through the sheaths of actions and the external existence. Having wakened up the self, the yogi comes upon the symbol of the Supreme Being, called in common man's language (Parlūk), the other world. It is said that in the samādhi when breath is stopped, the individual dies to the external world and becomes, in common parlance, actionless. In this state, it is said that he becomes conscious of an infinitely tiny dot of light in the Navel region above the Mūlādhāra. The Kuṇḍalinī is awakened! This is said to be the stage when the yogi has much to exert to raise

1. See footnote to V.77. Commenting on the Brahma-Sūtra, Swami Vireshwarananda says: "An inquiry into Brahman is desirable because ... the result of the true knowledge of the Self leads to liberation, and so serves a very, very fruitful purpose."

Brahma-Sūtra by Swami Vireshwarananda, p. 21
Also see note to verse 82.

the Śakti and help it ascend, piercing[1] through the disc of the 'Sun' in the Navel region, up to the abode of Parama Śiva in the Sahasrāra (in the cerebral region). That is the way of attaining Mukti or freedom from the fear of death. Once the Union of the individualized self and the Universal Self is attained, the chain of birth and death is automatically broken asunder.
automatically broken asunder.

That is the Yogeśvarī's experience, faith, and lesson to the aspirants. In explicit terms she teaches the art of yoga-practice and explains the means of achieving emancipation from birth and death. It is, indeed, a daring lesson and a dangerous one too for an uninitiated person. No monkeying is safe, unless undertaken under the guidance and supervision of an accomplished Siddha Guru. Lalla has spared no pains in emphasising the importance of a Guru, an accomplished preceptor. And it has already been said that coming upon a Sat-Guru is entirely a matter of God's grace.

The precepts are hammered down into our acceptance by the strong arm of an experienced practitioner of yoga. She had solved the problem of "death" for herself and gladly would she teach others to follow her example. Her confidence and her eagerness to help become evident from the following verse.

97. Jñānaki ambar pārith tane
Yim pad Lali dapi tim hrĕdi aṅkh:
Kārana Pranavaki layi kŏr Lalle
Tsĕth-jyoti käsan maranañ shĕṅkh.

ज्ञानुक्य अम्बर पूरिथ तने
यिम पद ललि दंप्य तिम हृदि अङ्क
कारणु प्रणुवुक्य लयि को_र लले
च्यथ-ज्योति कासुन मरनुञ शङ्क ।।९७।।

Note:—Reference to death does not pertain to the body.

1. "When Kuṇḍalinī rises up this canal (Virajā or the innermost part of Suṣumnā), the budlike nervous tissues turned downwards open up and give way to Her upward march, the process is known to yogis as षट्चक्रवेध i.e. *piercing* through the Six cakras. *Devātma Shakti* ch. VII p. 61.

Donning the clothes of knowledge,
Stamp thou thy heart with the vakhs which Lalla sang;
With the Instrument of Praṇava (Oṃ), Lalla has dissolved her self into
The All-Experiencing Light, and done away with the fear of death.

Conviction engendered by personal experience seems to impel her to sing this message for universal good. Altruism trickles from every pore of this vakh. Spiritually she had ascended to the state of union with the Cosmic Self. She would gladly lift up others too to that blissful state. Shelley's skylark sings from his ethereal heights and inundates the earth with joy: Lalla sings from her mystical heights and seeks to raise mankind to a condition of perennial bliss.

This vakh carries an added importance. Unequivocally Lalla refers to the Bīja-mantra, Oṃ, and its efficacy in the field of Yoga. Her Guru had given her *the Word.* She had acted on it and achieved her goal, and brought about "deathlessness" for herself. So she lays down the importance of *Oṃ as the mystical key to yoga.* Yoga, it is assumed, brings a promise of eternal life. Death dies. This is the lesson for all seekers after "life".

Like all saints, sages and mystics, Lalla was gifted with an abundance of goodwill for mankind. The peculiarity of her message is that she throws definite and unequivocal cues for attainment of practical yoga, to the aspirant. Those who study her vakhs with an appreciative, critical understanding, will not deny her a very exalted place not only among the philosopher-poets of the world but also among the saints and seers of the highest attainment. Surely, "time will not wither, nor custom stale" the practical significance of her mystical verse.

19

REALIZATION IN RETROSPECT

There is a peculiar flavour of exultation about a few vakhs which appear to have been sung in retrospect. An aura of self-satisfaction hangs around them. She had solved the problem of earthly life, and as it were cut the Gordian knot by sheer force of determination and past karmas. God's grace and human will had coalesced in building the superstructure of mystical knowledge on the granite foundation of spiritual impressions (saṁskāras) she had gleaned during her previous sojourns on the earth. The shadow of death had finally disappeared. On the phenomenal plane, it was natural that she should rehearse the drama of the Spirit, which she had hitherto acted solo, for the benefit of man in general.

The finale of her mystical accomplishment leaves one breathless. She too may have been staggered by the dimensions of her own Self-experience. But more than most, the plausible explanation of the vakhs uttered in retrospect is the revision of the glorious glimpses of Self she had had already. *She ponders over these aloud.* These vakhs are not only an after-taste of blissful experiences she had but also a tempting treat for the aspirants and neophytes.

Recapitulating the happy state of Samādhi, she says:

98. Dīshi āyas dasha-dīsha tīlith,
Tsalith tsŏṭum shūnya ada vāv,

Shivay dyūṅṭhum shāyi-shāyi mīlith
Shĕh-ta-trĕh träpimas ta Shivay drāv.

दीशु ग्रायस दशु-दीशु तीलिथ
चलिथ चोदुम शून्य ग्रदु वाव
शिवुय ड्यूंठुम शायि-शायि मीलिथ
श्य-तु-त्रेह त्रांपिमस तु शिवुय द्राव ॥६८॥

I came from my Country and wandered about far and wide in ten different directions,
I sped like a hurricane through ethereal voids,
Shiva did I find everywhere, embodied in everything!
I shut up the nine apertures,[1] and lo! I found none but Śiva within me.

Post-realization vision of Śiva pervading everything, not only the world of perceptible phenomena but also the ethereal expanse and voids beyond, ramified in all possible directions, confirms her attainment of the Self. The undercurrent of spiritual satisfaction is evident from the vakh. The yogic union of the individual self with the Supreme Śiva had become a matter of course for her. The organs of sense perceptions could be suppressed at will and the qualifying modes of the self set at naught to gain the blissful experience of union with the Self. It is just a verification of her previous achievements. She had realized Śiva, as the Essence of everything that exists. Whatever she turned her mystical gaze upon, it turned out to be Śiva.

It is not merely a case of realization recapitulated and ruminated over in solitude: Lalla's yoga had become second nature with her. "Yoga comes and goes". So it was not a state of meditation but that of perfection. The mystical height she had gained would not suffer reversion; the realization had become an irrevocable condition of her self. For her nothing existed but Parama-Śiva omnipresent.[2] One wonders whether such

1. Cf. *Kaṭha Upanishad* II. 5. 1. Also *Śvet. Up.* III. 18 and *Shrimad Bhagvadgītā* V. 13.
2. *Shrimad Bh. Gītā* V. 19.

certitude is discernible in any spiritual poetry elsewhere. Śaivaism includes pantheism, and Lallayogeśvarī talks of it as a matter of personal experience.

A few more vakhs are given here to support this view. She says:

99. Svan drāv vahani ta mal gav vathith,
Yĕli mĕ analāha dhyutmas tāv;
Katur zan gayas lola vĕglith,
Yĕli kaṭhakŏsh tsŏl nishi rav drāv.
Lal bŏh ruzas tĕli shihlith,
Yĕli tsĕtas pĕv bŏh Tas nāv.

स्वन द्राव वाहनि तु मल गव वथिथ
यलि म्य अनुलाह् द्युतुमस ताव
कतुर ज़न गयस लोलु व्यगुलिथ
यलि कठकोश चोल निशि रव द्राव
लल बोह रुज़ुस त्यलि शिहिलिथ
यलि च्यतस प्यव बोह तस नाव ॥९९॥

The impurity of gold burnt away, when
Putting it in the crucible, I heated it in the forge;
As a frozen sheet of water, I melted by the fire of love!
When the frost was gone, the Sun rose betimes.
I, Lalla, was quite at peace
When I recollected that I was but His name.

As a result of severe trials, the impurities of the limited self had burnt away. Austere living and yogic practice had enlightened her of the real nature of the Self. The frost of ignorance and uncertainty had melted away and the Sun of true knowledge shone warm and bright. The darkness of Māyā, the enveloping blanket of obscuration, had been dissipated in one sweep. Her conflicts and confusions of the early days had been resolved. The last traces of duality had been wiped out. She had realized that Prakṛti was only the shining forth of the Supreme.

This vakh testifies that her realization of oneness with the Supreme Being was perfect and in retrospect it is an admission that not a shadow of doubt was left in her mind regarding the identification of Śiva in everything, including herself. She was herself Śiva, under the name of 'Lalla'.[1]

Philosophical monism may not, perhaps, be asserted with greater conviction or in stronger language. Lalla identifies herself with the Absolute Being.

In these vakhs, the undercurrent of satisfaction rises to the surface. It is not an expression of conceit but a word of encouragement to the aspirant on the path, when she says:

100. Shunyuk maidān koḍum pānas,
Mĕ, Lalli, rūzam na bwad na hosh;
Vĕzay sapanis pānai pānas,
Ada kami hili[2] phŏl Lalli pamposh!

शून्युक मैदान कोडुम पानस
म्य ललि रूज़ुम न ब्वद न होश
व्यज़य सपनिस पानय पानस
अद कमि हिलि फोल ललि पम्पोश ॥१००॥

Travelling through the vast expanse of the Void,
I, Lalla, lost my intellectual power and consciousness of body;
(Benumbed that way) I became aware of the secret of my Self.
Behold! For Lalla, the sedge flowered forth the Lotus!

1. "As pure water poured into pure water remains the same, thus, O Gautama, is the Self of a thinker who knows", said Yama to Naciketa.
Kaṭha Up. II.4.15.

2. 'Hil' and 'gil' are two variants. Hil — Sapless plants growing under water, usually in standing water of lakes and ponds of Kashmir. They grow in large clusters and the branches are full of short spindles of soft, horny shoots. The Dal lake is full of 'hil'. The botanical equivalent of the plant is 'Potomogeton Crispus' and 'Potomogeton Natans'. 'Gil', on the other hand, is a Persian word not in everyday or even general use in Kashmiri. Its Kashmiri equivalent is 'rab' which means mud. The lotus roots do grow in the muddy bottom of lakes and pools, where the water is not very deep. In this vakh 'hil' is preferred to 'gil', because the former is a Kashmiri word and the whole text of Lalla's verse shows that Persian had not made much impact on her poetic diction.

She had had a hard time of it like the Magi of the East, journeying through sun and rain. The magi had taken all the trouble to pay homage and offer gifts to Christ at his nativity. Lalla's journey however, was performed on the subtle mystical plane, through the Voids of Being, and entirely on a different level of consciousness. The Lord was birthless and deathless, ever there to be recognized and realized. It is the Lord who makes the ultimate warp and woof of the universe. On that plane, intellectual dialectics and physical powers had ceased to be of any avail to her. The realization of unity in diversity had literally stunned her, exalted as her consciousness was. She had obtained the key to the secrets of the Self. She had understood the nature of the Being with which she had the blissful experience of merging. She had realized the Brahman in the transcendental state and, in that event, the lotus of true knowledge had blossomed for her. From the sedge, or alternatively 'mire', of her earthly existence, she had stalked up into the rarefied plane of mystical understanding of the Truth. The Lotus of Self-knowledge bloomed for her for ever and for ever.

'Śūnya'[1] is not to be taken for nothingness. In Lalla's terminology Śūnya is equivalent to the Absolute. Hence, travelling through

1. Refer to footnote to vakh 41. *Śūnya* is not empty space or vacuum. Lalla had not had to face *emptiness*. One is inclined to interpret it as 'Ākāśa', as the concept is defined in the Upaniṣads. In mystical terminology it may be the equivalent of the Transcendental Śiva:

(a) Vācaknavi Gārgi asks Yājñavalkya: 'O Yājñavalkya, that of which they say that it is above the heavens, beneath the earth, embracing heaven and earth, past, present and future, tell me in what it is woven, like warp and woof ?'

Yājñavalkya said: 'That of which they say that it is above the heavens, beneath the earth, embracing the heaven and earth, past, present and future, that is woven like warp and woof is the *Akāśa.*' *Bṛhad-Upaniṣad.* III. 8. 344.

(b) श्राकाशस्तल्लिङ्गात् ॥ २२

Brahma-Sūtra, Swami Vireshwarnanda, p. 49.

Ākāśaḥ:—(The Word) Ākāśa *Talliṅgāt,* on account of the characteristic marks of that (Brahman).

"(The word) Ākāśa (ether) is Brahman on account of the characteristic marks of That (i.e. Brahman) (being mentioned)."

(c) "What is the goal of this world ? 'Ākāśa', he replied. For all these beings take their rise from Ākāśa only and dissolve into it. Ākāśa is greater than these. It is their ultimate goal. It indeed is the Supreme Udgītha...... He who knowing this as such meditates on the Supreme Udgītha......"

Chand Up. 1.9.1-2

[contd.

expanses of the Void may be interpreted as getting absorbed in the state of samādhi wherein the microcosmic self was experienced as getting dissolved in the Macrocosmic Self. Overcoming the stumbling blocks of the limited self, stuck into the quagmire of the conditioned physical life like the roots of the lotus plant, she had struggled and risen into the sunshine and bracing air of realization. Naturally, the flower of knowledge bloomed with all its pinky glory. In this behalf, we may quote Dr. Radhakrishnan: "Gorgeous flowers justify the muddy roots from which they spring!" Lalla had become a very gorgeous Lotus, indeed!

The change was felt by her quite tangibly. She sings of the change in the vista of her mystical perceptions, of the change wrought within and without her. She had become a different person, altogether. Her spiritual metamorphosis was complete. She says:

101. Tsĕth nŏvuy tsandram nŏvuy,
Zalmai dyūṅṭhum navam nŏvuy
Yana pĕṭha Lalli mĕ tan-man nävay,
Tana Lal bŏh navam navay chĕs!

च्यथ नो़वुय चन्द्रमु नो़वुय
जलमय ड्यूंठुम नवम नो़वुय
यनु प्यठु ललि म्य' तन-मन नोवुय
तनु लल बो़ह नवम नव़ुय छ्यस ॥१०१॥

(d) The word Ākāśa refers to Brahman and not to elemental Ākāśa (ether). The word Ākāśa is also used for Brahman in other texts:
"That which is called Ākāśa is the revealer of all forms and names."
Chānd. Up. 8.14.

When Yājñavalkya says that "that is woven like warp and woof in Ākāśa", we have to recognize the fact that Ākāśa is not distinguished from Brahman as a separate entity, in so much as that would lead to *duality*. Ākāśa does not, therefore, refer to the atmosphere or ether in the physical sense, but to the transcendental entity identical with Brahman or Śiva. Lalla's voyages through Ākāśa, therefore, clearly refer to her sublime mystical experiences of identification with the Absolute Being. In the blissful states of samādhi, the attributes of the embodied Jīvātmā, Buddhi and Mind, and consciousness of the body automatically disappeared. The Lotus of the Sahasrāra, the seat of Parama Śiva, in the microcosm, blossomed out.

There is a tinge of humility in her reference to 'hil' as the symbol of her humble beginning of spiritual aspiration, which had been more than fulfilled.

My Citta is new and so is the Moon!
Flushed with water, I see all (Nature) fresh (and green)
Since I, Lalla, cleansed my body and mind,
How different and fresh am I !

Retrospectively, Lalla, the Yogeśvarī, sings of the complete sea-change she had undergone. No longer was she Lalla, the seeker. She was a perfected Soul, emancipated from the fear of birth and death. The field of her consciousness was different now. The impurities or 'malas' had been burnt down. The function of the mind had been raised from the phenomenal world and the limited self of ego-consciousness to the sublime heights of the consciousness of The All-pervading, All-enveloping, All-inclusive, All-experiencing Being. She was one with the Lord!

The external (Prakṛti) Nature was no longer the same as she had viewed it in the beginning of her life. It was pulsating with life — the essential spirit that is Śiva. The phases of the Moon were no longer ordinary phases of the planet with respect to earth. The cosmos was represented in the microcosm. The 'Moon' in the Sahasrāra was quite a new phenomenon unbounded by and un-connected with the Solar system. The arid dryness of the physical perspective had changed into a fresh and green spiritual view of Nature abounding in 'water' of life. *'Water' as the symbol of Śiva's benign grace permeated everything in Nature,* not only cleansing impurities, but also enlivening the whole panorama of existence. As a perfected Yogeśvarī, she perceived Śiva in every blade of grass that grew around her. Doubtless it was now quite a New World.

Lalla leaves no room for more direct and forthright admission of the fact that since the day she had had the good fortune of her triumphant mystical experience of the communion with The Eternal Being, after she had purified her body and mind of the defilements and limitations attendant on them, she was a completely changed person. She had realized the Self and had become a Jīvanmukta, freed from the inexorable Laws of Karma. Without the least taint of duality, basking in the ever-effulgent light of Parama Śiva and conscious of oneness with Him; unfettered and uncircumscribed by the relativities of Time, Space, Kala etc. (the six principles of subjective Limitation);

without subservience to her Ego, Intellect and Mind; taking the sense organs and their functions in their stride as but the Lord's instruments of manifestation; without the compulsion of the individual will for or against anything, the Yogeśvarī, though still apparently, for all worldly intents and purposes, an individual, living her earthly allotted days like any other individual, had attained her mystical perfection and was verily a *Changed Personality.*

"Self-transcendence is the watchword of the Upaniṣads and the Vedânta,"[1] says Mahendranatha Sircar, and one might aver that self-transcendence is the goal of Mystical Discipline. Lalla had followed this path and gained the highest of ends—the state of blessedness. The last vakh categorically declares that with the purification of her Antaḥkaraṇas, the light of the Lord shone within her. The sense of alienation which had cast a gloom over her once had totally disappeared from her mind. "Mysticism is to be defined as the direct awareness of reality conceived as Truth".[2] Lalla's awareness of Reality was evidently complete. She lived in a sublime state of consciousness of the all-pervading Being. She had discovered her self as the Cosmic Self, as Sat-Cit-Ānanda—and she everafterwards lived in that state. "God is the poet, the world is the divine comedy. Those who have eyes to see can see the living God through it!".[3]

1. *Hindu Mysticism.* Introduction p. 2.
2. *Ibid.* p. 8.
3. *Ibid.* p. 11.

20

A NOTE ON THE FORMAL ASPECT OF THE VAKHS

Apart from their mystical content, the Vakhs of Lalla-ded provide ample formal interest to the critical eye. One may presumably suggest that the gushing inspiration of Lall-ded could not issue but in the form of a *vakh* which has assumed in Kashmir a peculiar connotation of its own. A vakh and mystical matter have become almost synonymous, interchangeable terms. A vakh has come to mean metaphysical knowledge expressed in verse, and it stands for a unique species of poetical language that touches the deeper chords of the listener and communicates to him depths of subtle consciousness, both uplifting and soothing.

'Vāka' is a Sanskrit word meaning speaking,[1] and 'Vākya' means speech, words, a sentence, a saying. It also means an argument or syllogism, a precept, rule or an aphorism. It is in the sense of an argument, a precept and, more than anything else, in the sense of a short pithy saying that a vakh comes very close to vākya. Most of the vakhs of Lalla-ded are aphoristic in style. They resemble Sūtras, enclosing a sea of meaning in a nutshell, leaving much to be filled in by the reader or listener. One may dwell on the following lines and even expound them into an elaborate treatise on metaphysical philosophy.

(i) Shiv chuy krūṭh ta tsen vŏpadīsh (v. 29).
(ii) Mŏtiyay kuṅh ta suy vŏpadīsh. (v. 40).

1. *A Sanskrit-English Dictionary*, Sir M. Monier-Williams p. 936.

(iii) Tsèth gŏl tai kěṅh ti na kune,
Gay Bhūr, Bhuvaḥ, Svaḥ věsarzitḥ kèth. (v. 45).
(iv) Nishi chuy tai dūr mo gārun,
Shuněs Shunyāh mīlith gav. (v. 43).
(v) Kar manas ta pavanas saṅgāṭh. (v. 55).

Besides, the argumentative pose is present in the vakhs. A syllogism comprises three propositions: the two premises and the conclusion. A Lalla-vakh has a variant of four lines; the first three propound and develop a problem and the fourth makes the conclusion, buttressed by profound conviction. Vakhs 7, 22, 23, 26, 27 and 48 may illustrate this. The last line of each vakh winds up the thought process into a categorical assertion. As precepts, the Lallavakh are a splendid vehicle of didactic poetry. With their compressed content the lessons come home. Verses 5, 43, 73, 74, 82, 84, 85, 86, may be cited as examples.

Each vakh is a quatrain in which the first and the third, the second and the fourth lines rhyme together. There are, however vakhs in which only the second and the fourth lines have rhyming end-words and this may be so because the natural flow of sense would not be sacrificed for the sake of introducing a rhyming word. The following examples will illustrate this.

(a) Gwaras pritshām sāsi late
Yas na kěṅh vanān tas kyāh nāv,
Pritshān pritshān thacis ta lūsas:
Kěṅh-nas nishi kyāhtaṃ drāv.

(b) Tsa na bŏh na dhey na dhyān,
Gay pānai Sarvakrya mashith:
Anyav dyūṅtḥukh kěṅhti na anvai:
Gayi sath layi Par pashith.

It may also be pointed out that in mystical poetry, the onrush of inspiration takes precedence over the formal niceties. That a vakh is not found in rhyming lines does not detract from the substance of a Lalla-vakh its essential rhythm and import.[1]

1. "In 1917, Sir Aurel Stein ascertained definitely that in Kashmiri songs, the metre depended soley on the stress accent. In Lalla's verses four stresses go to each Pāda or line...Lalla's metre...is in fact very loose indeed. She starts really with an Indian dohā as her basis which is a purely quantitative verse, and then abandons quantity altogether and depends on stress-accent alone—in this she does exactly what the early Christian monkish writers did with their Latin Hymns."
The Word Of Lalla: Sir Richard Temple. p.1.

By and large, each line of a vakh breaks up into seven syllables. We may take the following for illustration:

(i) Shiv/vā/Kī-/shav/vā/Jin/vā
Kam-/laja-/nāth/nām-/dhā-/rin/yuh
Mĕ/a-/bali/käs-/tan/bawa-/roz
Su/vā/su/vā/su/vā/suh.

(ii) Mūḍ/zä-/nith/pa-/shith/ta/on
Kŏl/shru-/ta-/vun/zaḍ-/rūpi/ās
Yus/yih/da-/piy/tas/tiy/boz
Yu-/hay/tvata/vĕ-/dis/chuy/abyās.

(iii) Kĕṅh/chiy/nĕṅd-/ri/hati/vu-/di
Keṅ-/tsan/vu-/dĕn/ne/sar/pey/
Keṅh/chiy/snān/ka-/rith/a/puti/
Keṅh/gĕh/ba-/zith/ti/a/krey/

(iv) Abyā-/sī/sva-/vīkās/layi/vŏ-/thū
Gaga-/nas/sva-/gun/myūl/sami/tsraṭa
Shuñ/gŏl/ta/Ana-/may/mŏ-/tū
Yu-/hŏy/vŏpa-/dīsh/chuy/ba-/ṭṭa.

The vakhs have a flowing rhythm, but we are not able to classify the metre under any one of the known Sanskrit or Persian metres as applied to Kashmiri verse. (A few scholars and poets of Sanskrit and Kashmiri were approached, but they could not help denominating the metre.) It is likely that the Prakrit Kashmiri of Lall-dĕd's time had a verse metre of its own which suited the form and content of the vakh. Sweeping influence of Persian on the Kashmiri language in the later days, as Persian became the Court Language, changed not only the texture of Kashmiri but also brought about a sea-change in the intonation and accentuation of words. One cannot say by what angle the present-day recitation of Lalla-vakhs has deviated from its original position. The classical artistes of Radio Kashmir add an elongated lilt which resembles a wail. It is a wind-sound with a marked plaintive note. Often the artist mixes syllables and words so that it is hard to determine the accented and the unaccented.

Nevertheless, the nuances of tone and pitch are so delicately managed that a vakh, when sung in accompaniment with a musical instrument, 'Santoor', leaves a lingering ring of harmony in the ear. Over the centuries, the Vakhs and Persian Classical music have found an eager ear among the Kashmiris in general and among those of metaphysical bent in particular. The vakh, when recited, seems to act as a spiritual balm and brings solace to the careworn.

Despite the predominant wail as may aptly describe the pangs of separation from the Lord, there is a diversified mosaic of rhythm marking the various content of the vakhs. When she sings of her supreme success, the rhythm changes into one of jingling, sonorous harmony. It moves at a faster pace, as may be clear from the following:

(i) Tshāṅḍān lūsas päñi-pānas
Tshĕpith Jñānas votum na kūṅtsh
Lai karmas ta vätsas althānas
Bari bari bāna ta cĕvān na kūṅtsh.

(ii) Pānas lägith rovukh mĕ tsa
Mĕ tsĕ tshāṅḍān lūsum dŏh
Pānas maṅz yĕli dyūṅthukh mĕ tsa
Mĕ tsĕ ta pānas dyutum tshŏh.

The high water-mark of intellectual activity which had issued in the earlier centuries as the works of eminent sages and saint-philosophers like Kallaṭa Bhaṭṭa, Abhinavagupta, Kṣemarāja and others seems to have reached the lowest ebb by the time Lalla-dĕd came on the scene. Mystical poetry alone, which held up the candle of hope to the bruised heart of humanity wallowing in the mire of destitution and ignorance, could, perhaps, withstand the shattering blows of religious and socio-political upheavals. It is no wonder, therefore, that the Lalla-Vakhs and the 'Shruks' of Sheikh Noor-ud-Din are the only extant forms of our poetic heritage of those times.

The undefined metre, however, does not take away from the Vakhs their prismatic charm. Lall-dĕd sings in bold, concrete images and these are constructed out of the ordinary wares of a householder's life. The delicate, subtle and highly abstract thought comes home as it is moulded by her ingenious, plastic art into visual images: for instance, in the practice of Yoga she had to face immense difficulty in discovering, on the subtle plane of consciousness, the ineffable Nāḍīs. She seems to have been in a tight hole. It is a forbidding subject. It is an indescribable exercise to be conducted within oneself, and still more difficult to explain it to others. She concretizes the subtle situation in the following vakh.

Zānaha nāḍidal raṭith
Tsaṭith vaṭith kuṭith kleshı
Zānaha ada asta rasāyan gaṭith
Shiv chuy krūṭh ta tsen vōpadīsh.

The 'Kaleśas' are like herbs to be torn into smithereens, to be collected and pounded in a mortar with a pestle. The potion thus prepared is to be turned into a pasty pill to be swallowed and the Kleśas are done for. It is a vivid image of what is done at an apothecary's shop. The compression of the difficulties to be surmounted in yoga is drastic, yet the picture of frustration more than explains itself: Śiva is difficult to attain!

Again, for attainment of Self-realization, Prāṇa—the subtle vital air—must be brought under control. Ordinarily it may be beyond words to communicate the abstract process of dealing with the Will-o'-the-wisp, Prāṇa. Lall-dĕd finds an appropriate metaphor.

Dihaci lari dāri-bar trōprim
Prāna-tsūr roṭum ta dyutmas dam
Hradayici kūṭhari aṅdar gōṅḍum
Ōmaki cobuka tulimas bam.

The human body is a house and the apertures of sense organs are its doors and windows. Prāṇa is the recalcitrant thief. She shuts the apertures of sense organs tightly, so as not to leave even a chink open. The thief is overpowered and bound in the cell of the heart. He is then suffocated and lashed hard with the whip of Oṃ, the highest of Bīja-mantras. The image of breaking in Prāṇa is graphically perfect.

But when she takes to abstractions, she is ruthless and puts our faculty of limited understanding completely to rout. Take verse 39, for instance.

> Abyāsī svavikasi layi vŏthū
> Gaganas svagun myūl samitsraṭa
> Shuñ gŏl Anāmay motū
> Yŏhoy vŏpadīsh chuy baṭṭa.

It is not a child's play to realize what she means by

> "Abyāsi svavikas layi vŏthū
> Gagnas svagun myūl samitsraṭa."

We translate it: With constant practice, the One unlimited, unqualified Being spread out everywhere, rose to absorb the qualified (Being), i.e. the immanent Śakti aspect, the two coinciding with each other into a homogeneous whole and appearing like one mill-stone sitting smoothly on the other, the two becoming one block. And then the Void melted away: only the pure One remained!

What that adds up to only Yogis can tell. The awful abstract experience leaves one dumbfounded.

There are still other things to note in the vakhs. The concrete imagery sparkles with the ornaments of conscious poetic art. Alliteration, sound assonance, medial and end rhymes, personification, use of felicitous words and phrases and other adornments are employed to burnish and add lustre to the form. We may examine the following vakh.

> Damāh dam kŏrmas damanhāle
> Prazalyom dāph ta nañeyam zāth
> Aṅdaryum prakāsh nĕbar tshŏṭum
> Gaṭi roṭum ta karmas thaph.

Self-realization is an event of joy. Lall-dĕd appears to bubble with satisfaction at the great mystical achievement. Consequently the high sentiment is couched in a concrete figure glistening with ornaments. The bellows of respiration are restrained for a moment and the candle of Self blazes up! It is an occasion for fireworks and illumination. Scintillating images are conjured up. "Aṅdryum Prakāsh nĕbar tshŏtum"—I winnowed the inner light out in a cascade! "Gaṭi rŏṭum"—I seized the 'light' in the enveloping darkness. Could the mould have better glaze?

Let us look at the words: 'Damāh', 'dam' and 'damanhāle' in one line. It is an excellent example of alliteration and sound assonance. Use of mellifluous words like 'prazalyom,' 'nañeyam' 'prakāsh', still more honeyed with repeated liquid consonants like l, m, n is surely a feat of poetic artistry. One marvels at the choice of language as much as one is mystified by the indescribable subtle content of the vakh.

An acute strain of lyricism relieves the fatigue of concentrated thought. Here is an example.

Pŏt zūni vathith mŏt bolanovum
Dag lalanävam Daya-saṅzi prihe
Lal, Lal, karān Lāl vuzunovum
Mīlith tas shrotsyom dihe.

'Pŏt Zūni'—at the declining moon in the small hours of the morning—the two words suggest a highly romantic atmosphere most suited for lovers to meet. When the dust of the material world has settled down, the propitious hour to invoke the Lord is come. The emotion-packed heart (mŏt) bursts forth in melody: 'I am Lalla, the seeker! O, I am the seeker!' the same way as the nightingale sings to call its mate. 'Mŏt' appears to be a conscious selection, for there is no other equivalent Kashmiri word charged with amorous fondness to be used for a love-laden heart bursting with sweet pangs of love and almost in a state of desperation. 'Mŏt' has a delicate halo around it, differentiating it from 'Pāgal'—insane, become demented or gone crazy. Not seldom do we give this appellation to spiritual men or 'dervishes'. And Ruby (Lāl) is the word used for the Divine Beloved. The effulgence of the Ruby purifies her corporeal frame!

Examining the linguistic drapings, we cannot miss the medial rhyme of 'Pŏt' and 'mŏt'; the harmonious balance between 'bolanovum', 'lalanävam,' and 'vuzanovum', and the softness of 'shrotsyom', 'prihe',. 'dihe'. The repeated use of the honeyed letter 'la' as many as ten times in one quatrain lends the vakh a cloyingly sweet effect. It is a superb demonstration of the poetic art. Sublime mystical poetry is by its nature inspired, as all exalted poetry needs must be but inspiration does not rule out linguistic selection, trimming and lacing and embroidery.

Lastly, a word on her poetic *diction.* A large proportion of the words used by Lall-dĕd is Kashmiri very much in use today. The language though simple is selected to produce the maximum effect with minimum linguistic material. For instance, we take the following Vakh.

Āmi pana sŏdras nāvi chĕs lamān
Kati bozi Dai myon mĕti diyi tār
Āmĕn tākĕn poñ zan shĕmān
Zuv chum bramān gara gatshaha.

Om pan, sŏdar, nāv, lamun, bozun, tār dyun,
om tok, poñ shĕmun, zuv bramun, gara gatshun—not one of these words or phrases is un-common or unfamiliar; yet the selection and combination are obvious. Towing a boat on the high sea or river with an untwined thread is an exercise in futility. Pouring water into unbaked earthen plates demonstrates the same effect. When she means to emphasize the rigours of *patience,* she uses thundering, guttural words, as in the following :

Tsālani chai vuzamala ta traṭai
Tsālun chuy maṅdiñan gaṭakār
Tsālun chuy pān-panun Kaḍun graṭai
Hĕti māli santoosh vāti pānai.

Vuzamala, traṭa, maṅdiñan gaṭakar, kaḍun graṭa—it is the language of a storm and rumbling thunder. The diction and rhythm of the vakh conform to its sense and temper.

The Kashmiri language of her time has a fair sprinkling of Sanskrit words and not a few words owe their descent to Sanskrit. The following are examples of the Sanskrit words bodily used by her:

Nĕshbodh	from	निशबुद्धि	Lack of wisdom
Khīd	from	खेद	grief
Āgrai	from	अग्र	source
Santoosh	from	सन्तोष	Contentment
Makar	from	मुकुर	Looking-glass
Mal	—	मल	Defilement
Sahaz	—	सहज	Natural, easy, True
Kusum	—	कुसुम	Flower
Mūḍh	—	मूढ़	Dull of understanding
Jñāna	—	ज्ञान	Knowledge
Vĕbhava	—	विभव	Prosperity, earthly goods
Lūbh, būgh	—	लोभ, भोग	Greed, enjoyment
Va	—	वा	Or
Nāmdhārin	—	नामधारी	Named
Bawaroz	—	भवरुज	Earthly ills
Yudvanai or Yudvai or yud	—	यद्यपि [यदि+वै Vedic]	In case, if
Yuh	—	यः	Who
Tsĕta	—	चित्त	Consciousness
Broṅt	—	भ्रान्ति	Illusion
Vash karun	—	वशीकरण	To enthrall
Disha	—	दिशा	Direction
Desh	—	देश	Country
Sadai	—	सदैव	Always
Saṅdeh	—	संदेह	Doubt
Byŏn	—	भिन्न	Differentiated
Tsiṅth	—	चिन्त्	To think
Anād	—	अनादि	Without beginning
Tyaji	—	त्यज	To give up
Vākh	—	वाक्	Speech
Vatsun	—	वचन	Word
Kumbh	—	कुम्भक	Restraining breath
Kuṭith	—	कुट्	To break into pieces
Rasāyan	—	रसायन	Pasty potion
Yūzan	—	योजन	Eight miles
Āhār	—	आहार	Diet

And the following are a few examples of Kashmiri words which derive from Sanskrit or are corrupted forms thereof :

Hoṅd	होंड	from	हुड्डा	A ram
Nīlvat	नीलवट	from	वट	A round thing, stone
Bocha	बोछः	from	बुभुक्षा	Hunger
Harān	हरान	from	Sanskrit root हृ	To snatch away, to fall
Vāv	वाव	from	वात्, वायु	Air
Prāh) or) Prai)	प्राह् प्रय	from	प्री	To feel affection for, to love
Vĕzay	व्यजय	from	-वित्	Known, familiar
Sŏdar	सोद्र	from	समुद्र	Ocean
Bakhts	बखच	from	भक्ति	Devotion
Rotse	रोचि	from	रुच्	To like
Sware	स्वरे	from	स्वंर, (as verb)	To remember, to chant
Zaḍ	जड	from	जड	Lifeless
Sŏm	सोम्	from	सम	Balanced
Lalith	ललिथ	from	लल धातु	(to loll the tongue)
Swŏth	स्वोथ	from	सेतु	Bund, dam
Täṭhis	तांठिस	from	तिक्तं	Difficulty
Vagi	वगि	from	वल्गा	Bridle
Härinj	हांरिज	from	शरज्या	A bow-string
Kroṅt	क्रोंत	from	क्रान्त	To subjugate
Kartal	करतल	from	करत्री	A dagger
Taph	तफ	from	तप	Penance
Būdum	बूदुम	from	बुध्	To concentrate on
Khyŏd	क्ष्योद	from	क्षुत	Hunger
Varzani	वरजनि	from	व्रजन	Fast blowing
Hĕti	ह्यति	from	इति	In this manner
Mŏtse	मोचे	from	मुच्	To leave behind
Pashith	पशिथ	from	पश्य	To see

Häriṅj, būdun, hĕti, yuh, sadai are examples of words which have become obsolete.

In v. 10., Grierson uses the word 'kor' which means blind in Persian.

But MS, Śāradā Script, Research Library, Srinagar, Acc. No. 961 uses 'ŏṇ' (Śloka 80) which is the Kashmiri word for blind. Grierson's use of 'Kor' for 'oṇ' appears to be a later substitution. In the said MS. description of four types of blind-men is given and 'ŏṇ' is used repeatedly.

BIBLIOGRAPHY

Anand Kaul Bamzai: *Pandit*: Sayings of Lalleshwari, Reprinted from The Indian Antiquary, vol. IX, 1931 and vol. LXI, 1932.

Arberry: *A.J.*: Sufism.

A'zmi: *Khwaja Mohammad A'zam Dedamari* : Waqiat-i-Kashmir (History). 1747 A.D. R.L. Srinagar

Aurobindo, *Sri*: The Synthesis of Yoga: Shri Aurobindo Ashram Pondichery.

Bankey Behari: Sufis, Mystics and Yogis of India: Bharatiya Vidya Bhavan Publication.

Charagi, *Pandit Sarwanand* : Lalla Vakh.

Charanjitlal (*vānaprastha*): The Grandeur of Gayatri: The New World Publications, Lahore, 1946.

Chatterjee, *J.C.*: Kashmir Shaivaism: Cultural Academy Publication, Srinagar.

Chidbhavananda, *Swami*: The Bhagvadgita: Tapovanam Publishing House, Tiruchirapalli, Madras State.

Christopher Isherwood : Ramakrishna and His Disciples: Advait Ashram, Calcutta-14.

Donkin, *William* : Wayfarers (An account of the work of Meher Baba).

Elton, *Oliver* : Modern Studies (Chapter on 'A word on Mysticism').

Grierson, *Sir George*, & *Lionell D. Barnett* : Lalla Vakyani or The Wise Sayings of Lall-Ded: London, Royal Asiatic Society 1920.

Gopinath Raina: Lalleshwari Upanishad Vakya Rahasya: Srinagar.

Ghose, *Sisir Kumar* : Mystics and Society; Asia Publishing House, 1968.

Hassan, *Pir Ghulam Hassan Khuyihami* (1833-98): Tarikh-i-Hassan, vol. III, Tazkira Aulia Kashmir.

Hanuman Prasad Poddar: The Philosophy of Love, (Bhakti Sutras of Devarṣi Nārada): Gita Press, Gorakhpur.

Haridas Bhattacharya: The Cultural Heritage of India, vol. IV, The Religions: Kashmir Shaivism.

Huxley, Aldous: The Perennial Philosophy.

Inge, W.R.: Mysticism in Religion: Rider & Company, London.

Idries Shah: The Sufis: W. H. Allen, 1964.

James, Sir William: The Varieties of Religious Experience: Longmans, Green and Co., London.

Jia Lal Kaul Jalali (Pandit): Lalla Vakh, Srinagar.

Kirpal Sing (Sant): Godman: Ruhani Satsang, Delhi.

Kashur Samachar: A Monthly Journal, Delhi: Lalla Number, Jan.-Feb., 1971.

Khemraja: Parapraveshika: Translated into Hindi: Prabha Devi: Kashmir Shivadarshan Maṭhika, Srinagar.

Leidecker, Kurt F: Pratyabhijñāhṛdayaṃ (The Secret of Recognition): Translation and notes on Khemraja's Commentary in Sanskrit: Adyar, Madras.

Max Muller, F.: The Sacred Books of the East (Upanishads).

M. C.: Light on the Path and Karma.

Manuscript Lalavākya: Bhaskara: Śāradā script: Acc. No. 797: Research Library, Srinagar.

MSS. Lalavākya: Acc. Numbers 961, 1335: Research Library, Srinagar.

Nandlal Kaul Talib (Professor), *Jayalal Kaul* (Professor); Lalla-Ded: Cultural Academy Publication, Srinagar.

Nicholson: *R.A.*: Rumi, Poet and Mystic (Ethical and Religious Classics of the East and West): George Allen & Unwin Ltd., Ruskin House, London.

Nicholson: *R.A.*: Selected Poems from the Divani Shamsi-Tabrez: G. Allen & Unwin, London.

Nayanaponika Thera: The Heart of Buddhist Meditation: Rider & Co., London.

Osborne, Arthur: Ramana Maharshi And The Path of Self-Knowledge: Rider & Co., London.

Pandey, Dr. Kanti Chandra : Abhinavagupta: The Chowkhamba Sanskrit Studies, Varanasi-1

Paul Brunton, Dr.: The Secret Path; Rider & Co., London.

" Wisdom of The Overself: Rider & Co., London.

Ramjoo Malla: Pandit: Lalla A'rifa Saheba: Srinagar.

Radhakrishnan, Dr. S.: Religion And Culture: Orient Paperback.

Raushan Nath: *Yogi*; Flaming Faith: Rajiv Publications, New Delhi.

Rudrappa, Dr.: Kashmir Shaivism: Research Library, Srinagar.

Ramsay, Arthur Michael: God, Christ and the World: Scm Press Ltd., London.

Ruth Reyna: The Concept of Maya from the Vedas to the 20th century: Asia Publishing House.

Shankaracharya: Saundaryalahari : commentary in Hindi by Shri 108 Swami Vishnu Tirth ji Maharaj: Vignyan Press, Rishikesh (U.P.).

Sircar, Mahendranath: Hindu Mysticism: Kegan Paul, Trench, Trubner & Co., Ltd., London.

Temple, Sir Richard Carnac: The Word Of Lalla The Prophetess: Cambridge University Press, 1924.

Thornton, Edward: The Diary of a Mystic: George Allen & Unwin Ltd., London.

Vireshwarananda (Swami): Brahma-Sūtra: Advait Ashram, Calcutta-14.

Vishnu Tirth Ji Maharaj (Swami): Devatma Shakti (Kuṇḍalini): Shri Sadhan Granthmala Prakashan Samiti, Bombay-1.

Will Durant: The Story of Philosophy; A Washington Square Press/Pocket Books Publication, New York; 1961.

Wilson, Horace Hayman; Sanskrit Dictionary

Williams, Monier: Sanskrit-English Dictionary.

Woodroffe, Sir John: The Serpent Power And the Ṣaṭ-Cakra-Nirūpaṇa: Ganesh & Co., Madras-17

१. ॐ पूर्णमदः पूर्णमिदं पूर्णात् पूर्णमुदच्यते ।
पूर्णस्य पूर्णमादाय पूर्णमेवावशिष्यते ॥

INDEX